Land in Her Own Name

Women as Homesteaders in North Dakota

H. Elaine Lindgren

Foreword by Elizabeth Jameson

University of Oklahoma Press
Norman

Dedicated to my parents, Kenneth W. Wiederrecht and Beulah Ella Minder Wiederrecht, whose guidance during my eighteen years of growing up on an Iowa farm fostered my respect for the land and my appreciation for the rural way of life.

Library of Congress Cataloging–in–Publication Data

Lindgren, H. Elaine.
   Land in her own name : women as homesteaders in North Dakota / H. Elaine Lindgren ; foreword by Elizabeth Jameson.
      p.   cm.
   Originally published: Fargo : North Dakota Institute for Regional Studies, c1991.
   ISBN 978-0-8061-2886-3 (paper)
   1. Women pioneers—North Dakota—History.   2. Women pioneers—North Dakota—Biography.   3. North Dakota—Social life and customs. 4. North Dakota—Biography.   I. Title.
F636.L56   1996
978.4′0082—dc20   96–20628
                                                          CIP

On the title page: Pauline Shoemaker, courtesy Sheila Robinson

The paper in this book meets the guidelines for permanence and durability of the Committee on Production Guidelines for Book Longevity of the Council on Library Resources, Inc. ♾

Contents

Tables

Foreword

Land in Her Own Name records the stories of women we have seldom heard even though they helped write a familiar chapter of American history. Textbooks, movies, television, novels, and theme parks all present the sagas of American homesteaders who, spurred by the promise of "free land," helped claim the continent for the United States. These pioneers forged key American traits and values, such as self-reliance, independence, and democracy. The popular versions of western settlement, however, omit many of the real historical actors, including women who forged their own definitions of opportunity on western homesteads.

When Congress passed the Homestead Act in 1862, it envisioned a nation of family farmers, where husbands and wives would work as partners. Our most common images of women who homesteaded are of wives and daughters, like Caddie Woodlawn, or Laura and Caroline Ingalls of the "Little House" stories.[1] But the Homestead Act also allowed women, for the first time, to claim an independent stake in the land. Women as well as men could homestead if they were single or heads of households, at least twenty-one years of age, and citizens or immigrants who had filed for citizenship.

The federal government distributed almost 250 million acres to private individuals between 1868 and 1955. Congress defined the exact requirements in a series of laws beginning in the 1840s. The details varied over the years, but the outline was the same. The government offered a homesteader part of the public domain—usually 160 acres, and more, eventually, in arid areas. In return, the homesteader paid a small filing fee, built a home, and lived on the land and improved it for a specified time—usually five years.[2]

Homesteading offered an unprecedented opportunity for women, and thousands took it. What they sought and how they won it recasts the familiar story of western pioneers. Despite the historic provision of the Homestead Act, few historians, until quite recently, explored its significance for women. In 1976, Sheryll Patterson-Black published a pathbreaking article, "Women Homesteaders on the Great Plains Frontier." Using land office records from Lamar, Colorado, and Douglas, Wyoming, for the years 1887, 1891, 1907, and 1908, Patterson-Black calculated that an average of 11.9 percent of the homestead entrants were women, and that 42.4 percent of the women "proved up" and received title to their claims, compared with 37 percent of the men. Her work sparked further research and a lively debate about what land ownership meant for western women.[3]

Elaine Lindgren's study of North Dakota women as homesteaders confirms much of what we have learned about women who homesteaded and their relative success. The period from 1900 through 1915 marked the peak years for homesteading in western states. During this period, too, increasing numbers of women filed for land. Always a significant presence on western agricultural frontiers, they ranged from about 5 percent of all homesteaders in early settlements to some 20 percent after 1900. But until *Land in Her Own Name* was published in 1991, we had no in-depth study of homesteading women that told the story of how they filed for land, how they organized their work and their relationships, and what homesteading meant to them. Lindgren provides a nuanced profile of a large population of women who homesteaded, using case studies of 306 North Dakota women. Interviews and correspondence with nineteen women add depth and detail to this collective portrait, as do land records, news articles, documents, and pictures provided by the women and their acquaintances. From this rich array of sources, Lindgren draws the most comprehensive picture to date of homesteading women, embedding her valuable statistical profile in an engrossing and readable text. The analysis never over-shadows the women, whose own words and photographs evoke a qualitative sense of people, place, and lived experience rarely achieved in social histories.

Lindgren has distilled patterns from the considerable variety of individual experience, patterns that will provide a basis for comparison with other rural women and other parts of the West. Women of all ages, races, ethnicities, and backgrounds homesteaded in North Dakota. Most, however, were young and single, and came from the upper Midwest or from Europe. More women, proportionately, homesteaded after 1900 than before. But even in the far eastern counties of North Dakota, the areas of earliest Euro-American settlement, thousands of homesteading women demonstrated that women could "make it" on their land. They became visible models of what was possible for the next generation of homesteading daughters.

The ways they "made it" add new dimensions to the story of American pioneers. This is not a simple story of how women, like men, found opportunity in the "free land" of the American West. There were any number of people in North Dakota, of course, whose histories did not fit the familiar pioneer saga—American Indians whose land became the "public" domain for others to claim, for instance, and the majority of homesteading hopefuls, men and women alike, who lost their land to debt, drought, grasshoppers, and large-scale commercial agriculture. Their lives, certainly, challenge the mythology of western opportunity. But even for the Euro-American settlers of the traditional western story, the ones who succeeded and won title to their land, the stories of the homesteading women offer new perspectives on what free land promised.

The ways that women succeeded reveal a great deal about gender in western agriculture, and about the meanings of "opportunity" and "liberation" for different westerners. Single women who homesteaded forged cooperative relationships with friends, family, and neighbors as they managed their own land. Few were isolated individuals, rugged or otherwise. They, like family farmers, allocated much of their daily work by gender. Many women worked in other occupations while homesteading. Some traded domestic work for help with field work; some rented their fields, or paid men to cultivate them. But virtually all managed their own land, and used it to enlarge their own possibilities.

This book, like most good women's history, brings new perspectives to men's lives and to our collective past. We discover that the men who homesteaded depended on nearby women with whom they traded work and built local communities. And the different ways women used their land suggest that we need to reevaluate traditional measures of homesteading achievement. Generally, "success" meant winning the land and staying there; leaving was a sure sign of failure. By those criteria, forty percent of women who won their homesteads really "succeeded" and lived on their claims longer than the five years required to "prove up." For the remainder, their land was an asset that provided other opportunities—money to start a small business, education for themselves or other family members, or funds to buy land elsewhere. For all homesteaders, as for the women in this book, persistence on the land is an inadequate measure of its promise. Many people who left their homesteads used them as investments to acquire their own versions of success. Many who stayed, no doubt, lived with pain and difficulty.

Land in Her Own Name expands the meanings of opportunity in the American West. Readers will glean their favorite images and stories from this richly textured book. As we see new actors in the familiar pioneer tale, the story achieves added depth, complexity, and humanity. The homesteading women do not take us to a female version of a heroic West. They offer us instead a history that illuminates the interdependent West we inherit.

Elizabeth Jameson
University of New Mexico

Notes

1. Both authors wrote for children, providing stories of self-reliance against the backdrop of the 1930s Depression. Carol Ryrie Brink, *Caddie Woodlawn* (New York: Macmillan, 1935). Laura Ingalls Wilder, *Little House in the Big Woods* (New York: Harper & Brothers, 1932); *Farmer Boy* (New York: Harper & Brothers, 1933); *Little House on the Prairie* (New York: Harper & Brothers, 1935); *On the Banks of Plum Creek* (New York: Harper & Brothers, 1937); *By the Shores of Silver Lake* (New York: Harper & Brothers, 1939); *The Long Winter* (New York: Harper & Brothers, 1940); *Little Town on the Prairie* (New York: Harper & Brothers, 1941); *These Happy Golden Years* (New York: Harper & Brothers, 1943).

2. Homestead figures calculated from *Historical Statistics of the U.S.: Colonial Times to 1970. Bicentennial Edition* (Washington, D.C.: U.S. Government Printing Office, 1975), 429. For homestead laws, see Chapter 2 and James Muhn, "Women and the Homestead Act: Land Department Administration of a Legal Imbroglio, 1863–1934," *Western Legal History* 7, no. 2 (summer/fall 1994): 283–307.

3. Sheryll Patterson-Black, "Women Homesteaders on the Great Plains Frontier," *Frontiers* 1, no. 2 (spring 1976): 67–68. See also Paula Nelson, "No Place for Clinging Vines: Women Homesteaders on the South Dakota Frontier" (master's thesis, University of South Dakota, 1978); and Katherine Harris, *Long Vistas: Women and Families on Colorado Homesteads* (Niwot, Colorado: University Press of Colorado, 1993). For published reminiscences of homesteading women, see Edith Eudora Kohl, *Land of the Burnt Thigh* (1938; reprint, St. Paul: Minnesota Historical Society Press, 1986); Martha Ferguson McKeown, *Them Was the Days: An American Saga of the 70s* (Lincoln: University of Nebraska Press, 1961); Elinore Pruitt Stewart, *Letters of a Woman Homesteader* (Lincoln: University of Nebraska Press, 1961); and Elizabeth Corey, *Bachelor Bess: The Homesteading Letters of Elizabeth Corey, 1909–1919*, ed. Philip L. Gerber (Iowa City: University of Iowa Press, 1990).

Preface

"What are you doing this summer?" a friend asked casually as we passed in the hall outside my office at the university. I told her about my exciting new project, collecting information on the experiences of women who filed claims in North Dakota under their own names. "Oh! Did women homestead?" she asked. After a prolonged pause, she answered her own question. "Of course they did; my grandmother homesteaded."

This encounter illustrates what was to become a common response to my work. For the most part, people do not think of women as early landowners. Historical accounts as well as popular literature focus on men as the primary actors in the drama of settlement. Thus, because it was assumed that women performed only secondary or "helpmate" roles, much of the reality of the lives of many women settlers either has been ignored or overlooked.

Although women sometimes have received credit for strength and courage within the domestic sphere, their roles often have been distorted, even to the point of the absurd. In *Prairie Women*, Carol Fairbanks discusses some particularly disparaging remarks of noted authors:

> Walter Prescott Webb, the respected historian, devoted less than two pages of his book *The Great Plains* (1931) to the topic "What has been the Spiritual Effect of the American Adventure in the Great Plains on Women?" He observed that men who settled on the prairie found "zest to the life, adventure in the air, freedom from restraint; men developed a hardihood which made them insensible to the hardships and lack of refinements." He claims that women, on the other hand, experienced fear and distrust of the land;

they were lonely and missed the comforts of former homes and the cultural activities of former communities (505). This attitude persists. For example, in the 1970s a Canadian literary critic, Eric Callum Thompson, affirms the opinion of a 1930s novelist, John Beames, who wrote this in his novel *An Army Without Banners:* "It is not in women that the pioneer spirit stirs; the horizon does not beckon them; hills and rivers are to them a barrier, not an invitation to explore. It was the men only who pressed on across the great plains; the women had little more to say than the horses who drew the wagons in which they sat. Where women had the deciding word no move was made" (quoted in Thompson 216). Thompson responded thus: "Beames makes an astute comment on the different attitudes held by the sexes." He accepts the myth of the female as reluctant pioneer.[1]

As scholars have begun to look more carefully at the actual roles women of the plains played, descriptions such as those of Webb, Beames, and Thompson seem based more on outmoded stereotypes of gender roles than on historical fact. Nevertheless, it is important to realize how much these stereotypical accounts have shaped public awareness. My friend's difficulty in remembering her grandmother's role as a landowner is typical. Other common responses indicate no recognition of women as landowners and even disbelief that they "really homesteaded." Yet thousands of women's names appear on the land records, too many to consider these women as exceptions.

The purpose of my project was to provide information that could be used to better understand the contributions made by a specific group of North Dakota women, contributions that furthered agricultural development and the growth of new communities in this region during the settlement period. It is only a beginning. Resources limited this study to those women who acquired land through federal legislation related to preemption, homesteading, or timber culture.

Although these procedures were differentiated legally, many of the regulations governing them were similar; and throughout the book, I often have referred to women in all three categories as homesteaders. Unfortunately, those women who purchased land from a former owner, who took charge of a claim held in a man's name, or who were involved in the acquisition of land through some other means could not be included.

My data did not support Beames' contention that "it was the men only who pressed on across the great plains." Getting to know some of the women who helped to settle the plains, a few directly through personal interviews and many others indirectly through friends and relatives, has been a privilege. These women were not the pathetic creatures Webb, Beames, and Thompson described.

Undoubtedly some women had little to say about the direction of their lives, but their circumstance has been taken as commonplace. Most women in my study were actively involved in the decisions that affected them. Although many women endured hardships, the women in my study were active and decisive. These women were visionaries as well as community builders. The same challenges that brought their male counterparts to the "garden of the world"[2] drew the women. A quarter section of virgin land promised independence, freedom, and security.

The information for this volume comes from three major sources: (1) women who homesteaded, (2) friends and relatives of women who homesteaded, and (3) land records. In the fall of 1983, North Dakota State University issued a press release that I was searching for information about women who had filed on claims in their own names. Responses came from many people throughout North Dakota, as well as from people who had moved out of state but whose relatives had homesteaded in North Dakota.

A few of the respondents were homesteaders themselves. I interviewed 15 of these women and corresponded with 4 others. Most of the information, however, came from friends and relatives of women who are no longer living. These respondents completed a questionnaire and sent written accounts, documents, news articles, and pictures. The personal interviews and the information from relatives and friends formed the basis for 306 case study files.

All these women took land in North Dakota, except for Mary Dooley Bartels. Mary homesteaded in South Dakota, but because I was able to interview her personally and because her account was of such detail and similar to the North Dakota experience, I included her in the study.

Information on age, marital status, and ethnicity for this sample does not represent the North Dakota population as a whole. Nevertheless, it does help us to understand who the women were who took land.

I was interested not only in gathering anecdotal material but also in determining what proportion of people who filed on claims were women. For this information, I depended on land records. Where county histories were available, I calculated proportions of early landowners from printed maps. Some individuals who had compiled maps contributed their documents. I used microfilmed land records in the *United States Bureau of Land Management Tract Books* (also called *Federal Land Office Homestead Tract Books*), which are located in the Chester Fritz Library at the University of North Dakota, Grand Forks. These records were useful in determining percentages of women landowners and in verifying the locations and dates of acquisition of the claims of women included in the case study files.

Throughout this volume, material from the personal case study files is quoted extensively. Unless a source is cited, the quotation has been taken from unpublished material in these files. Quotations have been reproduced in their original form. Alternative forms of spelling and grammatical usage have not been altered. Access to these files is possible through the Institute for Regional Studies, North Dakota State University, Fargo.

Many of the women in this study took land as single women and later married. Some of those who were widows remarried after living on their claims. Throughout their lifetimes, many of these women had more than one identity. I have, for the most part, used the name entered on the land records when referring to individual women unless the information was taken from recollections made after marriage. The appendix consits of a list of all the women included in the case study files. Their names are listed alphabetically according to the name which appears on the land records, but subsequent name changes due to changes in marital status also are provided.

Acknowledgments

Through the efforts of many people, this book became a reality. About 325 friends and relatives of women who filed on claims provided me with information. This book is about their grandmothers, mothers, aunts, cousins and friends. Fifteen women who had homesteaded themselves graciously invited me into their homes and shared their adventures; four others corresponded with me. I shall never forget the warm friendship and hospitality that has been extended to me over the past six years.

Others, too, have been generous with their help. William C. Sherman, who first brought to my attention the number of women who filed on claims, has provided continuing support throughout the project. Bill G. Reid suggested funding sources when it became apparent that I could not personally cover the mounting expenses. James Muhn, of the Bureau of Land Management, provided valuable resources and advice for the chapter related to land policies. EunSook Park spent endless hours searching through microfilm records to establish what proportion of homesteaders were women and to verify the claim locations of women in the case study files.

Additional contributions to the collection and interpretation of the data were made by Jeannie Dettmann, Sybil Hopkins, Robert Thompson, Mary Dunlava Tellefson, Laura Mitchell and the Pembina County Pioneer Daughters, Dan Rylance and the staff of the Special Collection Division of the UND Chester Fritz Library, John Bye and the staff of the NDSU Institute for Regional Studies, Michael Miller, Timothy Kloberdanz, and Joy Query. Many county auditors and registers of deeds and their staffs helped to verify the locations of certain claims. Their knowledge of county records is certainly one of North Dakota's important assets.

A special thank you to Kate Ulmer, who steered the manuscript through many revisions without losing a single computer file.

Elizabeth Arnold and the staff of the NDSU Media Center skillfully reproduced the original photographs and prepared them for publication.

I particularly want to thank my sister, Lois Wiederrecht-Finke, and colleague, Charlene Lucken, for reading several drafts of the manuscript and for their thoughtful ideas and suggestions. Comments from the co-editors of the Institute for Regional Studies, David Danbom and Michael Lyons, and Catherine Gjerdingen, copy editor, further refined the manuscript. Designers Mark and Heather Strand combined their remarkable talents to produce the final work.

I am grateful for the support of the College of Humanities and Social Sciences, under the direction of Dean Margriet Lacy and former Dean Archer Jones, the Agricultural Experiment Station, under the direction of Dean Roald Lund, and the Institute for Regional Studies whose financial resources made this project possible.

And finally a thank you to my daughter, Ann, son, Ken, and husband, Jon, who have always encouraged my academic pursuits.

1

They Staked Their Claims

Oh, I was anxious to go. I don't know but I just had a feeling I wanted to get away from my former home and go out in this world. All I had was a desire to go and I did. . . . It was not so easy. I didn't have water on my place. My brother had filed on that homestead but he relinquished it to me. He didn't want to live there. The shack was full of mice. I could hardly sleep the first night. I set traps all the time and I got rid of them.

— Christine Larson Tollefson

"I want to take a homestead so bad," wrote Effie Vivian Smith in a letter to her cousin, Mary Eaton, in Iowa. Effie had come with her father and brother from Iowa to her father's claim near Bowbells, North Dakota, in 1902. In 1905 she filed on her own claim southwest of Bowbells.

Effie was one of a remarkable group of women who took a chance, investing in the future of a portion of the northern plains called Dakota. Who were the women who chose this course of action? Did they come alone? How many of them were there? And what motivated their decisions?

The backgrounds of women who took land varied widely. Most immigrants came from European countries, some by way of Canada. Other women, native born of foreign-born parents, traveled to North Dakota from Minnesota, Iowa, and South Dakota. Some women's parents had arrived in the United States several generations earlier. These women were more likely to have come to the state as small children, and a few were born in North Dakota. Some came from aristocratic families with bountiful resources while others had few financial assets. Whatever their point of origin, ethnic heritage, or material resources, those women who chose a life on the plains embarked on their adventures filled with anticipation and hope.

THE JOURNEY

Once the women decided to take land, they had to establish a residence. For those who already were living and working in the area, the adjustment was minimal— it was a matter of moving a few miles and assuming a life-style similar to what they had been used to. For others, it meant departing from a family home, undergoing tedious travel, enduring severe weather and homesickness for the first time, and acquiring new skills.

As the tracks were laid across North Dakota, the train became an indispensable part of the journey. Some settlers rode most of the way in passenger cars, with their possessions shipped as freight; but it was common for families and friends to rent an entire car, the "immigrant car," as it was called, fill it with their possessions, supplies, and even live animals, climb in and ride as far as the rails would take them, completing the trip by stage, wagon, or buggy or on foot.

The following accounts are several women's recollections of their journeys to their claims and show the variety of reactions these women had to their new homes.

Ada Kelsey homesteaded near Alexander in McKenzie County in 1908. Her sister, Mabel, was to receive $100 for staying to help. Their father, Alex Kelsey, staked out the ground and built their shack. The two women left their home in Granville, 25 miles east of Minot, boarded the Great Northern Railway bound for Williston, where they took the stagecoach to Alexander. "From that point on, whether we were women or still little girls would be decided."

The stage tossed and rocked as it raced over the dusty dirt road. A few miles of that ride found Ada and me stealing glances at each other—each wondering how the other was enduring. As our eyes met we would smile bravely, then look out the window as if we were enjoying the view.

We finally arrived at the banks of the Missouri at Indian Hill. Indian Hill was an important landmark and a good example of the rest of the Badlands—rough, rugged, uncivilized—yet unnaturally beautiful.

There on the riverbank, the infamous Bell's Ferry awaited us. It was a flat raft with side-rails. It was big enough to hold one stagecoach or two buckboards or buggies. It was pulled across the river by pulleys. Riding that ferry was some experience! I never could figure out why the horses didn't panic, because I easily could have.

From there we bounced down the trail into Alexander. One glance at tiny Alexander would have caused one to get right back on the stage and return to Williston, and I didn't doubt we both had thoughts in that direction.

If we didn't have thoughts of giving up at Alexander, I'm sure we did when we transferred our supplies to a buckboard and started toward the homestead. The bumps on that trail were the same as on the stage route, only we were going slower, the more to get full benefit of having no cushion on the seats as we had had in the stagecoach. Deeper and deeper into the Badlands we rode.

. . . we followed the trail to our claim and finally, from Dad's description of the cabin, we knew we had come to the end of our journey.

I'll never forget that cabin as long as I live. It was a one-room shack, eight by ten feet and sided with clapboard.

There was a door in the center and a small window at each
end. The boards of the curved roof were covered with
tarpaper. Dad had dumped a load of coal on the ground to
last us our stay. A few feet away stood a small outhouse
made from scrap boards and covered with burlap.

    For a moment we just sat there in the buckboard and
quietly stared. I think even the horses wanted to go back.[1]

Mary Dunlava Tellefson recalled the time her widowed mother
decided to sell her farm in the Red River Valley and move west, where
she, too, took a homestead in McKenzie County's Alexander area.
Mary states, "Mother had the pioneer spirit having moved from
Pennsylvania to Ohio, then Michigan, Minnesota, and coming to
Dakota Territory where she spent 27 years in Cass County earning a
living from the soil." In 1906, a year after her husband's death, Clara
Fuller Seager Dunlava left Cass County with her children in search of
free land.

    In Williston we engaged a Mr. Anderson, who
was in the livery service, to take us to Alexander. He
drove a two seated spring wagon, it had to be a sturdy
vehicle to stand those river bottom roads. The trees and
brush were still there, so the driver had to guide his
team as best he could but he couldn't possibly miss all
the stumps.

    My first view of Alexander will always remain in
my memory, as we came over the divide that was later
known as Peterson's Hill, I saw Alexander. A trail wound
down the valley with buttes on all sides and that trail led
through what is known as main street today. There were
two or three buildings to be seen, the Dakota Trading
Company's store and the Stone Bank. As we came closer
in we could see the Log Cabin at the spring and a four-
room shack which was Art Maderson's hotel. It was a

desolate sight and as evening settled down we wished we were anywhere but in Alexander. The driver took us to the four-room hotel; a dining room, kitchen and two bedrooms, one for the men and one for the women. Mrs. Maderson was not there when we arrived and two men cooks were in charge. They were having a drunken brawl and were throwing canned tomatoes at each other. The place didn't appeal to we easterners and we started looking about for possibilities of another lodging place, to no avail. There were cowboys riding their bucking broncos up and down the trail through town (main street). When time came to settle down for a nights rest the men's bedroom was taken over by the cooks and the "westerners" who weren't to our liking and so it was that beds were made on the floor in the women's bedroom for the men in our party and our driver. The next day our party, all except the driver and I, went out to look at land. They engaged John Martin, a locator, who would show them the land open for homesteading and arrange for their filing on same.

That fall my mother, sister, and brother Leslie, returned to establish their residence of their homesteads and make the necessary improvements. My brother built my mother's homestead shack which was larger than average, 14 x 20 feet and a story and a half. He then built smaller shacks on his and my sister's homesteads, all three homesteads joining.[2]

Mary Dooley's experience was quite different from that of women who were accompanied by their families. She was teaching school in Iowa when she decided to put her name in a lottery for land in South Dakota. Her brother had talked about getting land in the West, and she was intrigued by the possibilities for herself. At this point, her father was not in the least supportive. He said, "Oh, you are just throwing your money away, Mary." She responded that it was not much money because she could get to Dallas, South Dakota, on the train for $10 to $15 . She took two days off from school and boarded the train. This trip was required to register for the lottery. If her number was selected, she would have a chance for land.

W ednesday evening I was off! . . . I took the train to Des Moines and there at my sisters we called the various depots for travel information. I was to leave from the old East Des Moines Chicago North Western depot at 3:00 A.M.—an ungodly hour. We arranged for a taxi to call for me. . . . I lay down and set my alarm. Driving down in that eerie hour alone in the back seat of the taxi—having heard many tales of Des Moines taxi drivers—was an unforgettable experience.

The train people sold me my ticket to Dallas, South Dakota, but no one seemed to know what route would get me there. . . . I was informed I would have to change trains at St. Paul, Minnesota, so I settled down in my coach seat to sleep the hours away. When the conductor woke me and said, "You have to change trains here at Ames, Iowa" I said sleepily, "No, I'm going to St. Paul!" He said, "You're going to Dallas, South Dakota aren't you?" I acquiesced. So he insisted I must change trains right now. "Oh, me, an eerie cold dark place they put me off and I had to walk what seemed blocks in between tracks to a waiting train. Of course, it turned out to be that good old double track across Iowa North Western road out to Missouri Valley, which I became very familiar with in later years. I covered my face with my newspaper and slept the early morning away. . . .

Trains were crowded and running late these last few days before that drawing ended. And it was nearing midnight before we reached our destination. Coming across Gregory County after dark rumors began to spread. "You shouldn't go on to Dallas, you should get off the train at Gregory, and register there." If you went to Dallas you probably couldn't get anything to eat. It was so crowded

6

there were no accommodations. They even had to haul their water. Rumor said you couldn't get water to wash your face. One enterprising bartender had spring water at 5 cents a glass. . . . Many passengers were convinced these were all true and they left the train at Gregory.

I came on to Dallas, that was supposed to be the head-quarters of the land drawing, so I didn't look for anything too bad, but really those rumors were a little frightening to a perfect stranger as we were. But alighting from the train the bright lights were glaring and the crowds were going busily about as if in day time. My seat mate kindly asked to escort me to my stopping place. I had him pretty well sized up by that time and decided it was alright.

I said, "The first thing I'm going to do is register, if I can, then I'll leave on the train in the morning." . . . There were several notary public offices open where we could register. Then you took your own document, a sealed envelope, up to headquarters and dropped it into the slot yourself. Anyway we did this.

Then I immediately made an effort to find myself a room. The young gentleman politely carrying my suitcase in my search. I asked at so many places for a room, none available, all filled.... I finally ended up in a sort of barracks, a bare boarded up place, filled with cots for ladies. The proprietor was about to turn me away from there, but finally said there had been one empty cot and his wife was tired and she had gone to bed in it. But he went and called her and she got up and gave it to me. The bed was already warmed up for me! The cots, occupied by sleeping women, were so close together you could hardly walk between them and there was much giggling going on among some of the non-sleeping girls. . . . I got very little sleep.

In the morning we stood up on our beds to dress ourselves to keep out of each others way, there wasn't room to stand on the floor. There were similar barracks for the men also we understood.

At daybreak, I boarded the train again for the journey home. People on the train were exchanging addresses and promising to write and tell each other whether they drew a claim number or not. . . . I was back in my school room in Iowa to teach Monday morning after my adventurous weekend to register.

Not long afterward, Mary learned of her success in the drawing. "When I got to the house, my mother, my sister Margaret and my brother Bert all stood looking at me and then looking at each other. *The Des Moines Daily News* which they received that day carried the names of the early winners and 'sure nuff', my name Mary A. Dooley, drew No. 663. Well I was a really surprised gal! This was probably October 23, 1908. The registering closed Oct. 17th. I had registered October 16th. . . . 114 ,679 persons had registered for the 6,000 homesteads."

As did many people, Mary used the services of a locator, who charged a fee for helping homesteaders find suitable land. She made another trip to South Dakota to choose the land and returned to Iowa to finish her school term before settling on her claim. "I had picked a fine 160 acres of gently rolling almost level table land covered with beautiful salt grass hay."

Emma Bublitz traveled by train from Winthrop, Minnesota, to Dickinson, North Dakota. "First I got to Dickinson on Friday by train. And I found out that the stage wouldn't leave until the following Monday. Was I ever homesick! I almost went back." When asked why she did not go back, she responded, "Well, I guess it was coming so far and spending all that money." While she was staying at the hotel, Emma met another young woman.

She was crying. I asked her what was the trouble. She had come out to file on a homestead and was going back home until she had to return to live on the land. She had expected money from her folks for her return ticket to be at the hotel but it wasn't there. I said, 'How much would you need?' 'Eight dollars.' I gave her eight dollars and she went home. She said, 'I'll send the money to you as soon as I get home.' A perfect stranger, you know. I didn't have too much with me, myself. ... She sent it as soon as she got home.

On Monday Emma boarded the stage and began a tiresome, dusty, and bumpy two-day ride. "It was New England the first day by horses. I stayed over night and the next morning I took another stage. The horses were fresh and rested and we got to Stillwater. My brother was out here." Emma worked at the Stillwater Cafe for six months before she moved out to her claim.

Anna Koppergard, along with her sister, Vighild, and cousin, Martha Kjerre, began her journey to North Dakota from a port in Norway. The ship made a brief stop in London and landed some time later in Boston. From there she boarded the train, arriving in Grafton, North Dakota, on June 10, 1907.

My Uncle, Nils Koppergard, was to meet us, but he didn't think we were coming until the eleventh. We didn't know what to do, so we went to a hotel and found some people who spoke Norwegian. They understood we were newcomers and we told them of our plight. One man said he knew there was a fellow in town from that direction, who had hauled in a load of pigs. He left and brought this man back and it was Henry Lee, and what a coincidence that was. Uncle had obtained jobs for all three of us and it was at his farm I was to work. We all got in his lumber wagon and rode the seven miles to their home.[3]

Pearl Robertson's mother ran the newspaper office that published the *Graceville Phenix* in Graceville, Minnesota. Neither Pearl nor her mother had lived on a farm; but in August 1902, they took the

Soo Line Railroad to Kenmare where they hired a horse and buggy and drove over the land until they found a suitable spot for a homestead. Afterward they returned to Graceville to prepare to move. In November, they returned to the claim in a lumber wagon with material to build a shack.

In the summer of 1907, Mary Ann Murray accompanied her son, Paul, who had already filed a claim, to locate a homestead for herself. They rode the train from Minnesota to Dickinson and from there took a 90-mile, two-day trip southward by horse and buggy across country to Rhame. Mary Ann filed on a piece of land close to Paul's and returned home to prepare for the move. In 1908, she leased an immigrant railroad car to haul their belongings to western North Dakota. Her 15-year-old son, Frank, rode along in the car from Foley, Minnesota, to Rhame, a trip that took 10 days instead of the usual seven because of rerouting.

> The car was crowded and stuffy. It contained a wagon, a walking plow, a team of horses, "Doll and Barney," two cats (that turned out to be the original ancestors of the present-day Rhame cat population, other settlers moved in catless), a batch of ducks, seven cows, roughly 25 chickens, china dishes, tools, and lumber and nails for starting a tar paper shack on Paul's quarter. . . . Young Frank arrived at Rhame on March 27, 1908.[4]

The unloading was completed the next day and the items were stored at the Frank Bacon ranch until buildings were erected on Paul's homestead. In May, Mary Ann arrived by train with her daughter, Florence, and son, Allen. "A courageous mother, $40 in a tattered handbag and a determination to carve a living from this new land was all that separated her family from success or failure."[5] In late summer, a sod house was constructed on her quarter section. About a year later MaryAnn's daughter, Olive, who had been attending Normal College at St. Cloud, came out and bought a relinquishment (land given up by another homesteader) next to her mother's claim.

Neighbors' talking about North Dakota land got Clara and Mary Troska and their two cousins, Helen and Christine Sonnek, "interested and excited about this new country and we decided to go at once."

Mary, Helen, Christine and I packed our suitcases. I took my mandolin, Christine took hers and her rifle. The boys paid us our shares of the farm and away we went by train to St. Paul. There we got land seekers tickets (one cent per mile). Many people were headed for Dakota and Montana. On August 20, 1905 we were on our way to Minot....

The trains were packed. Everyone was very friendly and we met people from all over and all talking of the adventure of going to a new country opening up for settling. When we arrived at the west border of Minnesota we met many long trains of immigrants. Many families had all their possessions—cattle, furniture, etc. and lived right in the box cars. There were diners on the passenger trains. Travel was slow because of the long train.

Arriving at Minot many passengers disembarked. We had to walk down the streets to the hotel. The hotel was very large with a big dining room and so crowded we had to stand in line to get a room. After washing up and changing clothes we went to the land office. The man in charge showed us a large plat or map of the land. All the land on the flats was taken so we picked [a site] on the rolling hills. We tried to locate as close together as possible. We had to answer many questions.

When we got to Bowbells the livery man, George Hedwen, took us in a three seated buggy to the locator, Chris Iverson. The locator found the cornerstones. Mary and Helen were real close but Christine and I were about a

11

half mile apart. The soil was wonderful. Some lakes and sloughs—desirable for ranching and farm land. Seven of us were looking for cornerstones. Helen would get out to examine the soil. We were too tired and sleepy to care. Mr. Hedwen was very considerate as we all had some trouble (Minnesota two step and Dakota trots). The alkali water affected everyone, and we would run behind the hay stacks for relief. At least we had a little privacy. After our business was finished, back to Bowbells we went.

There was a great demand for domestic workers. Mrs. Anderson, a widow that Mary knew let us stay at her place for a few days. We bought food and cooked there. We all got work at the hotel, Helen as a cook, Christine and I as waitresses. There was no writing down orders those days— you had to remember everyone's order. With everyone yelling at once I got so confused I started to cry. Men apologized—they were really very kind.

There would be quite a bit of added expense at the end of our stay so the money we earned would come in handy.

Weather sometimes added to the difficulty of getting started. Nancy Smith settled on a western North Dakota homestead about 12 miles from Sentinel Butte in 1904. Her father and a neighbor helped her haul lumber out to the shack site.

They happened to hit a rainy spell so they found hard going. Leaving Sentinal Butte about four o'clock in the morning, they then kept to the top of the hills as much as possible—there was no road to follow, anyway—but even so, it took them 'til sundown to cover the 12 miles to her homestead. The team would pull until they couldn't pull anymore then have to rest.

When they reached the site she had chosen for her house, rain was still pouring down. They couldn't go back to town that night so they sat under their load of lumber. Father tied each horse to the others tail. That way they could eat, but they couldn't run off.

Although the wagon kept the rain off them, to a measure at least, the ground was as wet as any place else, so Nancy tried crawling up on the wagon reach. But that was too hard, so she had to go back to the ground. It was a miserable night, but there was nothing to do but stick it out.

They had only taken lunch for noon with them so they had no supper and no breakfast the next morning. Nevertheless they went ahead and framed up the shack before they went back into town. They stayed in the hotel until the shack was ready for occupancy.[6]

Snow hindered Isabel Peterson as she traveled to her claim. The sun was shining when she, two brothers, and another relative left Epping for Grenora Township; but the Dakota weather changed rapidly, and snow began to fall thick and fast. During the three-day trip they sometimes had to abandon the wagon and travel on foot.

While some women had support and encouragement from their families, it was not always possible for family members to locate on nearby homesteads. Lottie Walker McGrane could never forget her mother, Martha Ann Smith, telling about her first day on the claim.

In the morning the buckboard was packed with provisions and she and her folks set off for the claim winding 14 miles in and around the red scoria buttes. By mid-afternoon they reached the shack, hastily unloaded, her mother hugged her goodby with a promise to be back in two to three weeks. She felt like a little kitten that had been dropped off in a wilderness. The weeks ahead were an eternity. She was homesick for the Minnesota farm, her married sister and all her close friends she had left behind.

13

Andrea Farland's children "cried bitterly and wished they were on their way back to South Dakota." Courtesy Amanda Winkjer.

Eleanor Green filed on her land sight unseen. Courtesy Ruba Paulson.

The feelings of loneliness and isolation from family and old friends were not restricted to adults. Amanda Farland Winkjer recalled how difficult it must have been for her mother, Andrea Farland, when she came as a widow with her young children to homestead near Wildrose. Amanda and her sister, Mabel, sat by the side of the house and cried bitterly, wishing they were on their way back to South Dakota.

It was common practice to locate a homestead and then return "home" to make plans before actually establishing a residence. Some adventuresome souls, however, filed on land sight unseen. Eleanor Green, a single woman 32 years of age, came to North Dakota from Minnesota in 1907. Her daughter, Ruba, remembers her mother's recounting her first glimpse of the land she had taken. "[She] saw a mass of rolling acres of dry, dead grass, and rocks, rocks, and more rocks." Undaunted by this spectacle, Eleanor pressed forward, purchasing a claim shack another woman had vacated after receiving a patent for her land on a claim about a mile away. She had the shack moved to her claim and set up housekeeping with the belongings she had brought with her from Minnesota.

Even if such matters as choosing land were not left to chance, other contingencies befell beginning homesteaders. Margaret McDermott Jennings and her daughter loaded their belongings from the freight car to a wagon and trusted the driver to take them to their claim near South Heart. Toward dark, the driver informed them that he was lost. He managed to find the home of some of his relatives who lived nearby, and there they spent the night. The next day they located the claim only to find the house was not finished as expected but was still being built.

Margaret McDermott Jennings and her daughter at their claim near South Heart.
Courtesy of Mary Irene Berrigan.

Initial encounters with homesteading ranged from the stunned silence or eager anticipation of inexperienced newcomers to the easy transition of young people who had grown up in homesteading families or who were at least familiar with farm or ranch life. But it would be a mistake to judge the adaptation of settlers to the plains by their initial reaction. Even though some expressed dismay at their first encounter, for a variety of reasons they persevered and changed their attitudes as the plains "caught hold" of them. Too often present-day analysts dwell on negative first impressions and assume that all women continued to find the plains a hostile place. In fact, many women, even those who at first expressed disappointment, eventually developed strong bonds to the land. The transition from dismay to allegiance will be discussed in a later chapter. Men were not the only ones to establish bonds to the soil as authors such as Webb and Beames would have us believe.[7]

WHO WERE THEY?

As would be expected, many young, single women were among those establishing claims. Surprisingly, land ownership also appealed to other women: older single women, widows with small children, widows accompanying their grown children, divorced or deserted women, and even a few married women who were consid-

15

ered the heads of their households because their husbands were ill or incapacitated.   In fact, Horace Greeley, well known for imploring young men to go West, did not limit his invitation to men.   "Young men! Poor men! Widows! Resolve to have a home of your own! If you are able to buy and pay for one in the East, very well; if not, make one in the broad and fertile West!"[8]

Anne Furnberg was a widow with a claim near Fargo. She crossed the Sheyenne River by crawling on a log. Courtesy Marvyl Nielson.

Anne Furnberg, a widow, was one of the early settlers in Dakota Territory. She came in 1871 along with some of her Minnesota neighbors who were looking for land. Anne had immigrated from Norway only two years earlier and had married, but her husband died shortly after the birth of their first child. She and her son, Christian, started out from Minnesota in a covered wagon drawn by oxen. Their first home was a log cabin about five miles west of Fargo. Anne had a cow and some chickens and sold butter and eggs in Fargo to make her living. Because there was no bridge across the Sheyenne River, Anne crawled over on a log. In 1875, when she was about 38, Anne took up a claim of 80 acres 5 miles south of Fargo. Her 11-year-old nephew, Ole, cared for Christian and cooked meals while Anne farmed.[9]

Annetta Erickson's shack was a center for gatherings and parties. Courtesy Lila Erickson.

Annetta Erickson was born of Swedish parents in 1879 in Chicago. The family came to the Bismarck area when Annetta was only five years old. She filed on her own claim in 1900 and proved up in 1906. According to a relative, all the young people in the area knew where Annetta's shack was; it became the center for many gatherings and parties. Annetta remained single and eventually returned to live with and care for her parents.

Caroline Gunvaldson left New Prairie, Minnesota, at age 27 to join her brothers and a sister who had preceded her to North Dakota. She took a homestead in Ward County in 1902 and taught school while she proved up. After she married, she and her husband made their home on her land.

Caroline Gunvaldson was 27 when she took a homestead in Ward County in 1902. Courtesy Clara Hall.

Margaret Madson Shaski originally came from England, first settled in South Dakota, and later moved to Montana. After her husband deserted her, she brought her baby daughter, Romaine, to a homestead in the Badlands near the Little Missouri River to start a new life. Margaret was 26 years old when she filed on her claim. In England she had completed a three-year apprenticeship as a seamstress. This training came in handy on the homestead, enabling her to earn extra money sewing for others. She lived on her homestead for almost 11 years.

Margaret Madson Shaski homesteaded and earned extra money as a seamstress. Courtesy Romaine Clouse.

Kari Skredsvig was a widow with seven children. She was advised to put her children in an orphanage, but she kept her family together and ran her homstead in Burke County the remainder of her life. Courtesy Margaret Lien.

In 1900, shortly after being widowed, Kari Skredsvig brought her seven children to North Dakota from Minnesota. Kari was 38

years old, and her children ranged in age from two to 10. A friend had advised her to put the younger children in an orphanage and go "out" to work. Instead, she preferred to keep her family together. Kari's neighbor remembered her as "a hard worker." She washed clothes for others, cleaned and cooked ducks for hunters, cared for the sick, and carried the mail on a Star Route to supplement her income from the land. Her 160-acre homestead in Burke County remained her home for the rest of her life.

Karoline Holen was 64 when she homesteaded in Williams County. Courtesy Mrs. Carl Larsen.

Karoline Holen was 64 years old when she filed on her land in Williams County in 1906. Her husband's death had prompted her to move further west and take a homestead near her two sons and a daughter. She remained on the land for nearly 12 years.

Anna Hensel was 67 when she came to the United States from Bessarabia, South Russia. A year later, she declared her intent to become a citizen and applied for a homestead. She stayed on the homestead for 11 years, making a home for her daughter and son-in-law and their children.

Anna Hensel came from Bessarabia, South Russia, when she was 67. She stayed on her homestead 11 years. Courtesy Loraine Stindt.

Even members of religious orders tried their hands at taking claims. Sisters Mary Stanislaus Rafter and Mary Augustine Enright, American-born members of an Irish foundation of Ursuline nuns, arrived in Grand Forks in 1883. The two took claims on Stump Lake about 60 miles from Grand Forks. Sister Augustine shortly thereafter transferred her title to a Sister Louise.

18

$\rm O$ct. 19, 1883. M. Stanislaus and M. Augustine left Grand Forks to go to their claims on Stump Lake. . . . On Sat. 20 went to their own shanty, walked around the claims and selected the site for the future Mother house of the Order in North Dakota. Spent Saturday night on the claims each in her own shanty.[10]

Age

Table 1 shows the distribution in my case study sample of the ages of the women taking claims. The majority of those claiming land were younger. Just over half (53 percent) were between the ages of 21 and 25, and 17 percent were between 26 and 30. Even though the legal age for filing was 21, 6 percent apparently misrepresented their age and filed before their twenty-first birthday. This was not an uncommon practice. Thirteen percent were 31 to 40 years old with smaller percentages in the older categories.

Valberg Redahlen was 25 when she filed on her claim in Divide County in 1908. Courtesy Alice Schulz.

TABLE 1		
Age of Women Taking Claims		
Age	Percent	Number
under 21	6	16
21-25	53	128
26-30	17	40
31-40	13	32
41-50	4	9
51-60	5	11
over 60	2	5
	100	241*

*Information was not available for all cases.

Marital Status

The marital status of women in the sample is illustrated in Table 2. Most (83 percent) were single, but 15 percent were widows. Only 1 percent had been divorced, separated, or deserted, and 1 percent proved up land their husbands had filed on before their untimely deaths. Unless a married woman was considered the head of the household, she was ineligible to acquire public lands. The regulations regarding the disbursement of public land are discussed in Chapter 2.

Dorothy Russell came from Iowa in 1893 when she was 64 to homestead near her son. Courtesy Raymond Russell.

TABLE 2

Marital Status at Time of Land Entry

Marital Status	Percent	Number
Single	83	239
Widowed	15	42
Divorced or separated	1	4
Married; husband died before proof	1	2
	100	287 *

*Information was not available for all cases.

Ethnicity

The rich heritage of North Dakota derives partly from the diverse national origins of its people. The nationalities of the women in my sample can be found in the appendix. The majority either had Anglo-American or Scandinavian roots, though many other groups are represented. Table 3 shows that 6 percent of the sample immigrated to the United States with their parents, 29 percent came as adults, and 65 percent, or the majority, were native born. Many of those in the native-born category were children of immigrant parents.

TABLE 3		
Women Taking Land Who Immigrated to U.S. as Children or Adults and Those Native Born		
	Percent	Number
Came to U.S. as children	6	16
Came to U.S. as adults	29	77
Native born	65	175
	————	————
*Information was not available for all cases.	100	268*

Julia Moen was born Gunhild Gulbrandsdatter. A teacher suggested the name Julia; her family chose the surname Moen. Courtesy Esther Johnson.

Table 4 gives the point at which the women's migration began. Many moved more than once. For example, some started in Norway and immigrated first to Minnesota and then to North Dakota. In this case, the point of origin would be considered Norway rather than Minnesota. Many of those in the sample immigrated to the United States from Norway. Minnesota was the most common point of origin for those who were native born. Only 8 percent of the women in the sample were born in North Dakota.

Clara Blegen was seven when she came to Churchs Ferry, N.D. with her parents. Courtesy Lola Ruff.

The case study sample is not representative of the state's ethnic population in that Norwegian and Anglo-American groups are overrepresented. Other sources of information indicate that women from most ethnic groups present in Dakota took land there. Land records that list original landowners include the names of women from many different ethnic backgrounds. A recent study of original landowners in 43 North Dakota townships found women from 13 ethnic groups; there were Anglo-Americans, Norwegians, Swedes, Danes, Finns, Hollanders, Icelanders, Germans, German-Hungarians, German-Russians, Bohemians, Poles, and Ukrainians.[11]

TABLE 4			
Place of Origin of Women Who Took Land			
Origin	Percent	Number	
State			
Minnesota	35	92	
North Dakota	8	21	
Iowa	7	19	
South Dakota	3	9	
Wisconsin	3	8	
Illinois	3	7	
Other	7	19	
Country			
Norway	24	65	
Canada	5	13	
Sweden	3	9	
Other	2	6	
	100	268*	

Aase Jorgenson came from Norway with her parents to Minnesota and then to North Dakota. Courtesy Mrs. Carl Larsen.

*Information was not available for all cases.

The research of William C. Sherman provides information on small enclaves of two additional ethnic groups: Lebanese and Jews (Tables 5 and 6).[12] Among the Lebanese, religion may have been an important factor in determining whether women took land. One Christian settlement with 12 homesteaders had no women homesteading.

The Pierce County settlement had 8 percent and Williams County 18 percent. The high percentage found in Williams County is consistent with that of other groups in that county; the average percentage of women taking land in the entire county was 18. In the Moslem settlement in Mountrail County, however, no women homesteaders were among the 71 persons taking land. In Jewish settlements, women accounted for 9 to 16 percent of the homesteaders.

TABLE 5			
Women Who Took Land in Lebanese Settlements			
County	Religion	Percent Women	Number of Women/Number of Settlers
Williams	Christian	18	14/80
Walsh	Christian	0	0/12
Pierce	Christian	8	6/76
Mountrail	Moslem	0	0/71

TABLE 6		
Women Who Took Land in Jewish Settlements		
County	Percent Women	Number of Women/ Number of Settlers
McIntosh	14	12/85
Ramsey	16	15/95
Burleigh	9	7/79
Bowman	14	15/104

Some black women took land in North Dakota. In an extensive study, Tom Newgard reported a number of blacks homesteaded in North Dakota.[13] Among them were at least five women. Georgia Fuller homesteaded in Mountrail County in 1907. Lizzie Reidy took her claim in 1906 north of Alexander in McKenzie County. Three other women, Jennie Bryant Banner, Gertie Johnson, and Sarah Johnson, were members of a group of black land seekers who settled in Moline Township in McKenzie County.

Some women from almost all ethnic groups settling in Dakota apparently took land. Whether their ethnic heritage was a factor that encouraged or discouraged them cannot be determined here.

23

THE LONE ADVENTURER: MYTH OR REALITY?

Anna Enstulen home-steaded near her brothers, Anton and Ole, in McKenzie County. Courtesy Adeline Ley.

Did these women come to their claims to live solitary lives far removed from family and friends? This perception of isolation is a common one reflected in the question, "How did they survive out there all alone?" This question is posed by many who look back from today's vantage point and think about how it must have been around the turn of the century. Although the initial experiences of homesteaders varied considerably, few women or men struck out on such an undertaking literally by themselves. Settlers likely came in pairs or groups with family or friends and settled near one another.   These settlement patterns moderated the isolation of the plains which novelists and poets so graphically describe.

Many of the women in this study had brothers homesteading nearby. Lena Carlson and her brother had adjoining homesteads in Benson County. They shared a team of horses and worked the land with a breaking plow. Anna Enstulen homesteaded near two of her brothers, Anton and Ole, in McKenzie County.

Two, three, and even four sisters often claimed adjoining land. Minnie and Lydia Lavalle settled near Newburg in Bottineau County. "The land they chose was rich and flat, covered with grass that had waved for eons in the brisk prairie winds sweeping down from Canada."[14]

While Eva Popp was eager to homestead in Bowman County, her sister, Ida, was not as enthusiastic. Their mother insisted that they undertake this adventure together, and both saw it through and proved up.

Two Linn sisters, Elise and Lena, filed on claims in McLean County in 1902. A third, Emelia, joined them in 1905; and a fourth,

*Minnie and Lydia Lavalle
settled on land near
Newburg in Bottineau
County. Courtesy
May Shipton Girard.*

*Four of the five Linn sisters took homesteads. Lena, front, left; Emelia, front,
right; Inga back, first from left and Elise back, right. Courtesy Ruth Bernsdorff.*

Inga, followed in 1906. Inga was frail and suffered from tuberculosis; but in spite of her failing health, she bravely undertook the task of homesteading.   Unfortunately, her health continued to deteriorate, and she died before proving up. Resources indicate that only the women of the Linn family were interested in homesteading. Apparently none of their brothers took claims.

Parents and children often combined homesteading efforts. Some adult children accompanied their parents to North Dakota, the parents' taking one claim and the children's finding claims as close as possible. Sometimes a young woman would come with her father, and the rest of the family would join them later. Lena Norby's parents homesteaded just across the section line from her own property; her three brothers had claims in the immediate vicinity. Through homesteading, older widows could provide a home for themselves and still be close to their grown children who were also homesteaders.

Thora Sanda's brother, Knute, was the first to come from Norway to Northwood, North Dakota. Later he invited Thora and their mother to follow.
Courtesy Helga Norgard Anderson.

Table 7 shows the extent to which homesteading was likely a family affair. Of the women in my study, 74 percent took land near an immediate family member. If more distant relatives such as uncles and cousins are included, 81 percent had family nearby. Only 4 percent already had marriage plans and settled on land conveniently close to their future husbands.

26

Anna, Emma, and Thina Thingvold (Laura, far right, did not home-stead) and five of their six brothers came from Norwegian Grove, Minnesota, to homestead in North Dakota. Courtesy Norma Good.

TABLE 7

Women Who Took Land Alone or Near Relatives or Friends

Claim Located Near	Percent	Number
Father, mother, sister, brother, adult children	74	146
Other relatives	7	14
Husband-to-be	4	8
Friends	8	16
Came alone	7	14
	100	198*

*Information was not available for all cases.

Friends also played an important role. If family members could not be counted on, a friend might be persuaded to join the adventure. In many cases, friends and family members took part in the effort and settled in the same area. Gelina and Julia Lyngen joined a group of 12 young people who came from Watson, Minnesota, and homesteaded in Adams County. Others came in smaller groups. Marie Holen and three of her friends homesteaded in Williams

Karen Olsen Storberget, a widow, seated at lower left, and her three daughters, Bertha, upper left; Maren, upper right; and Karen, lower right, all homesteaded near each other in Grainfield Township in Towner County. Courtesy Edmond Strand.

Gelina Lyngen and her sister, Julia , were part of a group of 12 young people who came from Watson, Minnesota, to homestead in Adams County. Gelina is shown here on the left with her sister-in-law, Annie Hilden Stolee. Courtesy Helen Hilden Cusher.

County. The four women jointly owned a cow. Marie's mother and brothers were about 20 miles away. Hattie Jones came to North Dakota from Nebraska with her best friend, Marie Dunn. They homesteaded adjoining quarter sections. Other friends were located four or five miles away.

A few women, about 7 percent of those in this study, fit the definition of the lone adventurer. With little support from family or friends, these women had to establish a support network with neighbors soon after they arrived on their claims.

Hattie Jones was 21 when she came with her best friend from Nebraska to North Dakota. Courtesy Edna Thoreson.

Both Kirsten Knudsen and Eliza Crawford had only themselves to depend on. Kirsten left Norway with two other young women but came to North Dakota alone. She did not know anyone in the United States nor could she speak English, but she carried a letter of introduction to an attorney from someone who was a mutual friend.

Eliza, while living in Cooperstown, North Dakota, was called upon to nurse a Mr. Wilson, who planned to open a land office in Dickinson for people seeking claims. He persuaded her to take a claim in a part of what is now Adams County. She left Cooperstown with her young son, leaving behind an eight-year-old daughter to finish

Top: Anna Kringen, right, is seated in front of her shack with her homesteading friend, Augusta Halvorsen. Courtesy Anna Sanda.

Bottom: Ada Asch came alone from South Dakota, but she could get advice from a relative who lived nearby. Courtesy Clement Rush.

school. Eliza apparently knew no one besides Mr. Wilson. In her diary she relates an incident that occurred while she was waiting to make her land entry in the local office.

> That day I sat in Mr. Wilson's land office—and it was full and we were obliged to take our turn. It rained hard all day. No one seemed to wear rubbers and every one's shoes were wet and muddy. Finally in came a man with patent leather shoes on (they were stylish then) and as clean and shiny, as tho there was no mud. He sat down beside me. We were almost the last ones to be called, for the room was getting empty. . . .
> After I had been home quite a while, I received a letter, one day, from a strange place, one entirely new to me. I hurriedly opened to see whom it could be from. I read these words: "I am the man with the shiny patent leathers." It made me laugh. Then he went on to say that his wife was nearly crying her eyes out because she had to go out on a claim: "There will be no one but men there," she said. He told her that he had met a very nice lady (ha! ha!) in Dickinson and she had filed on a claim so close to theirs that we could be neighbors.[15]

Eliza did become a very good friend of her neighbors, Mr. and Mrs. Mike Nevelle.

❦

Although the experiences of Kirsten and Eliza show that the lone adventurer did exist and could be successful, these women were the exceptions. The majority of those who came, women and men, were part of a supportive network of relatives and friends.

WHY DID THEY TAKE LAND?

We know that women took land. What prompted their decisions to do so? In general, the climate of the times was favorable.
Dakota Territory was being portrayed as an exciting place with a
bright future. The railroads were particularly zealous in their attempts to increase business and, accordingly, published a variety of
ads and pamphlets designed to encourage both women and men to
initiate settlements. Other commercial interests stood to gain from an
influx of population as well, and enthusiastic reports were presented
in the national press. Columns in local papers targeted young women
as appropriate candidates for taking land. In 1883, the *Sunday Argus*
(Fargo) reprinted an article from the *Pierre Journal* that outlined what
young women might expect:

A few years ago a well known hotel man of this
city brought to Dakota six girls from Iowa. They were all
engaged in his dining room, but inside of one year all had
"proved up" on valuable "claims," and were presiding over
their own households. It must not be taken for granted that the
men who are opening up this great territory and building cities
are rough and uncultured and do not appreciate a good and
true woman. The men of Dakota are from all portions of the
United States, and for manliness, intellect and business enterprise, are without a peer. They have come out it is true to bear
the hardships and toils incident to frontier life, but this has only
increased their admiration for the girl who comes to the frontier, and is willing to undergo the discomforts of a western
town. . . .
A few miles from Pierre a number of young ladies from
Indianapolis have filed on land and boys are seeing to it that the
requisite number of acres are plowed, and assisting in many
ways to make their life in the little shack enjoyable. Girls, come

to Dakota, and we will vouch for it that in a few years, you will not regret having made the change.[16]

In one sense, this article implies that if women will just come to the territory, the men who are opening up, building, and developing the land will take care of them. At the same time, it suggests opportunities for women on the frontier.

Residents who already had settled in the territory made appeals not directly associated with commercial interests. Linda Slaughter, wife of a military surgeon, was a well-known advocate for Dakota Territory. Her lively stories of frontier life, published in several Eastern journals, may have inspired many to come West.[17]

The climate is eminently healthful, the atmosphere being clear, bracing and singularly free from moisture. No diseases occur that can be fairly charged to locality. . . .

The soil is a rich, black loam about eighteen inches deep with an indurated clay subsoil from eleven inches to three feet deep and under that about seven feet of gravel forming a soil not easily affected by drought or continuous rains, and excellently adapted to farming purposes.

The farms which have been opened in the vicinity of Bismarck have proven highly productive, the soil being kept moist by frequent rains. Vegetables of all kinds are grown with but little trouble. . . .

Water is abundant and of the purest quality, the wells which have been dug yielding an apparently inexhaustible supply. . . .

The water of the Missouri river is quite turbid particularly in the spring, but when allowed to settle, it becomes quite clear and pleasant to drink. . . .

The forest growth is not extensive and the open plains are destitute to great extent of the nobler forms of vegetation. Between Fargo and Bismarck, two hundred miles, there is no timber except that skirting the rivers. . . .

At Burnt Creek are groves of the Wild Plumb, the fruit of which is delicious, being juicy and well flavored. . . .

Coal is in great abundance, and of good quality if found on the Missouri River. . . .

Elk, Black-tailed Deer, Long-tailed Deer and Mule Deer, Antelope, Black and Cinnamon Bear, Beaver, Otter, Wildcat, Panther . . . are the animals native to this region.[18]

While the glowing reports from writers and the information sent out by the railroads, land companies, and other commercial interests may have enticed some individuals to venture to Dakota Territory, the impact of letters and personal contacts

Emma Beske expressed a love of adventure. Courtesy Catherine Haugen.

among relatives and friends should not be underestimated. Undoubtedly, a letter from a brother or sister or good friend could be quite convincing.

As women contemplated taking a claim, a number of factors must have entered into their final decision. Why did they find themselves caught up in the rush for land? Emma Beske expressed a love of adventure, and it was surely this that beckoned some toward new horizons. Anna Chermak came with friends from Minneapolis seeking a new lifestyle. Pauline Shoemaker remarked, "I've done everything else I might as well try homesteading."

Anna Chermak came from Minneapolis in search of a new lifestyle.
Courtesy Ruth Hinkley.

Lucy Goldthorpe described how she envisioned herself to be part of a great historical event as she prepared to leave her home in Iowa and take a homestead near what was soon to become the town of Epping: "Even if you hadn't inherited a bit of restlessness and a pioneering spirit from your ancestors it would have been difficult to ward off the excitement of the boom which, like the atmosphere, involved every conversation. Here was probably one of the last opportunities to become a part of the development and growth of this great country."[19]

Cora Barnfather told how she got caught up in the excitement of it all. "A lot of land was just opened up and Williston had just gotten a land office and everyone was doing it and I had just come 21 years old." After proving up, she left the homestead and began teaching in Williston, but she still had title to the land when I corresponded with her in 1985.

Hulda Krueger's decision to homestead was a bit of a lark, an adventure to be relished. She referred to her acquisition of land as "a stroke of luck.... I did it to see if I could win something, I think." When reservation land was opened up for homesteading, Hulda and five of her friends registered in Plaza. "I was the only one who got a lucky number on the land." She soon bought a second quarter-section and rented both to neighbors. The land was still in her name when I interviewed her in 1987. She proudly stated, "I still own the land. I never borrowed a cent against it in my life."

Given the incomplete nature of anecdotal accounts, it is impossible to determine all the factors that may have influenced individual women to take land. Almost half of the case study files provided some specific factors. Although adventure was an important element, it was evident that a number of women based their decisions on more practical grounds.

First and foremost, these women expected a financial return on their investments. For some, the claim became a permanent home, thus fulfilling the spirit of the Homestead Act of 1862, which Congress had enacted to provide land and consequently subsistence to those of little means. For others, probably the majority, the land represented a speculative venture. Once title had been acquired, the claim became an asset to be sold at the market price or traded for something of equal value.

Some women expected quick profits, but others saw the venture as a long-term investment of time and energy with more modest returns. Some women actively sought land while others simply happened to be in the right place at the right time. Encouragement from relatives, particularly fathers and brothers, and friends had a major impact on the decision of many women to homestead.

Louise Karlson expected a financial return on her investment. Courtesy Merv and Doreen Wike.

Kirsten Knudsen ventured forth from Norway planning to make a fortune in America and then return home. Instead she married after proving up and remained in Mountrail County, living on her homestead for almost 13 years.

To Louise Karlson, homesteading sounded like a good investment. "When in 1908 I heard about the homestead land one could get for free—just live there part of the time and work out the rest of the time, I thought, 'here is my chance.' Some of my girl friends told me

36

one could sell a homestead and get as much as $2,000 and that sounded like what I was looking for."[20]

Isabel Peterson felt homesteading would be more profitable for her than hat making. Her sister, Sophia, also was interested in such an investment. In 1903, Sophia wrote to a third sister, Ida, to convince her to homestead in North Dakota rather than seek employment in the state of Washington. Ida had wanted Sophia to accompany her to Washington. All three sisters proved up claims in Williams County.

Isabel Peterson felt homesteading would be more profitable than hat making. Courtesy Harriet Graupe.

I think you would do wiser to stay here and go up North Dak. and locate land and work a little . . . and after some years sell it and then make a call on Washington. So I will not be going now and you will have to decide for yourself whether you want to go or not. . . . if you did not go out there we could go up N. D. thords [sic] fall and earn each 2 dollars a day. Cook together in cooking car. . . . Pete [brother] cooked alone for three weeks and had $3.25 a day. They gave $4 if they baked the bread but he could not do that so they hired a woman near by to do it. Now that would be $44 a month for each of us but do as you wish.

Cecil Nickelson and her older sister, Susie, were good cooks. They cooked in restaurants at Lake Metigoshe and in Bottineau, but during the fall they usually worked in the cook cars, preparing meals

Cecil Nickelson at her claim with a young boy sent to keep her company for a week or two, 1908. She heard about land in McKenzie County while working in a cook car. Courtesy Maxine Carley.

37

for men who were harvesting grain. It was on one of these runs that they happened to hear about land available in McKenzie County. "They were thrifty, had saved their money and were looking for a chance to own some land. With the encouragement from a brother-in-law and some friends they decided to try it."

Katie Gramling considered herself fortunate to get a homestead in Burleigh County. It took persistence to find one, and she was disappointed on her first attempt. "I wanted to homestead but I couldn't find one. I had heard about 80 acres. . . . Somebody told me I could have it if I filed on it. So I went down there. It was quite a ways." Unfortunately, one of her relatives mentioned to a neighbor that Katie was going to file the next morning. That night, the neighbor left for the land office and filed on the land himself before Katie could. Finally Katie found someone willing to relinquish his claim. "All I had to do was go ahead and do it and there was $250 to pay and I could move right in. Father thought that was cheap so he loaned me the money." Katie rented her land to neighbors. She made her home on the claim, teaching during the years that she proved up.

Nora Pfundheller told why she homesteaded: "Well I was 21 and had no prospects of doing anything. The land was there, so I took it." Her parents' claim was five miles away and closer to the school where she taught, so she lived in their home during the week, residing in her own shack only on the weekends.

Nora Pfundheller: "Well I was 21 and had no prospects of doing anything. The land was there so I took it." Courtesy Nora Pfundheller King Lenartz.

Christine Larson filed on a piece of land her brother relinquished to her because he did not want to live there anymore. She was ready to leave home and try something new. The land was about 300 miles from her family.

A visit to relatives living in North Dakota led some women to stay and take a homestead. Sara Isaacson had not considered homesteading when she accompanied her mother on a trip from their home in Wisconsin to McKenzie County to visit two of Sara's sisters. During the visit, she learned teaching salaries were higher in North Dakota than in Wisconsin. A teaching position was open, and Sara could draw a teaching salary, acquire property, and rent the land to her brother-in-law, all at the same time.

No, I didn't come out to homestead at all. My two sisters came out here and homesteaded. And one of them got married here and my Mom and I came out to visit her. And we came out here and we found out that you could get a 9 month term [teaching] at $45 a month and back in Wisconsin, there was only 8 months at $35 a month and down in Bismarck they were willing to transfer my diploma. So I got it transferred for a school year and rode horse-back to school. . . . And that's why I took up the homestead to help out my brother-in-law and his brother. . . . My home-stead was in a Z shape. This way forties would be isolated and no one would file on forty acres. Then the ranchers would buy these isolated forties. They were put up for auction but I can't recall anyone bidding against them [the ranchers].

☙

Hilda Paulson and her sister were enroute to Oregon when they stopped in western North Dakota near Cartwright to visit an uncle, who persuaded Hilda to take a claim.

Me and my sister took a notion we would come out here to visit Uncle. We were really on the way to Oregon. We just wanted to get out. Move away from Grafton, that's all. But we got stuck here. . . . I wasn't gonna have it, ya know, but he had that piece of land and he said I should have it. Well, he says its one easy way to make a few pennies if you need it. . . . And I needed the money so I thought

39

if I proved it up I'd have a little money. . . . I thought, well, I'd just take and file on a homestead and if I liked it I'd stay there. I didn't look forward to the future at all, I just looked forward to proving up.

Hilda Paulson (both photos) and her sister were enroute to Oregon when an uncle persuaded her to take a claim in western North Dakota near Cartwright. Courtesy Hilda Paulson Oakland.

Emma Bublitz was not at all interested in homesteading, but she had a brother who persuaded her to come to Slope County and take a piece of land near him. "I had no intention of coming out here. He kept writing to me all fall. He said that there was a homestead I could get that joined his, if I wanted to come out." Her mother encouraged Emma to take up her brother's invitation. "And Mother was in favor of it but Dad didn't like to see me go so far. Mother came out to visit me after I got settled. She kind of liked it, the prairies, and hearing the coyotes, and all, at night."

Their brothers persuaded Gertrude Sheidamantel and Hannah Hylden to homestead. Gertrude's brother died suddenly after living on his claim about two years. She carried on alone, proving up after about six years.

Mary Lien's opportunity came as a result of another's failure. Her two brothers came with a friend to Walsh County from Wisconsin.

40

The friend later decided to return to Wisconsin, telling the brothers to let someone they would like for a neighbor know about the available land. The brothers asked Mary to come.

Gertrude Sheidamantel came to homestead near her brother, but he soon died; and she proved up after his death. Courtesy Gertrude Sheidamantel Wenck.

Hannah Hylden: "When my brother came home for the holidays he wanted me to go out to Williston and file on a quarter." Courtesy Melvin H. Anderson.

Mary Dooley's brother influenced her decision to take a claim in South Dakota. "Sitting around the porch of our big old Iowa farm home in the dusk of the midsummer evening in 1908, the family listened to my big brother George tell of his plans to come out west to register for a claim. . . . He said to me, 'Mary, why don't you register?'. . . after George left his words kept coming back to me."

A married sister already living in North Dakota persuaded Clara Cumming to file on land in Ward County. Later another sister, Mary, joined Clara and homesteaded next to her quarter section.

Anna Koppergard's uncle, who was already in North Dakota, persuaded Anna and a cousin, Martha, to come from Norway to homestead. "He thought it would be better than Norway. I was kind of anxious to see how it was here."

41

An uncle persuaded Thea Thompson to file because she was the only child in the family old enough to qualify. "My uncle was out there and there was a relinquishment. Claims were mostly taken up around there when I got there but then there was this relinquishment and he told me about it and I was just old enough to claim it. Otherwise it would have been my brother going, you know.... I stayed there just long enough to prove up."

Relatives were not always encouraging. A brother persuaded Anna Stenehjem to file on a quarter section near Arnegard; but, she remarked, "Some of my family and friends thought it was ridiculous."

Although immediate family members had the greatest impact on decisions, some women were influenced by other relatives. It was a distant relative, Josie Danielson, who encouraged Betsy Aslakson to file in Williams County.

Friends provided important information and were often supportive. Pearl Robertson talked with Mrs. Dalrymple, who had homesteaded years earlier in the Red River Valley. She was impressed with the opportunities and convinced her mother that they should both go to Renville County to homestead.

An unlikely acquaintance suggested that Thora Johanson take a homestead. Thora knew the wife of the Divide County State's attorney in Crosby. The State's attorney mentioned to his wife that land was available near Thora's mother and asked if she thought Thora would be interested. His wife suggested that he call Thora who responded positively, "Sure, I said, why not, because it was close to my mothers, just a mile . . . so he made out the papers."

Many children over the age of 21 homesteaded alongside their parents. Resources could be shared, making the venture more economical for all. Mr. and Mrs. Pat Sheridan brought their family from Dexter, Minnesota. They and five of their eight children, including three daughters, Nell, Mae, and Margaret, all filed on claims in Renville County November 29, 1901.

Luella Rodenbaugh and her father came to Logan County from South Dakota. She cooked for the men who were hired to build a house for her parents and shacks for her, her sister, and her brother. "Well, as soon as school was out, my Dad and I came up. He had the

Nell Sheridan   Margaret Sheridan   Mae Sheridan

For the Sheridans, homesteading was a family affair. The parents, two sons and three daughters all filed claims in Renville County. Courtesy Sheridan Hopkins.

carpenters build the house, a two-story frame house with a big window in front. . . . I did the cooking for all those men and when somebody would run short of something when they were working, I had to drive to Napoleon to get the supplies."

In some cases, children took land to provide a home for their parents. Ruth Abbott and her brother filed on homesteads to provide a fresh start for their family, who had suffered hard times in Larimore.

Some women homesteaded at the request of their parents. Flora Whittemore was not excited about this prospect, but she felt compelled to follow the suggestion. "At the time I worked at Donaldson's [Department store in Minneapolis]. . . . I was an apprentice in a big shop. That's where I got my training. I was quite unhappy that they wanted me to come home and file on land."

Luella Rodenbaugh cooked while a crew built shacks in Logan County for her, her sister and brother and a house for her parents. Courtesy Luella Rodenbaugh LeBarron.

Flora's parents wanted her claim to provide them with a home. They had already acted on their right to a homestead in Minnesota and therefore could not obtain another homestead themselves. Flora complied with their wishes, even though she hated to leave Minneapolis. When asked why she did not return to the city, she replied, "I was too busy after I got out on my claim. There were too many things to worry about and too many things to do."

43

Cora Newnam, right, with her parents, Mr. and Mrs. Frances Newnam.
Courtesy Susie Ella Lindley Newnam.

Ruth Abbott and her brother filed on homesteads to provide a fresh start for their parents. Courtesy Philip Haug.

Hattie McCombs homesteaded to gain more land for her father. After she received the patent, she deeded the land to him. Maria McElwain's father farmed her acres, though she later sold the land to someone else. Lizzie Larson's father promised her $250 if she would homestead a quarter section next to her brothers.

Anna Jensen's father picked out land for her adjoining his. "There was another man that wanted it but he said that as long as just a young girl wanted it, why he would let it go." Her father took care of the land, and she sold it to him not long after she had proved up.

Some women decided to homestead after they arrived in North Dakota to help relatives with domestic work. Sarah Knutson, Lillie Tysver, and Olga Trygstad all came to North Dakota to keep house for their brothers. Nora Johnson's brother asked her to help care for his children because his wife was ill. When the opportunity came to homestead, all of these women took advantage of it.

44

Nora Johnson came to North Dakota to care for her brother's children. Courtesy Gillferd Rust.

Fannie Overstreet had three brothers in North Dakota when she came from Indiana. Later her parents, two more brothers and a sister came , too. Courtesy Pat Henry.

Olga Trygstad and her brother, Julius. Olga came to North Dakota to keep house for two brothers. Courtesy Helen Hauge Jouhnson.

45

Marie Jensen Burns' return to North Dakota resulted from a complicated series of events. She had come to the state originally as a child. An uncle who had homesteaded near Abercrombie had returned to Norway to bring about 50 relatives, including Marie and her family, back with him. As a young woman, Marie went south to be with a sister. While there, she married and had a son, but then tragedy struck. A doctor attending to her baby treated the boy's eyes with a medication that resulted in his blindness. Marie's husband refused to pay the bill, and, in a confrontation, the doctor shot and killed him.

Widowhood forced Marie to take a job demonstrating flour, which required extensive travel through Alabama and Georgia. Under those conditions, she could not take care of her son. Her sister assumed responsibility for the child and later refused to give him up. Marie returned to North Dakota to help her aging mother and her sister and brother-in-law who encouraged her to file on a piece of land that was good for grazing and had a coal mine on it.

Young widows, in particular, were forced to think of the practical side of homesteading. These women had to provide a home for their children. In response to the query, "Why did she homestead?" one grandson responded, "Well to tell you the truth, she was expected to take care of herself and her children. The relatives of her husband were probably glad to have her off their hands."

Kari Skredsvig, who brought her seven young children to North Dakota, had to provide for her family. Margaret Madsen Fjelde homesteaded with three daughters and a young son. Nellie Oslund Lauzon decided to homestead after her husband was killed by a team of horses. She came to North Dakota as a seamstress but ended up filing on a claim as well.

Mr. and Mrs. George Funston encouraged their friend, Carrie Johnson, a widow with two young children, to file near them. They needed the 80 acres adjoining their place for pasture, and they wanted Carrie to take the land because her children were about the same age as theirs and could be playmates for them. Carrie undoubtedly saw this as an opportunity to provide for her children as well as to be close to her friends.

Tyra Mattson Schanche became a widow quite suddenly. She was born in Sweden. Her parents were a part of the Swedish military aristocracy. Tyra met and fell in love with Henrik Schanche, a Norwegian medical student. After their marriage, the couple immigrated to North Dakota on the advice of Dr. Tronnes of St. Luke's Hospital in Fargo. The two men had been students together at the University of Oslo. Tyra and Henrik had three daughters during the time he practiced in Portland, North Dakota. Then he moved his practice to the Minot area where tragedy struck. Henrik contracted spinal meningitis from a patient and died within five days, leaving Tyra with three young children, Bergloit, age 5, Herdis, age 4, and Vera, age 3.

While the Schanche family lived in Portland, Randi Garmann immigrated to North Dakota from Norway to work as Dr. Schanche's nurse. Dr. Schanche was convinced that Norwegian nurses' training was the best available, and he wanted an assistant with such a background. Randi grew up in Bergen and was trained in Norway as an international nurse. She could speak German, French, English, and Norwegian.

With the death of Dr. Schanche, Randi was without an employer and Tyra without a husband. Neither woman had relatives in the United States. When a friend in Minot encouraged Tyra to file on a homestead claim, she and Randi decided to make it a cooperative venture. Their claims were adjacent, and the shacks were built close together.

Homesteading offered a young widow a second chance and an opportunity to control her own destiny. The older widow could have a home, often with the bonus of its proximity to her grown children. Caroline May, whose married daughter was homesteading in Dunn County, made a home for herself on land nearby with the help of her adult son.

A few women began the homesteading venture with their husbands, but the husbands died. Many of these women continued to homestead and received the patent for the land in their own names. Hanna Amanda Boesen Anderson took over the homestead when her husband died of tuberculosis, and Clara Rowe took charge after her

*Karoline Holen
decided to venture
west from
Minnesota after her
husband died.
Courtesy
Mrs. Carl D. Larsen*

*The death of Henrik Schanche left his wife and three small children without support.
Tyra (left) joined her efforts with Henrich's nurse, Randi Garmann, and the two took
adjoining homesteads in Williams County. Courtesy Bergliot Schanche.*

husband drowned while attempting to cross the James River.

In only five of the case studies could it be determined that the woman was planning to homestead as a joint venture with a future husband. Each of these women married shortly after filing on her land; she received title to the homestead in her own name, even though she was married. By scheduling the marriage after she had filed on land, a woman could retain the right to homestead property if her husband was not proving up at the same time. After 1914, both could prove up simultaneously if they had already lived on their separate claims for one year.

Annie Koehmstedt married a few months after filing on her land in Cavalier County. Mary Belle Hanson entered her claim in Benson County January 11 and was married on January 23, 1897.

The fact that there were so few of these cases casts doubt on the popular notion that many women filed on their land just before marriage to expand the couple's landholdings. While this was the motivation for a few women who took land, it was much more common to decide to marry after deciding to take land.

Although health was not mentioned often as a reason for homesteading, it did influence some decisions. Anna Erickson, frail after a bout with scarlet fever and diphtheria, mentioned being impressed by the invigorating air of the prairies.[21] Addie Lindsley developed health problems while living in Jackson, Minnesota, and the doctor recommended a change of climate and outdoor living.[22] Anna Aaberg Jacobson's young daughter was ailing, so Anna decided to take both her children to visit her parents in North Dakota. She loved the plains and, at the suggestion of her father, decided to file on a claim.

Some women took claims to escape abusive situations; however, information in this area is scarce and difficult to substantiate. Relatives with whom I talked concerning this issue could only speculate that abuse was a factor in the decision to homestead.

Of the many possible reasons why women took claims, the primary one clearly was economic. Land ownership offered an investment that might provide financial gain as well as security. Some used the original quarter section as the nucleus of a larger enterprise.

The majority who proved up, however, sold their land to those remaining and invested elsewhere.

For many women, sheer adventure was an additional incentive. This was particularly true for young, single women, but no one regardless of age or marital status was immune from the excitement and challenge of seeking land.

The decision to take land often was made at the urging and encouragement of family and friends. Fathers, brothers, and uncles were the most likely to give such advice, but mothers, sisters, aunts, and other relatives were sometimes influential. Some families undertook settlement as a unit, with parents and siblings who were of age all claiming land in the same area. Others came in pairs or smaller groups, and a few braved the venture alone. Young widows with dependent children looked to a claim as a chance to be self-sufficient and to provide for their children. Older widows could homestead alongside their grown children, contributing to the family enterprise yet maintaining their own homes. A few women took land in response to a parental request; but even in these cases, the agreement usually included some financial gain for the women.

Health considerations were mentioned occasionally, and escape from abusive situations probably motivated some to take claims.

Little evidence supports the notion that women homesteaded to gain property that would make them more desirable marriage partners. While a woman was undoubedly aware that owning land made her a "desirable catch," her own motivation more likely was financial gain rather than matrimony.

In reviewing the reasons and circumstances that influenced women to take land, one has to be impressed by the initiative required to undertake such a venture and the practical approach with which the women carried out their plans.

HOW MANY WERE THERE?

Ruth Abbott. Annie Koehmstedt. Ella Reetz. Mary Anderson. Hester Lewis. Susan Ficker. Hildur Erickson. Anna Mathilda Berg. Mayme Sisco. These names and others, handwritten on the pages of the Federal Land Register, stand as a testimony to the individual women who took up the challenge and filed on claims in North Dakota. Names of such women appear on the land lists of nearly every township in the state. But the question still remains, "Just how many were there?" Did only a few women, or "girl homesteaders" as they were called then, fulfill these aspirations? How common was it to find a woman in charge of a claim? My data would indicate that in the area that is now North Dakota, thousands of women took land.

Since anecdotal material cannot provide this type of information, maps and land records were used to determine what percentage of claimants were women.[23] The nine counties selected for the sample included some that were settled before 1900 and others settled after 1900. The state's major ethnic groups were represented in these counties.

Hildur Erickson's name was one of the thousands of handwritten names in The Federal Land Register. Courtesy Jean Trueblood Bye.

Because of the nature of the available sources of information, the percentages calculated for women taking land should be considered approximate rather than exact figures. Some of the landowners listed on maps in county histories may have purchased their land from original homesteaders or other entities. A few names could not be classified as male or female; it is possible a few were misclassified. In spite of these drawbacks, the sources used were the best available, and the final figures should be reasonably accurate.

Table 8 shows for each of the nine counties the percentages of claimants who were women, the major ethnic groups represented, and the approximate time major settlement took place. Percentages of women filing for land range from a low of 6 percent in Pembina County to a high of 20 percent in McKenzie. The average for the nine counties was 12 percent. Counties on the eastern side of the state, which were settled very early, had the lowest percentages of women taking land, while those in the northwestern part of the state, settled primarily after 1900, had the highest percentages.

TABLE 8			
Percentage of Claimants Who Were Women in Selected Counties			
County	Predominant ethnic groups[a]	Approximate time of settlement	Percent women
Burke	Norwegian Swede Dane	After 1900	14
Foster	German Norwegian Anglo-American	1880s-1890s	11
Grand Forks	Norwegian Anglo-American	1880s	8
Kidder	German Norwegian Anglo-American	1880s-1890s	10
McIntosh	German-Russian	1880s-1890s	8
McKenzie (28 of 89 townships)	Norwegian Anglo-American	After 1900	20
Pembina	Anglo-American (Canada)	1870s-1880s	6
Sheridan	German-Russian	After 1900	11
Williams	Norwegian	After 1900	18

[a] There were many other ethnic groups represented in these counties

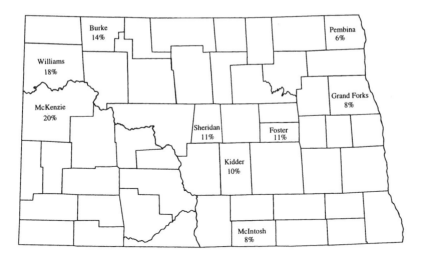

Percentage of women who took land in selected North Dakota counties.

Map of North Dakota indicating percentage of women who took land in selected counties.

If townships are considered individually, the range of percentages is somewhat wider but still consistent. Of the 300 townships included in the counties studied, only two could be found in which no women took land; only five had percentages of 30 or more (30, 30, 31, 32, 32).

These figures for North Dakota are similar to figures for other areas. Records from land offices in Lamar, Colorado, and Douglas, Wyoming, show that an average of 11.9 percent of the homestead entrants were women. Here, too, the time of settlement was an important factor: percentages range from 4.8 in Douglas in 1891 to 18.2 in Lamar in 1907. In Logan County and Washington County, Colorado, percentages were 12 and 10, respectively, before 1900 and nearly 18 after 1900.[24]

It is interesting to note that Emma Haddock in 1886 reported the proportion of women taking government ment lands in the "West" to be about 5 percent,[25] a figure comparable to the 6 percent that was found for Pembina County, which was settled at about the same time.

Although counties that were settled early tended to have low percentages, individual townships sometimes deviated from the expected pattern. In Lovell Township in Dickey County, 16 percent of the homesteaders were women, a high percentage for an area settled in the early 1880s. These women, all of Anglo-American heritage, did not come together as a group. They migrated from a number of different points of origin.[26]

Ingrid Kapseng came from Norway to North Dakota in 1893 with her brother, Knute. She and Knute broke much of the sod on their homesteads and built the shack on the section line, half on her land and half on his. Courtesy George Dybing.

The reasons for the consistent increase in numbers of women taking land in the later settlement period were undoubtedly many and complex, but both demographics and changing attitudes toward the roles of women must have been important influences.

Changes in migration patterns meant increasing numbers of women were coming to the plains. The proportion of women to men continued to increase throughout the settlement period. The demand for schoolteachers, housekeepers, cooks, and women in other acceptable female occupations grew, opening up opportunities for employment. These occupations could be pursued simultaneously with the taking of a claim.

During this period, women continued to work toward suffrage and equality under the law. In the later years, taking a claim was likely more socially acceptable for women as their arguments for equal rights became more persuasive.

As settlement progressed, young people who had come to Dakota as young children with their parents turned 21 and were eligible to take land. Many of these children, girls as well as boys, grew up on homesteads and were familiar with the demands of rural living. They had families who could provide them with the financial, material, and social support needed to set up their own homesteads.

When considering the question of how many women took land, it is useful to look at numbers as well as percentages. Although only 6 percent of those taking land in Pembina County were women, that percentage represents about 250 individual women. In Williams County, 18 percent represents nearly 1,500 women. The number of landowners in the areas included in Table 8 totals over 4,400 women.

2

The Land and the Law

It was all prairie as far as you could see. And then here and there were the little shacks of the other homesteaders.... There were wild herds of horses that roamed over the prairies, and cattle. I remember one time a herd of cattle came and rubbed on the shack. We thought they were going to tip it over.

— Nora Pfundheller King Lenartz

It was a place to stay and it was mine. I think I would homestead again. I was pretty interested in it and had quite a bit of ambition.

—Katie Gramling Stewart

The laws, and their interpretations, that laid down the procedures for acquiring public lands changed continuously throughout the settlement period. Determining the specific requirements for particular individuals is complicated and confusing.

Providing a comprehensive review of all the relevant legislation and administrative interpretations related to the distribution of public lands would be impossible here. Instead, this chapter will outline only major pieces of legislation that affected land seekers in the northern part of Dakota Territory both before and after statehood in 1889. This primary settlement period occurred roughly between 1870 and 1915.[1]

All of the public land in Dakota Territory was considered unoffered, that is, the land was not sold at public auction but could be acquired only through settlement laws.[2] Before 1891, most of the public land in North Dakota was acquired through the laws governing one of three procedures: (1) preemption, (2) homesteading, and (3) timber culture. Some individuals managed to take advantage of all three. Both the preemption and the timber culture laws were repealed in 1891, leaving the Homestead Act of 1862 and related legislation as the major means for acquiring public lands thereafter.

No matter which policies were in effect, essentially the same categories of people were eligible for public land: single men and women who were at least 21 years old, married men, widows, and women who were considered heads of households. Head-of-household status was granted only to women who were separated from their husbands, who had been deserted, or whose husbands were severely handicapped or physically or mentally ill. This meant that most married women living with their husbands could not make an entry on public lands. Widows or widowers who had children did not have to be 21 years old, since they qualified by virtue of their status as head of household.[3] If applicants were not citizens of the United States, they had to declare their intention to become citizens.

Most land parcels consisted of a quarter of a section (160 acres), although some individuals received allotments of 80 or even as few as 40 acres. Some of the later legislation allowed for larger tracts.

Regardless of whether an individual sought land through preemption, homestead, or timber culture, title to the land could not be acquired until surveyors had established the section lines. Those who established residence in the public lands before the surveyors came through were known as squatters. These people rushed ahead of the surveyors to pick out the choicest land and establish the right to make entry as soon as the lands became available.[4] Women as well as men were among these early hopefuls. Engeborg Lindstrom and her son, Christian, came to Antelope Valley in Benson County

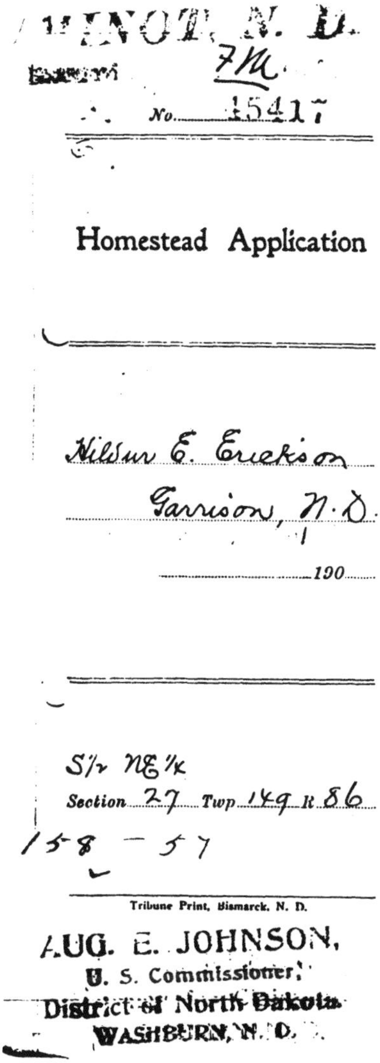

MINOT, N. D.

No. 15417

Homestead Application

Hildur E. Erickson

Garrison, N. D.

_____190_____

S½ NE¼
Section 27 Twp 149 R 86

158 — 57

Tribune Print, Bismarck, N. D.

AUG. E. JOHNSON,
U. S. Commissioner,
District of North Dakota
WASHBURN, N. D.

Hildur Erickson's homestead application.

during the spring of 1884. At this time Engeborg was 52 years old and divorced from her husband. That fall, when the land was finally opened for filing, several squatters went to Devils Lake to file on their claims. "As a matter of courtesy to a woman, the settlers from Antelope Valley all agreed to allow Engeborg Lindstrom to make the first filing in what later became Oberon Township."[5] Five women squatted in Lovell Township, Dickey County: Mrs. J. M. Wilkens, Nellie Canfield, Pamela Woodward, Susan Holcomb, and Christina Trauger.[6] These women were representative of many others who established their rights to land as soon as it was available.

Preemption legislation, repealed in 1891, provided a means of land ownership to only the earlier settlers of the area that became North Dakota. The term *preemption* referred to the rights of the occupant to purchase land at a minimum price.[7]

Throughout the 1800s, a series of laws pertaining to preemption were enacted, but the basic elements of this procedure were laid out in the Preemption Act of 1841. With this legislation, Congress at last regarded the settlement of the public domain as more desirable than the revenue the land might generate. Legislators intended that the domain be divided into small farms so cheap land could be extended to the largest number of individuals; they desired that settlers be protected from intrusion, and they allowed a reasonable time to pay for the tracts. Land could be purchased at the government minimum price of $1.25 per acre, except in the case of the government's alternate sections within the limits of land grants to railways, which could be preempted at $2.50 an acre.[8] No more than 160 acres could be claimed.

Preemption required that the claimant establish residence, build a dwelling, and improve the land. After 1880, specific procedures required that for surveyed lands not offered at public sale, "the claimant must file his declaratory statement [stating his or her intention to settle on the land] within three months from the date of settlement, and make proof and payment within thirty months after the expiration of the three months allowed for filing his declaratory notice, or, in other words, within thirty-three months from the date of settlement." To complete the process, the claimant had to testify along with witnesses that government regulations had been met. Although many people took advantage of the time allowed for payment, a few filed their statements and paid for their land at the same time.

Early interpretations of the Preemption Act by officials of the General Land Office discriminated against both married and single women. The legislation described those eligible to take claims as "every person being the head of a family, or widow, or single man, over the age of twenty-one years, and being a citizen of the United States, or having filed his declaration of intention to become a citizen."[9] The General Land Office interpreted the phrase "single man" literally and would not accept applications from single women.

Everett Dick suggests that to circumvent this ruling, a single woman sometimes would adopt a child temporarily, would be classified as head of household, and then would return the child after securing her land.[10] This early interpretation did not really affect those settling in Dakota Territory because in 1867 land officials liberalized their interpretations to include single women as well as single men, and in 1875 a revised statute changed "single men" to "single person."[11]

The Preemption Act and its amendments allowed individuals to purchase government land at minimum prices, but the Homestead Act of 1862[12] went even further, eliminating the purchase price in exchange for an extended period of residency. Settlers were required to establish and maintain a residence and improve and cultivate the land, as in preemption, but they had to reside on the land for five years.

Originally the Homestead Act required the applicant to appear personally at the district land office to present his or her application. Later modifications allowed a person, who was prevented from getting to the district land office by distance, bodily infirmity, or any other good reason, to make a preliminary affidavit for homestead entry within his or her own county. The application was to be made honestly and in good faith for the purpose of actual settlement and cultivation, not for the benefit of any other person, persons, or corporations.

A settler had six months after making entry to establish actual residence in a house built on the land. This gave him or her time to attend to other responsibilities and prepare to relocate. Meeting this deadline was usually no problem; but for some people, unexpected difficulties arose. After filing on a claim in McKenzie County, Rachel Taylor returned to Steele County to teach a session of school and visit friends. As the deadline for establishing her residence on the claim drew near, she set out for her new home. To her dismay, the river had risen and was too high to cross. She waited three weeks. Finally her friends arranged for her to cross the high water in a rowboat so that she could arrive on her claim in time.[13]

After a five-year residency period an applicant could make final proof of his or her compliance with the law. In some cases, the claimant could extend the time required by obtaining an approved leave of absence. Generally leave was granted for up to two years, although even longer leaves were given for sickness, crop failure, devastation of grasshoppers, and other unavoidable calamities. Isabel Peterson received approval for a leave of absence in 1911 to enter a TB sanitarium. She returned after a year and proved up her claim in 1915.

On January 24, 1907, the *Williston Herald* reported a blanket leave of absence necessitated by the severe weather: "A leave of absence has been granted settlers in this part of the country of three months from the 18th of January." This action was unusual since weather was ordinarily not considered a legitimate basis for a leave of absence.

Once an applicant for a tree claim, a preemption, or a homestead had complied with government requirements, he or she had to file a written notice with the register of the appropriate land office. The register arranged for publication of the notice in a newspaper at the expense of the applicant. The pronoun used to refer to women in these public notices seems to differ with the register. Some used the masculine pronoun for both women and men; but, in some instances, the feminine pronoun was used for women. Since women were sometimes employed as clerks of the register, they may have been the ones who were inclined to substitute the feminine pronoun where appropriate.

The following notices, which illustrate both formats, show that women as well as men served as witnesses. While Caroline Budke had four male witnesses, Mary Collier's witnesses included both men and women.[14]

Land Office at Minot, N.D., Jan. 24, 1905.

Notice is hereby given that the following
named settler has filed notice of his intention
to make final proof in support of his claim, and
that said proof will be made before Register
and receiver U.S. Land Office at Minot, N.D.,
on March 24th, 1905, viz:
    Caroline Budke, H. E. No. 8131
For the NW1/4 Sec. 21, T. 162N. R 85W

He names the following witnesses to prove
his continuous residence upon the cultivation
of said land, viz:
Fred Zurburg, Albert Hamerly, Joe Bollwerk,
Ole Druvduhl, all of Whitney, N.D.

                  R. C. Sanborn, Register

Notice: Land Office at Aberdeen, Oct. 6th 1884.
Notice is hereby given that the following named
settler has filed notice of her intention to make
final proof in support of her claim, and that said
proof will be made before Register or Receiver
of the U.S. Land Office at Aberdeen, Dakota, on
Nov. 25th 1884, viz:
          Mary Collier
for the S.W. 1/4 sec. 19 Tp. 129 R. 59.
She names the following witnesses to prove her
continuous residence upon, and cultivation of said land
viz: Tillie Kleutgen, Thomas Hanlon, Sarah J. Nason
and Harry Donovan, all of Ticeville, D.T.

                  C. T. McCoy, Register

H. A. Tice, Atty.

Land Office at Minot, N. D., Jan. 24. 1905.
Notice is hereby given that the following named settler has filed notice of his intention to make final proof in support of his claim, and that said proof will be made before Register and receiver U. S. Land Office at Minot, N. D., on March 24th. 1905, viz:

Caroline Budke, H. E. No. 8131

For the nw¼ sec 21, T. 162 N. R. 85 W.

He names the following witnesses to prove his continuous residence upon and cultivation of said land, viz:

Fred Zurburg, Albert Hamerly, Joe Bollwerk, Ole Drevdahl, all of Whitney, N. D.

f17m24   R. C. Sanborn, Register.

Caroline Budke filed notice of her intention to claim land near Minot in 1905. Note the official reference to her as "him." Courtesy Aurora Seehofer.

Publication was the last opportunity for another party to contest the applicant's claim to the land. If such a complaint was filed, local land officials heard the case. Their decision could be appealed to the Commissioner of the General Land Office and, in extreme cases, to the Secretary of the Interior.

If all went well and the claim was uncontested, the applicant had to appear with at least two of the named witnesses before the officer designated to make proof. After approval at this level, the application was sent to the General Land Office in Washington, D.C., where final approval was given and a patent issued. Another factor affected the length of time that elapsed between making an entry on the land and the receipt of a patent. The requirements for residence set by Congress dealt with the time between making an entry and making final proof. Local land office officials passed upon final proof and gave the claimant "equitable title;" but after this action, there could be substantial time lags.

Clerks in the General Land Office had to approve the entry before a patent was issued. This was a bureaucratic procedure, and inadequate staffing plus heavy workloads caused many delays in this final step. The act of March 3, 1891, declared that uncontested entries were entitled to a patent issued within two years after receipt of the final certificate.[15]

For example, records show that Caroline Peterson filed on her land in McHenry County June 13, 1904. She received her final certificate June 21, 1909, and the patent was issued June 14, 1910. For many of the women in my sample, the patent was issued about a year after the date of the final certificate.

In the final analysis, although the specific procedures differed, acquiring public lands involved three major steps: (1) making entry on the land, (2) final proof, which was the local officials' issuing the final certificate, and (3) receipt of the patent, or actual title, to the land, which was issued by the General Land Office in Washington, D.C. The second step or final proof generally was known as proving up. In other words, at this stage the claimant had proved to local land officials that he or she had met government requirements and was entitled to a patent. Federal officials later issued the patent.

Government land records usually show the dates of entry and final certificate and sometimes the date of patent for homestead and tree claim entries. If both the final certificate date and the patent date are listed, the final certificate date usually is labeled "F.C." and the patent date "Pat." If only a single date is listed and no designation given, that date is usually the date the final certificate was issued. For preemptions, often only one date is visible on the microfilmed records, the day the claimant paid for the land.

Included in the Homestead Act of 1862 was a provision allowing commutation which established a process much like that of preemption. The five-year residency requirement was waived upon payment for the land at the same rate that applied to preemptions, $1.25 to $2.50 an acre. At first, commutation was allowed at any time before the expiration of the five years. In 1869, an administrative ruling sought to ensure the good faith of entry persons making commutation proofs by initiating a six-month residency and cultivation requirement. Since this was an administrative action, the requirement could be waived; and, in some instances, homesteaders were allowed to commute before the six-month period had elapsed.[16]

The Public Land Reform Act of March 3, 1891, increased the required time of residency and cultivation to 14 months from the date of entry; but, since six months were allowed to lapse before the establishment of actual residency, a person could still meet requirements for commutation with only eight months actual residence. Stricter requirements were enforced with the act of June 3, 1896, which required that the 14-month residency begin at the date of settlement instead of the date of entry.

During the early years of the Homestead Act, few entrants — about 4 percent — chose the commutation privilege. After 1880, however, the situation changed. Benjamin Hibbard attributes this modification to a change in the motivations of the settlers. Those taking land in the earlier years were more likely genuine settlers. Later, the increasing productivity of the land made it more appealing to speculators. "Thus a veritable multitude of farmers' sons and daughters, and servant girls, as well as ne'er-do-wells, have sought lands in the Dakotas."[17]

Agnes Lamb the day she filed on her homestead near Washburn. Courtesy Kathy Crary.

Knowing how many of the original homesteaders intended to make the homesteads their permanent homes is impossible. With prices for a quarter section ranging from $400 to $2,600 during the early part of 1900,[18] the homesteaders certainly had an incentive to commute their homesteads as soon as possible and sell for a profit.

If a homesteader did choose to commute his or her claim, and many North Dakota women did, the wording on the final patent can be misleading. Instead of making reference to land received under the provisions of the Homestead Act of 1862, the phrase "according to the provisions of the Act of Congress on 24 April 1820 entitled 'an act making further provisions for the sale of the Public Lands' " may be found on the final patent. Commuted homesteads became purchases of public lands and, therefore, were patented under the provisions of an act pertaining to public land sales rather than to homesteads. Whether the land was originally entered as a homestead can be determined from the *United States Bureau of Land Management Tract Books*.[19]

In the later stages of settlement, the advantages of commutation were reduced with the passage of the Three-Year Homestead Act of June 6, 1912. This action shortened the residency requirement from five years to three and allowed leaves of absence of five months each year. This meant the time spent living on the claim could be as little as 21 months and the title was gained without payment other than the fees for initial and final proof.[20]

A number of other legislative acts modified the original homestead act. A homesteader, under the act of May 14, 1880, could, if desired, use as the beginning of the five-year requirement the date when actual settlement commenced rather than the day the application for the land was made. Consequently, a person who had lived on unsurveyed land for five or more years could make a homestead entry and final proof the same day. On June 13, 1912, North Dakota was added to the states provided for in the Enlarged Homestead Act of February 19, 1909. This act allowed homesteads of up to 320 acres instead of 160.[21] However, by this time, much of the land available for homesteading in North Dakota already was taken.

Some homestead lands that opened up on Indian reservations were distributed by lottery. An interested individual was assigned a number. If the number was selected, he or she could choose a homestead.[22]

During the time in which the Preemption and Homestead acts were simultaneously in effect in the United States, an applicant could take advantage of both policies. A person could acquire 160 acres through a preemption and an additional 160 acres by homesteading, although this could not be done at the same time because both acts required residency on the land.

Some settlers were able to add a second or third quarter section under the Timber Culture Act of March 3, 1873. The original bill was designed to encourage the growth of timber on western prairies. Title was given to any person (but not to a married woman unless she was

TIMBER CULTURE.—NOTICE OF INTENTION TO MAKE PROOF.

United States Land Office,

Devils Lake N.D.

June 11th 1901, ~~188~~

I, Karen Ronning of Jackson N.D.

who made timber culture application No. 3063 on the 28th day of July 1888, for S.E.¼ N.E.¼ W.½ N.E.¼ and S.E.¼ N.W.¼ Sec. 17 - Tp. 154 - R. 66. hereby give notice of my intention to make final proof to establish my claim to the land above described before the Register and Receiver at Devils Lake N.D.T., on Monday, the 22d day of July 1901 ~~18~~, by two of the following witnesses:

Gorger G. Garnik of Jackson N.D.

Jens Halvorsen of " "

Lars O. Ostegaard of " "

Ole S. Nestegard of " "

Karen O Ronning
Signature of Claimant.

Notice of intention to make proof as above must be published for not less than thirty days in a newspaper to be designated by the Register as published nearest the land, and must also be posted by the Register in a conspicuous place in the land office for the same period.

UNITED STATES LAND OFFICE,

Devils Lake N.D.

June 11th 1901 ~~188~~

Notice of intention to make proof as above will be published once a week for six consecutive weeks in the Churchs Ferry Sun, printed at Churchs Ferry N.D., which I hereby designate as the newspaper published nearest the land described in said application.

Ole Serumgard *Register.*

Copy –

Timber-Culture Certificate No. 1771
APPLICATION 3063

THE UNITED STATES OF AMERICA,

To all to whom these presents shall come, Greeting:

Whereas There has been deposited in the GENERAL LAND OFFICE of the United States a CERTIFICATE OF THE REGISTER of the LAND OFFICE at Devils Lake North Dakota, whereby it appears that, pursuant to the Acts of Congress approved March 3, 1873, March 13, 1874, and June 14, 1878, "To encourage the Growth of Timber on the Western Prairies," the claim of Karen Ronning has been established and duly consummated, in conformity to law, for the South East quarter of the North East quarter the West half of the North East quarter and the South East quarter of the North West quarter of Section seventeen in Township one hundred and fifty four North of Range sixty six West of the Fifth Principal Meridian in North Dakota containing one hundred and sixty acres, according to the OFFICIAL PLAT of the Survey of the said Land, returned to the GENERAL LAND OFFICE by the SURVEYOR GENERAL:

Now know ye, That there is, therefore, granted by the United States unto the said Karen Ronning the tract of Land above described: To have and to hold the said tract of Land, with the appurtenances thereof, unto the said Karen Ronning and to her heirs and assigns forever; subject to any vested and accrued water rights for mining, agricultural, manufacturing, or other purposes, and rights to ditches and reservoirs used in connection with such water rights, as may be recognized and acknowledged by the local customs, laws, and decisions of courts, and also subject to the right of the proprietor of a vein or lode to extract and remove his ore therefrom, should the same be found to penetrate or intersect the premises hereby granted, as provided by law.

In testimony whereof I, Theodore Roosevelt, PRESIDENT OF THE UNITED STATES OF AMERICA, have caused these letters to be made Patent, and the seal of the GENERAL LAND OFFICE to be hereunto affixed.

GIVEN under my hand, at the CITY OF WASHINGTON, the seventeenth day of May, in the year of our Lord one thousand nine hundred and two, and of the Independence of the United States the one hundred and twenty sixth.

BY THE PRESIDENT: T. Roosevelt

By F. M. McKean, Secretary.

Recorded, N. Dakota, Vol. 131, Page 350.

C. H. Brush, Recorder of the General Land Office.

Top: Notice of Intention to make proof.
Bottom: Patent for a timber culture claim.

considered head of household) who would, for 10 years, plant, protect, and keep in healthy growing condition 40 acres of timber.

Amendments were passed on March 13, 1874, and June 14,
1878. The required acreage of trees was changed to a more realistic
pattern of planting, and the number of years required for title was
reduced from 10 to eight. Land granted under the Timber Culture
Act did not have a residency requirement, so it could be acquired at
the same time as a homestead or a preemption. Termination of the
Preemption and Timber Culture acts in 1891 ended the practice of
individuals' making two or three separate entries.

Trees planted on homestead of Susie Wells in Oliver County. Courtesy Leora Conn.

Many North Dakota claimants acquired public land through
the process of relinquishment. A common phrase found in many of
my case studies was, "She bought a relinquishment." Some parcels of
land changed hands several times. Claimants would make entry on
the land and later sell their rights to others. This informal process
violated both the letter and the spirit of the public lands legislation,

which was enacted to encourage actual settlement rather than specu-lation. The exchange of money for rights to public land was a private affair between the buyer and the seller, the price being determined by the willingness of the buyer to pay. Relinquishments in North Dakota in the 1880s sold for as much as $700 or as little as $5 and a shotgun.[23]

Since the government did not approve of or officially recognize the process of relinquishment, the party relinquishing the land com-monly declared his or her intention to the officer at the land office and the party wanting the land would be standing next in line to assure his or her rights to make entry on the land. A person buying a relin-quishment could not reduce the required residency by the amount of time the original homesteader had lived on the claim; he or she had to reside on the land for the required time.

Relinquishments by some meant opportunities for others. Barbara Stracker bought a relinquishment in Slope County in 1911 when she was 50 years old. She was interested in a permanent home, not speculation, and resided on the land for 26 years.

From this brief review of preemption, homesteading, and timber culture policies, the question "How long did they have to live on the land?" cannot be readily answered. Some set-tlers squatted on land, filed, and paid on a preemption as soon as the land was surveyed. Others gained title by living on a homestead for five years, and many commuted their home-steads by purchasing the land and reducing their residence requirements to only a few months. Still others took tree claims, which required a waiting period of eight to 10 years before title could be granted but did not require the settler to live on the property at all. The terms of residence were determined by the laws in effect at the time of entry and by the options individuals selected to meet the government's requirements.

Emily Johnson bought a relinquishment from a railroad man in Minot. She paid $200 for the quarter and the shack. Courtesy Mrs. Lloyd Colbenson.

Although the preceding discussion focused on the procedures most women used to become landowners, there were some other options. The widows of veterans had certain rights to public lands. The Soldiers Homestead Act of June 8, 1872, allowed the widow of a soldier to apply the length of her husband's military service to the homestead residency requirement. That is, if her husband had four years of military service, the widow would be required to live on the land for only one year.[24]

A woman whose husband filed on land but died before proving up inherited the rights to her husband's land if she continued her residence or, in some cases, if she simply continued cultivation. Such was the case of Hanna Amanda Boesen Anderson. After her husband's death, she continued to farm and commuted her homestead in 1902. Mrs. William Lindsay's first husband died after his intention to prove up had been published four times. The title to the land was issued in her name.[25] A few women acquired land as heirs of homesteaders. Libbie Ralyea inherited a homestead from her brother, Elisha. She proved up the land in her own name in 1889.[26]

Hanna Amanda Boesen Anderson took over the homestead after her husband's death and commuted the claim in 1902. Courtesy Myrtle Christensen.

Many women did not acquire land in their own names but were homesteaders nonetheless. These women had a share in the development of the land their husbands received. It is beyond the scope of this work to describe the many contributions of these women to settlement, but it is certain that many of them exerted considerable influence and contributed significantly to the success of their husbands' enterprises. Jennie Balls Baldwin Roberts provides a good example. Even though the homestead patent was issued in the name of her husband, Samuel G. Roberts, Jennie probably provided the $400 necessary to commute the land, which was located in what is now downtown Fargo. Jennie Roberts was known to have "a head for business." Over the years, she increased her landholdings, and many subsequent deeds refer to "Mrs. Roberts and spouse."

As mentioned before, the U.S. public lands policies discriminated against a married woman such as Jennie Roberts. Marriage usually resulted in the loss of any opportunity to gain title to public lands. None of the major legislation regarding the disposal of public lands allowed a woman to take land in her own name after she was married and living with her husband unless she was considered the head of household or the entry was made before her marriage. A married woman could purchase land but was barred from the "cheap" or "free" lands available through preemption, homesteads, or tree claims.

Jennie Balls Baldwin Roberts "had a head for business." Many of her deeds were in the name of "Mrs. Roberts and spouse." Courtesy Mrs. J. Robert Haggart.

Even though the public land laws in the United States restricted the access of married women to land, men and single women had equal privileges after the initial interpretations of the preemption laws were changed. Such was not the case in Canada, where women could purchase land regardless of their marital status, but the "free" lands acquired through homesteading were given almost exclusively to men.

Only three categories of women could qualify for homestead lands: "widows, divorcees, and, in scrupulously documented cases, separated or deserted wives—providing, that is, that they had children under eighteen dependent on them for support."[27] Organized attempts to change the laws were largely unsuccessful; and, in some cases, the legislation became even more restrictive. Single women as well as married women were barred from making applications for homestead lands.[28]

Georgina Binnie-Clark, an Englishwoman who immigrated to Canada and became a farm operator, expressed her dissatisfaction with the unequal treatment that women received under Canadian land policies:

But on every side my neighbors had obtained their land as a gift from the Government, or at least one hundred and sixty acres of it, and a further hundred and sixty had been added on the condition of preemption . . . in this way a farm equal to the one which had cost me five thousand dollars was to be obtained by any man for nine hundred and seventy dollars. So that allowing that a woman farmer is at a slight disadvantage in working out a farm proposition, she has the killing weight of extra payment thrust on her at the very outset. She may be the best farmer in Canada, she may buy land, work it, take prizes for seed and stock, but she is denied the right to claim from the Government the hundred and sixty acres of land held out as bait to every man.

I talked to every man about it, and almost to a man they said, "Too Bad!"[29]

Some of the restrictions against married women in the United States were changed over time, although most of these were related to the rights of women who married after making an entry on land, and many of the changes occurred after most of the public land was taken. The Homestead Act of 1862 excluded most married women from taking land. If the couple was married and living together, the man was the assumed head of household and as such was the only one eligible for a homestead.

Married women never were extended the homestead privilege unless they had been deserted or were considered for some reason the head of household. A Government Land Office ruling as early as 1864 stated "that a married women is *prima facie* incompetent to make a homestead entry. That to entitle her she must show that she has been abandoned by her husband without cause and compelled to support herself and her family."[30]

A decision in 1872 held that a woman would lose her preemption right if she married after filing: "I have to state that if a single woman marries after filing her D.S. (declaratory statement) she abandons her right as a pre-emptor under the act of 1841."[31]

A decision in 1874 stated clearly that a married woman could not claim land under the Timber Culture Act: "A married woman not the head of a family cannot make a timber culture entry. An illegal entry by a married woman may be cancelled, and her husband, if qualified, allowed to enter the land as a timber culture claim."[32]

Another decision, made in 1875, allowed a single woman taking a timber claim to marry without forfeit of her rights: "I have to state that a single woman, duly qualified, who had made an entry under the timber culture act and subsequently marries, is not debarred by reason of said marriage from acquiring title to the land at the expiration of the statutory period, provided she has complied with all the requirements of the act relating thereto."

The Department of the Interior and the General Land Office followed the same course for Homestead Act entries that they did in the 1875 ruling about Timber Culture Act entries. In fact, that rule was enunciated for women who had Homestead Act entries as early as 1870. Commissioner of the General Land Office William A. J. Sparks attempted to dispense with the rule in 1886 by declaring that a woman who married before final proof forfeited her right to acquire public land under the Homestead Law, but Secretary of the Interior Lucius Lamar reversed Sparks's decision and returned to the practice previously in force.[33]

The act of June 6, 1900, upheld the rights of women who settled on unsurveyed lands and married before the official entry could be made. Settlers could, under the act of May 14, 1880, settle on unsurveyed lands and receive credit for the time spent residing on and improving their claims. The secretary of the interior ruled in 1899 in *Heath v. Hallinan* (29 LD 267) that "a person seeking to make an entry must at time of application be a qualified entryman." A woman who married before making entry could not make entry unless she remained head of household or some other reason overrode her disqualification. The 1900 act changed that decision.[34]

Restrictions were reduced further in 1914 when legislation was approved, which provided that the marriage of a woman who had filed on land to a man who had made a similar entry would not impair the right of either to a patent as long as they had both complied with the residency laws for at least one year. The law did, however, designate the husband as the person who would decide on which claim the couple was to reside.[35]

Additional legislation in 1914 provided that a woman who married an alien would not lose her right to public lands and that a wife who had been deserted by her husband for over a year could claim their land in her own name if she could establish the fact of abandonment and if she completed the requirements for residence, improvement, and cultivation.[36]

Ann Eldred postponed her marriage so that she and her husband-to-be could both file on claims. Courtesy Shirley Brown.

Decisions in the early 1900s which were favorable to married women probably reflected attempts to bring the law more into line with reality. Many women who took claims married before they proved up. Having invested time and effort, they would not have easily given up title to the land. Rather, they would probably have been inclined to bend or violate the rules to accommodate the situation. Ann Eldred postponed her marriage so that she and her husband-to-be could file on claims in 1901. Their marriage took place in 1902, and she proved up in 1907. In her case, marriage did not result in the loss of her claim.

Given the changes in the laws and their interpretations, the rights of married women in relationship to their access to public lands was a topic of keen interest to homesteaders and public officials alike. The importance of these concerns is discussed in a news item that appeared in the *Jamestown Alert* on October 26, 1905.

New Land Office Ruling

Where a woman having an unperfected homestead
entry marries a man having a similar entry and
thereupon abandons her claim and resides with her
husband upon his claim until he offers final proof
thereon, and they then establish a residence on her
claim long prior to the initiation of a contest
against the same, she thereby, cures her default
in the matter of residence and is entitled to perfect
her entry.

The for-going is a recent ruling of the secretary
of the interior and it has created something of a
sensation among the attorneys practicing in the land
offices. The very reverse has been the ruling of
land office officials and there are several cases
recently appealed from the decision of the local land
officials which the ruling will affect.

For land office officials, attempts to ensure compliance with the public land laws must have been, at best, challenging and, in many cases, a losing battle. The government staff was inadequate for strict supervision, and many settlers bent and distorted the rules. The fraud and corruption that took place during the settlement period have been well documented,[37] although some analysts feel it has been overestimated .

Paul Gates suggests that "the discovery that millions of acres of land have passed into private hands by the fraudulent use of the settlement laws, have led historians to misunderstand and underestimate the role of the Homestead Law and related settlement measures." He blames the pervasiveness of these misconceptions on the reports issued by the commissioners of the General Land Office which were filled with stories of fraud and deceit.

"So absorbed were the Commissioners in their efforts to make homestead function as it was intended to, that they devoted the space allowed them for recommendations for future action very largely to the frauds and malfunctions of the system." According to Gates, commissioners' emphasis has biased historians, who have tended to dwell on those who violated the spirit and even the letter of the law.

The "hundreds of thousands of people successfully making farms for themselves" have been virtually ignored.[38] It is interesting to compare the commissioners' view, which saw fraud and corruption everywhere, with the observations of Eliza Crawford. She resented the strict enforcement of the homestead requirements, particularly when she did not observe that same conscientiousness on the part of those enforcing the laws governing saloons.

The Homesteaders law is the only law that is enforced in Dickinson. 11 saloons run wide open. The saloon keepers are all prosperous men of course, living off the fat of the land, having an easy time beside their warm fires.

The Homesteaders are in the main, honest people trying to earn a home for their family. But do you think for one minute that there is one letter of the law that they can break and keep their homestead? No indeed!

The Saloon Keeper can break the law every minute of every day and be a respectable citizen of Dickinson. But let a homesteader leave his claim a few weeks and he loses his claim or is placed under arrest for perjury to the US government. I certainly believe in obeying laws but why not have each and every one treated alike. Let all be law abiding.[39]

Even though the commissioners may have overemphasized fraud and corruption, many women as well as men were forced to establish their rights before General Land Office officials. Neighbors often acted indirectly as effective law enforcers for the federal government. If a claimant violated the government's requirements, it is likely that a neighbor who had an interest in acquiring the land for a relative or friend would file a contest challenging the rights of the claimant.

Many of the contested cases depended on whether the claimant had actually established a permanent residence on the land. Since many settlers left their land periodically to seek employment or to visit family, government officials often had to decide whether the regulations had been met. The decision often revolved around the issue of "good faith," that is, whether the claimant established a legitimate residence that he or she considered to be a permanent home.

Excerpts from a transcript of a contest to the land of Cornelia Honens by George Norman illustrate the attempt of Honen's lawyer to retain her right to the land and her adversary's attempt to prove she had none.[40] A description of the shack by one witness who testified against her emphasizes its abandoned state:

> Q. Describe the appearance of the inside of the shack as
>   it was at that time?
> A. There was a mattress rolled up in one corner, and
>   there was no stove, not anything else that I could see.
> Q. Did you see anything else in the shack.
> A. No.
> Q. Any dishes there?
> A. If I remember right there were two or three cups.
> Q. What did you say?
> A. Two or three.
> Q. Where were those cups?
> A. On the floor.
> Q. Did you see all parts of the inside of the shack at
>   that time?
> A. Most of the parts.
> Q. Where did you look in the shack?
> A. I looked through a knot-hole on the south side.

Testimony by Cornelia's father provided a contrasting picture: "Well, she had a spring bed and mattress and bedding, chairs, if I remember rightly, it was carpeted, table, shelf table with hinges that would drop down for convenience, when not in use. There were fixtures around the wall, decorations, I don't remember just what they were." But Mr. Honens did concede that his daughter rarely spent nights alone in her shack.

> Q. Did she on some of these occasions stay at your
>   house overnight and take meals there, just state fully so nearly

as you can, the conditions under which the frequency of those visits, which you say your daughter made you at your home?

A. I want to say that her mother never would allow her to remain over night on her claim without some of us being with her; she made the remark frequently she would rather see her lose her claim than to have her stay there alone, unprotected. Of course, she visited frequently at our place and stayed all night and took meals, which would be very natural.

Although it was obvious that Cornelia spent considerable time at her parents' home, the man who contested her rights was unsuccessful in proving that the homestead shack was not Cornelia's permanent residence. Cornelia did not, however, carry through with her residence and prove up. In 1903, she married and relinquished her claim.

Juliana Hagel faced similar accusations of being absent from her claim, although her situation was quite different from Cornelia's. A report from the Department of the Interior showed Juliana was apparently the sole supporter of her mother and three younger siblings. She was often absent from her claim, since she held other jobs to make extra money for the family. Her challenger also failed to prove a lack of good faith.

The contestant has raised the question of the good faith of contestee in making her entry and hence the burden of proof rests on him as to that, but the only evidence introduced was an attempt by contestant's attorney to show by the testimony of one Joseph Krenzel that the land now under contest was to be given to him as soon as proved up. In this, they failed entirely. The fact that a girl built two sod shanties and a frame shanty on said land during the four and one half years which she had it, had sixty-five acres broken and cropped, twenty-five of which were broken by her, cut hay on the land every year, helped in threshing, dug stones every year and for the last four years has farmed it with the help of her brother, a boy now only fifteen years of age, and in addition has slept and cooked and spent what time she could on the land, in fact all the time when she was not helping her widowed mother, shows conclusively her good faith and honest intent to comply with the homestead laws.[41]

Undoubtedly some of the contests, especially if they had little basis, caused hard feelings in the community. When Grace Jacobsen made her application for final proof, a neighbor contested. The hearing ended with a decision in Grace's favor, but it was an event that she remembered and talked about throughout her life. Grace questioned the motives of the neighbor and had difficulty respecting him after that. Although the procedure allowing claims to be contested was probably effective in ferreting out many settlers who were stretching the regulations too far, it was also used by the unscrupulous to "grab" land.

The regulations spelled out in the various land policies discussed earlier were complicated and changed continually. The discrimination against married women is evident. Yet the public land policies of the United States were far more favorable to women than were those enacted in Canada. Women took advantage of the opportunities made available to them. They participated in all of the federal programs, particularly those related to preemption, homesteading and timber culture. Many women whose claims were contested successfully defended their rights to their land.

This brief review of major legislation and administrative procedures affecting the disposal of public lands illustrates the difficulty in determining the exact requirements for specific individuals who acquired land through federal policies. An attempt has been made, not to cover all possible procedures, but to outline major legislation and indicate the often ambiguous position of women in terms of their rights to the public lands.

Regardless of what specific legislation was in effect at any particular time, many North Dakota women completed the requirements necessary to gain patents to land in their own names.

3

The Shack: A Home on the Plains

A man nearby had a sawmill. We said I should sleep on the land that night. He dug up some green cotton-wood boards from under the snow and built a 6 x 10 foot shack right on his bobsled. In the afternoon we went up to my land, cleared snow from a little spot and set the shack on bare ground, tar-papered it and I moved in and got the helpers lunch.

— Cora Barnfather Meglasson

I had some odds and ends of wall paper from home and I had about ten different kinds of wall paper on mine. Just to make them a little warmer. It was 10 x 12. No, they weren't very big homes but held everything we had, stove and the bed. I was pretty well off.

—Thea Thompson Johnson

Before homesteaders could "settle in" they needed a dwelling of some kind. Most of them started in humble circumstances. The dimensions of their first homes, referred to as shacks or shanties, could be as small as eight by ten feet. The government did not require the dwelling to be a specific size; it was more interested in the settlers' establishing a permanent residence. The shack symbolized this permanence. While the size of the shacks would seem confining to us, in none of the interviews or other accounts was space mentioned as confining or frustrating. In fact, the small house was sometimes considered "cozy" as well as easier to heat and take care of.

Shacks can be classified into three major types according to their construction: dugouts, sod shacks, and frame shacks. At first, some settlers found it necessary to take advantage of the natural terrain. They constructed dugouts or built their homes into the side of a hill. These structures were common in the earlier periods of settlement and later were used as storage cellars. In a land with few trees, the sod house was a common sight; but as the population increased and more lumber became available, a small frame building became the standard style. Only in a few areas where timber was plentiful did people build the log cabins that were so common in states to the east.

Soon after the exterior of the shack was constructed, several furrows of ground were plowed around the dwelling to serve as a fire break, since prairie fires could quickly sweep over the land. Within the walls of the shack, pioneer women used their ingenuity to create a home that was both appropriately domestic and expressively individual.

Anna Marie Bergan was one of those early settlers who spent their first winter in a dugout. Along with a sister, Bertha, their brother, Christ, and a hired man, she set out from Fargo for her homestead near Oakes in 1882. The men had purchased 16 cows and three yokes of oxen.

With one canvas covered wagon, piled high with household goods and farm implements they started out over the trackless prairie, the two girls driving the oxen and the men the stock. In the Sandhills, near Sheldon, the mosquitoes were so bad the cattle bolted and it took the entire next day to round them up. Two of the animals were lost for two years. At Lisbon they got more supplies and lumber for roofs. On reaching the James river their first thought was for a barn.

This was accomplished by digging into a hill side and facing up the front with rock. As this was September, the wild hay was brown and dry, but they cut it with scythes and piled it near the new barn.   In the meantime the girls worked on a dugout to serve as a dwelling. It was in a side hill, with a lumber facing, into which were set the doors and windows. It was plastered with clay and lime, which dried white, and was about 16 feet square. . . .

The girls had left Fargo in new dresses, but three weeks of living in them night and day, with wind, rain and sun taking toll, left them backless.

In their trunks they carried many other dresses, not suitable for a prairie claim. They had come from a European capital and the clothes they carried with them were of the mode of the moment.

It took two weeks to build the dugout. They had an excellent stove on which they cooked in the open, turning it about to suit the fancy of the wind. They had wonderful meals, for there was an abundance of fish, white ducks, geese and prairie chickens were there for the taking.[1]

Ingebor Larson, a widow with several daughters, homesteaded an 80-acre tract in the early 1880s. Their first home was also a dugout in the side of a coulee embankment near Petersburg.

An account describing the building of a sod house for Mary Ann Murray relates some of the steps necessary to construct this type of dwelling. "Sod was stripped from the prairie with the walking plow, cut into pieces 4" x 12" x 24" and then stacked like bricks to enclose the 12' x 14' house. A wood roof and floor was installed and wood-framed interior walls carried wallpaper and an essential shelf or two."[2]

Amelia Brennon (bottom) and her sister Lena (top) built shacks near each other and alternated residency, staying part of the time in each shack. They spent one winter in these sod houses. Courtesy Margaret Albrecht.

Top: Sod barn built for Tyra Schanche (left) and Randi Garmann (right). Courtesy Bergliot Schanche. Bottom: Sophie Rude (seated far right) with a group of friends. Her shack was typical, a small frame structure covered with tarpaper. The stacks of sod provided insulation and stability. Dimensions were approximately 12 by 14 feet. Courtesy Amy Baska.

Top: Kari Uleberg and her frame shack near Columbus, North Dakota. Courtesy Avis Busse. Bottom: Sjannette Corneliusen and her shack in Pierce County, about 1897. Courtesy Helen Heidelbaugh.

Anna Nelson described her part in helping to build her sod house. Her brother had brought some chunks of white lime and sand for plastering the walls.

> I did not have a trowel, so I made one out of a piece of leftover window casing, 4 inches wide and about 8 inches long. I nailed 2 strips across and one strip lengthwise for a handle. I must say it worked better than a steel trowel that I had tried before. I put two coats on, and it looked real good. I had trimmed off the sod by each window, so I had two nice window seats. I made a table bench out of left over lumber. I had a steel folding couch and an old stove that had an oven, so I was all set for the winter.

Not all went so smoothly. She also mentioned some problems with the sod roof. "We made one mistake, too much of a pitch of the roof, so the sods kept on buckling and finally started to fall down, but it was very nice while it lasted."[3]

As settlement progressed, small frame shacks, often reinforced with stacks of sod around the walls, became commonplace. As was the case with dugouts and sod houses, fathers, brothers, or other relatives often played a major role in constructing frame shacks for women who took land, even though some women helped to construct the exterior as well as the interior of the buildings.

Nora Pfundheller's father and brother framed up her homestead shack. Flora Whittemore's father took charge of building her dwelling, but as she said, "I helped right along with him, you know ... the siding and the roof and then we had the inside. The rafters were covered with blue paper." Gina Brorby helped to build her eight-by-ten foot shack, which was covered with tar paper on the outside and a heavy red paper on the inside.

Rosa Kateley and her brother built a dugout in McHenry County; later a neighbor woman helped her add a frame structure.

Top left: Nora Pfundheller's father and brother built her shack (top right). Four interior views are shown on the opposite page. Courtesy Nora Pfundheller King Lenartz.

Left: Marie Gjellstad's shack in McHenry County. Courtesy Verna Schock.

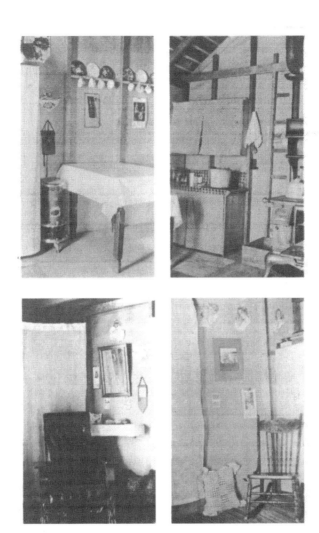

Nora Pfundheller photographed the four corners of her shack.
Courtesy Nora Pfundheller King Lenartz.

"She and her brother Erwin Kateley dug a basement on the southern slope of a hill and walled up around it two feet of sod. It had one window and one door. This answered as her home for several months, then herself and a neighbor woman started building a frame building, this was about 10' x 12' - and as the sod shack was about 10' x 12' - making a total space of 20' x 12'. She converted the frame part into a school room and taught the neighbor children." Rosa mentions in her diary, "I put tar paper on the north side of my shack last night."[4]

Sophia Peterson used the mail to send building suggestions from Minnesota to her sister, Ida, who was already working in Ray:

> You asked in Ella's letter about what shape of roof I would want on my house. Well I say make it the cheapest way but make it warm. I don't care how my house looks just so it is warm and good ventilation. Papa said you should buy all you could of the sixteen feet lumber as that was the nicest and best lumber. . . . Mamma said that you better make it 8 and 12 or it would be to small, and you shall have a cellar dug under the one standing on the highest ground so that we have some place to keep our vitals. Pa said it was better to have a cellar even if it should cost $5 more and you must not put the houses to far apart. But you must put them 8 or 10 rods apart and you must be sure that you get them one on each side of the line.

For those women who did not have relatives to give advice and help with construction, there were other alternatives. Gunda Ryen and her cousins, Petra and Caren Olimb, lived near one another. A neighbor helped the women build their shacks from lumber hauled out from Balfour in north central North Dakota, but they could not find anyone to help construct the barns. The three woman took over the task themselves, building a barn on each of their homesteads. "A neighbor, who spoke only German . . . came over and motioned to say

Marie Holen's brother built her eight-by-ten shack and ten-by-ten barn. Courtesy Mabel McLellan.

that they mustn't have a flat roof. Gunda tried to explain 'thresh-big stack,' which was to go on top. This satisfied him and he responded by clapping his hands."

In every part of the state, men made extra money by building shacks for homesteaders. Marie Holen's brother built several shacks in Williams County in addition to his sister's shack, an eight-by-ten-foot frame building with sod on all sides. A cellar three feet square was under the shanty. She also had a ten-by-ten-foot barn and a bucket well.

Many small towns had people who could advise homesteaders in need of a shack. Mary Dooley made all her own arrangements for building her shack, receiving advice from the proprietor of a local lumberyard. He helped her to plan the size and character of the house and provided information on costs. She had wanted a gabled roof but decided against it when she learned how expensive it would be.

I bought all the lumber and materials for my claim house, all the hardwood and furniture I would need and a six months supply of groceries. The manager of the lumber yard was very helpful figuring the entire bill, the plan and size of the house and how it should be built. He also recommended some freighter-carpenters who would haul all your stuff out. . . . You could go along, and they would put up your buildings while they were there before returning to town. . . . I was to pay each man $5.00 for his team and all their expenses during the trip. Meals, overnight hotel bill, livery barn expenses where they put up their teams over night and of course my own expenses. Then $5.00 per day per man while they were building and I had to cook for them. . . . They fixed a make shift tent for me to sleep under.

... I was able to put up a cot and my oil stove to cook on in there. It was a tarp thrown over the one lumber wagon, extending out on one side, and staked down out on the ground. The men slept in their blankets out under the prairie skies or under their wagons in case of rain. They built a stone boat (boards nailed across two runners) and showed me how to use it. . . . Sleeping that first night on my land I heard the howl of a coyote. Then I knew I was really "Out West." . . . By the end of the next day the floor was laid and the rough siding up so I could have my bed put up inside and sleep with no roof overhead. . . . After three or four days of hard work the men had their building work finished. . . . Next morning I paid them off and they left, leaving me alone "Queen of all I surveyed" with not a house in sight. Nobody there but me and God!

Soon other homesteaders moved in, and Mary was no longer alone on the prairie.

In many cases, a single shack served several owners. If the previous occupant had proven up or left in discouragement, his or her shack was often for sale. Gertrude Stevens was lucky. She received her shack as a gift from her uncle, Frank Banks, who had used it as a line shack for cowboys. It was moved to her claim near Ellsworth in McKenzie County.

Near Bowbells, Burke County, Clara Troska and her cousin, Christine, both bought secondhand shacks; another cousin, Helen, had to build her own.

I bought a second hand shack, 10 x 12 feet, with two windows and a door. It cost me $20.00 to have it moved to my claim. I bought new tar paper, a cot and a laundry stove with oven, put shelves on the walls for dishes and pans, a small table and a couple of chairs. Christine bought a second hand shack, too. Helen built hers, 12 x 15 feet. It had siding over paper on the outside, tar paper inside, and a peeked roof where ours was flat. Helen bought a range and we did our baking at her place. She was called Mom. The shacks were warm and easy to heat. We gathered dry cow chips for fuel.

No matter how the women acquired their shacks, many took an active part in the planning and some helped with the construction. All were responsible for furnishing the interior.

The dugout, with its sod walls and dirt floor, presented a difficult challenge for women who wished to make their shacks livable. However, some authors suggest that pioneer women's dugouts were transformed into comfortable living quarters; at times even resembling Eastern parlors.[5] And not just Dakota women used their ingenuity to create comfortable homes on the prairie. Evan J. Jenkins describes some of the interiors of Kansas dugouts:

> In one of those dug-outs which I visited on a certain rainy day, an organ stood near the window and the settler's wife was playing "Home! Sweet Home." . . .
>
> Many of those "dug-outs" . . . gave evidence of the refinement and culture of the inmates. . . . The wife had been reared in the older states, as shown by the neat and tastefully-arranged fixtures around the otherwise gloomy earth walls. . . .
>
> A neatly polished shelf, supported by pins driven into the walls contained the holiday gift books, album, and that indispensable household treasure, the family Bible.[6]

From descriptions and photographs, the interiors and exteriors of homestead shacks shared many characteristics, but the personal touches of their individual owners distinguished these homes.

Annie Andin's twelve-by-twelve-foot shack in Ward County was built by Ray Scurlock, her future husband. It had a small entryway and a trap door that led to a cellar. Another trap door led to a small attic. She had shades at the windows; and, while living there, she made curtains and rugs.

In her home she had a double bed with a straw mattress, a dresser, shelves with curtains for clothes and housewares. She had a table and some chairs, a trunk, a Singer sewing machine, which she had brought from Cherokee, Iowa, and a stove to cook on and to heat the house in cold weather. Her stove was a laundry stove which was adequate for a one person household. She also had a kitchen cupboard which had glass doors in the upper half and her own well and pump.

Nancy Smith's shack, located in Golden Valley, measured 10' x 14' on the outside. To save space, she had a bed frame nailed against the wall. The "spring" was a straw tick, the "mattress" a feather tick. . . . She dug her well, 18 feet deep, with a post hold digger. Since she didn't have money for a pump she just dipped her water out. Her "dipper" was a tomato can with a wire for a bail and a burr on the top edge to make it tip so the water would run in when it hit the water surface. It was slow work, lowering the can with a clothesline rope and pulling the water can to the top of the well, but she got by.[7]

The Shack: A Home on the Plains

Top: Margaret McDermott Jennings and her seven-year-old daughter homesteaded in this shack near South Heart. Bottom: two interior views of the shack's one room. Courtesy Irene Jennings Berrigan.

Top: Alma Anderson (center) while proving up. Her brother, Reuben, came to stay with her during the summer. Bottom: Interior of Alma (left) Anderson's shack. She is shown with Josephine Uleberg Anderson and baby Avis. Courtesy Avis Busse.

Top: Interior of Viola Lamb's shack, 1907. Courtesy Kathy Crary.

Left: Aagdt Bergsgaard (seated) inside her homestead shack. Courtesy Mrs. Herman Engh.

Lucy Goldthorpe, who settled in Williams County, described her shack as

Having walls of single board thickness covered with tar paper on the outside. Blue building paper covered every thing inside—ceiling, walls, and floor. To help seal out the cold, a layer of gunny sacks covered the paper on the floor and then homemade braided rugs went on top. "That first winter," she said, "was not only one of the coldest, but there was no storm entry at the door and the two windows were single. The two-lid laundry stove that served for heating and cooking, with an oven in the stove pipe, struggled to keep the place livable. Lignite coal, used for both cooking and heating, was stacked just outside the door within easy reach and to act as a banking along the wall. The temperature dipped to 40 below many times that winter."[8]

Eliza Crawford, who came to Adams County, instructed Mr. .Wilson to "have a folding bed frame made, and placed on the wall, just boarded up on the bottom, to take the place of the springs, and in place of interspings mattress, (ha! ha!). I had made a 'straw tick' and was able to buy hay (prairie grass) at Powell's Ranch to fill it."

Thus made our bed. Of course I took bedding. In one corner of the room a little corner cupboard had been made for our dishes and food. I hung a curtain in front of this, also one along the bed when it was up! During the coldest part of the winter I always kept it down. It got too cold, turned up. He also made a little table out of pieces of lumber left from the house. We bro't two chairs along with the stove.[9]

Hannah Hylden described how she fixed up her shack:

My stove was a small potbellied stove with only two cookholes and no oven, of course, so I bought a drum that was made to bake in, had it fastened to the stove pipe about halfways to the ceiling and had it fastened to the ceiling with wire that had to be fastened to the 2 by 4 in the ceiling. Was no trouble baking in it. Baked bread, cookies, cake, and pies, no trouble. For my table I nailed two boards together, then hung it on the wall, fastened to 2 by 4 with 2 hinges, then used a 3 in. board fastened to the front of the table with a hook, and then the other end of it was against the wall and the floor. So when it wasn't in use I could let it down and it hung on the wall. I made some corner shelves for my dishes. Also put up a board reaching from the shelves to the other wall, got some material and made curtains and hung them on this board so that was my clothes closet. . . . My bed was a couch that had a wing on each side to let down in the day time, and lift them up to make a bed at night.

Hannah Hylden at her shack with her neighbors, Walter Johnson (center) and Gust Nesseth (left). Courtesy Melvin H. Anderson.

101

Amanda Winkjer recalled the home she lived in as a child when her widowed mother, Andrea Farland, homesteaded in Williams County. It was larger than the ordinary shack.

Our living room was 14 x 16 and then we had a little lean-to on the north that was the shack that was there when they filed and then there was a little stairway to a room upstairs. We had two or three beds upstairs in that room. We had a davenport downstairs. And I think our mother slept there. Our mattresses were filled with straw which we harvested. . . . We'd take our old mattress out and empty the old straw and put in the new straw.

We would pick up cow chips. . . . There was a little hole under the floor in our shack . . . and we put the cow chips in there to keep them dry. When we had company my mother used to stand there on the lid so that nobody would open it and see what was under there.

Reta O'Neill recalled a special neighbor, Anna Marshall, a widow, whose shack near Velva had impressed her as a child.

Her house, to me as a child, was like a doll house. She brought many things from her Minneapolis home to beautify her North Dakota home. . . . She had flower beds that many families didn't have time to care for. We children loved to visit her and we were always treated to goodies served on pretty plates. Her cups and saucers were beautiful. . . . They were not the usual dishes of the average homesteader family.

For the most part, the homestead shacks served their purpose well. However, occasional comments indicate that the crude construction sometimes failed the occupants. Josephine Deming told of cutting up good shirtwaist dresses to fill cracks in her wall during a blizzard. Nora Johnson had the unique experience of watching as her shack sailed over her head during a severe thunderstorm. Her brother helped her to rebuild that same summer.[10] Mathilda Larsen, on the other hand, proudly related that after a two-day rainstorm her shack was the only one that stayed dry. All the bachelors in the neighborhood came over to dry out and eat.

Andrea Farland (near door) had a home larger than the ordinary shack. Courtesy Amanda Winkjer.

The shacks, of course, were not equipped with indoor plumbing. Although most of the photographs of the shacks do not picture the outhouse, it was ever present, built not far from the shack. Bergliot Schanche laughed when she told about "the sy-søti" (seventy-seven). "It was the best outhouse in the country." When Bergliot's mother, Tyra, and Tyra's friend, Randi Garmann, first took up homesteading together, they attempted to drill a well. The well drillers went down 77 feet without hitting water. The abandoned hole became the perfect site for "the seventy-seven."

The "sy-søti" (seventy-seven), an outhouse built on the site of a failed well. Courtesy Bergliot Schanche.

Talk of isolation abounds in pioneer literature, but for those settling the Dakotas from 1880 to 1915, an isolated shack was the exception. Families, friends, and neighbors usually built their shacks as close together as possible. Often four shacks would be sitting together on the adjoining corners of four quarter sections. Whenever possible, those who knew each other would select neighboring quarter sections and build close to or even right on the section line.

Mary and Clara Cumming built their shacks together, one on each side of the line. Minnie and Lydia Lavalle did the same thing, but with just one shack. They painted a thin, white line down the center of the floor directly above the East-West section center line. Each had a cot on her side of the shanty, directly upon her side of the dividing line. The little wooden table was also placed over the line, and at night each assumed her place on her own land."[11]

104

Marie Holen and three other young women built their shacks close together. The four jointly owned a cow, which they picketed on a rope. Mathilda Larsen built her shack close to her husband-to-be, Karl Froslie. Three other friends were close by. Soon after Lucy Goldthorpe settled in her shack, she became acquainted with two young women and two young men, all of whom had shacks nearby.

Throughout the settlement period, the simple, easily constructed homestead shack served its purpose. At best, it was a temporary home, a place to stay while getting settled and proving up. The structure was mobile and easily moved from one site to another. If the homesteader decided to remain on the land after proving up, the shack either was added to or replaced by a larger structure.

Friends and relatives often built their shacks on the corners of the adjoining quarter sections. Sisters Dorothea Hilden Lyngstad (left) and Marie Hilden (right) homesteaded with their brother Hans (center). Courtesy Helen Cusher.

105

Top left: Anna Koppergard Strand's shack, 1984. Some shacks survive today. Most are used for storage or are abandoned. Courtesy Melvin and Arthur Strand.

Top right: Agnes Lamb and her sister, Viola, built their shacks close to the section line. Courtesy Kathy Crary.

Eunice Divet Glynn, a widow with a young daughter, and her sister, Edith Divet, had this eight-room sod house built. Courtesy Fanchon Lien.

The Shack: A Home on the Plains

Top: These sod shacks belonged to Julia Lyngen, her brother, Peter, and their friend, Selma Swenson. Courtesy Helen Cusher. Bottom: Mary Belle Hanson and her husband, Olof Pierson, built this home in 1903 after proving up. The kitchen was built on her quarter and the rest on her husband's quarter. Courtesy R. Warren Pierson.

4

Patterns of Life

When my Dad and I came up, you see we were the only ones in that part of the country. Lots of times I was alone with no one inside. My Dad got a .22 rifle and told me to learn to use it. So I did. I could shoot those big gray gophers and I hardly ever missed one.

— Luella Rodenbaugh LeBarron

About once a week I went to Cartwright (about 7 miles). Sometimes I rode with the mailman and sometimes I went with neighbors. Or I would borrow a horse from my Uncle and ride there one day, stay overnight and come back the next day.

— Hilda Paulson Oakland

Although the little shack on the prairie became a permanent home for some, it was "home" to many settlers for a much shorter time. Residency was often intermittent. The time required to prove up, as discussed in Chapter 2, ranged from a few days to over 10 years, depending on which land policy was in place. After 1900, however, with amendments to the Homestead Act of 1862 in effect, the common practice in North Dakota was to pay cash and prove up within 14 months. A few individuals still chose to live on the land the full five years or took advantage of the later requirement of only three years; but the majority of the women described in this study took the shorter route and made payments to commute their claims.

Within the general residency requirements, the actual amount of time a settler spent living in the shack varied from a few days, now and then, to continual residence. Proximity to family and occupational commitments often regulated an individual's living pattern.

Olive Murray with her horse, Old Doll. She and her brother often spent time at their mother's place. Courtesy Mr. and Mrs. Allen Murray.

Mary and Anna Olson spent their summers working for wealthy families from Grand Forks at their summer homes in Detroit Lakes, Minnesota. Courtesy Jessie LaCombe.

Many young, single women and men spent considerable time with their parents, and it was not unusual to find the "homeplace" serving as the hub of activities. Children would spend a few nights on their claims but return to their parents' home regularly. Some spent the weekdays in their shacks and returned home for weekends or vice versa. Olive Murray and her brother spent most of their time at their mother's place. Nora Pfundheller lived with her parents during the week and spent the weekends on her own claim. Marie Burns told me that she lived with her mother and went out to the claim for a day or two at a time. Mary Lien went to her claim only once a month.

Many settlers coordinated their time on the claim with work elsewhere. Women as well as men worked off the claim a good share of the time.

A majority of single women who took claims eventually married, usually after they had participated in the paid labor force for some years. Many were in no rush to marry. In many cases, they were reluctant to marry. One interviewee put it this way: "Oscar had asked me to marry him and he wanted to marry right away but I was in no hurry. . . . I had a really busy winter and Oscar would write and say are we going to get married. He already had his wedding suit. I remember that he came out in February on horseback. He came riding up and had brought the wedding ring. . . . Oscar, I said, I don't know." She did eventually accept his proposal.

Unwanted suitors could be a problem. Kaja Kurz once turned out the lamp and waited quietly in her shack until the young man who had come to call left. A scorned suitor of Hester Lewis was so angry at her inattention that he refused to give her father a ride home from town, forcing him to walk the 10 miles home.

Table 9 lists the ages at which women who were single when they took land first married. The median age at first marriage was 27 for this sample, compared to a much younger median age of 22 for the general population of the United States in the years 1890, 1900, and 1910.[1]

TABLE 9 Age at First Marriage	
Age	Number
21	3
22	8
23	13
24	10
25	20
26	10
27	11
28	13
29	11
30	7
31	6
32	7
33	3
34	8
35	6
36	1
37	2
38	2
39	1
40	2
49	1
	145*

*Information was not available for all cases.

Louise Trenne proved up in 1909 and did not marry until 1912. Courtesy Helen and Vernon Porth.

111

Hilda Paulson had to find "short jobs" so she could remain on her claim. Courtesy Hilda Paulson Oakland.

Thora Sanda married in 1915, five years after she proved up. Courtesy Helga Norgard Anderson.

Another indication that many women did not hurry into marriage was the proportion who did not marry until after their land was proved up. I was able to determine for 167 women whether marriage occurred before or after proving up a claim. A majority, 57 percent, did not marry until after proving up, while 43 percent married during the period between filing and proof. Of 226 women who never had been married when they filed on land, 42, or 19 percent, remained single throughout their lives.

This tendency to postpone marriage, or to forego it, allowed women to practice a profession or work at other paid jobs. This meant adopting a schedule that would accommodate paid labor as well as other responsibilities. Teachers sometimes held classes in their own shacks, but more often they commuted to schoolhouses some miles away. Skilled seamstresses would visit families for a few days or a week to make the necessary garments and then return to their shacks. Some women ran small dress or hat shops or clerked in stores. Midwifery and nursing could be practiced with a claim shack as a home base. Shacks could double as homes and post offices or general stores.

Hilda Paulson mentioned working in Alexander and cooking in a cook car: "I had to get short jobs because I had to live on the claim." Kaja Kurz alternated her teaching sessions with time on the claim. Tillie Mostad lived in her shack on weekends, driving her horse and buggy the 15 miles to Minot where she worked as a dressmaker during the week.

Some settlers, like Katie Gramling, taught school or worked at other jobs close to their claims during the week but returned to their parents' homes on the weekends. Others planned their schedules around the seasons to avoid living in their tiny shacks during the harsh winters.

Anna Koppergard said she always tried to "work out" during the winter. Hulda Krueger spent weekends and summers on her claim, working in town the rest of the time. Miriam West spent summers on the claim, supporting herself the rest of the year by working at the Gladstone Hotel in Jamestown.

A number of women stuck it out the whole year. Lena and Amelia Brennon, who lived on adjoining claims, often shared chores and spent the night with one another. Together the two of them survived a winter on their claims. Their diet was limited, often consisting of peanut butter, biscuits, and tea. Neither woman cared much for peanut butter in later life.

Tomena Thoreson graduated from St. Cloud Teachers College, filed on a claim in 1902, and held her first class in her claim shack in 1904. Although space was at a premium she set aside an area for a dark-room, which allowed her to continue an interest in photography. Mary E. Wood lived on her homestead for about three years, teaching several sessions of school in a schoolhouse located on her land. Leah Carns taught school in Taylor and had to cover the 20 miles by horse and buggy.

Euphemia McInnis discovered there could be unwanted companions along the trail to school; she sometimes observed a coyote or two following her at a discreet distance. Weather conditions too had to be dealt with. While serving as principal and teacher at the Rhame school, Nell Elliott rented a room in town for emergencies; yet she was seen riding into town when the temperature was 30 below zero.[2]

Top right: Tomena Thoreson graduated from St. Cloud State Teachers College and taught her first class in her claim shack in 1904. She was also interested in photography, and the shack had space set aside for a dark-room. Courtesy Ruth Whiting Bernsdorff.

Middle right: Mary E. Wood (left) and sister, Inez, lived on her homestead three years and taught in a school on her land. Courtesy Rita Folkert.

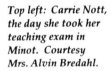

Top left: Carrie Nott, the day she took her teaching exam in Minot. Courtesy Mrs. Alvin Bredahl.

Bottom left: Mary E. Wood left her homestead to attend Valley City State Teachers College. She graduated in 1906. Courtesy Rita Folkert.

Bottom right: A souvenir for teacher Florence Hanson's students in Billings County, 1914. Courtesy David G. Davis.

114

Anna Thingvold (left) was the first member of her family to file for a homestead in 1900. Emma Thingvold (right) was a widow at age 22 with three children. Courtesy Norma Good.

Anna Thingvold (left) and her sister, Emma Thingvold Nelson (right), ran a millinery and dress making shop in Willow City for several years. Emma's daughter, Minnetta, is in the foreground. Courtesy Norma Good.

Seamstress Olive Roterud (right) traveled from family to family in a horse and buggy. Courtesy Mrs. Kenneth Hill.

115

Julia Pettingill (right, holding the horse) and her daughter (at wash tub) filed on adjoining claims. Sadie's shack (shown here) doubled as the Amanda Post Office, and she also taught school. Julia ran the Amanda store from her nearby two-room shack. She drove a team of horses 62 miles to Minot to buy supplies for the store. *Courtesy Mrs. John Holbach.*

Lillie Tysver earned income from nursing and teaching to pay for legal expenses, materials for her shack and seed for her crops. She is shown here with her nieces and nephews. *Courtesy Myrtle Ronnevik Lindstrom.*

Left: Kaia Johnson drove her horse and buggy 20 miles to Balfour to pick up laundry from the railroad workers. *Courtesy Lynn Lindblom.*

Right: Sjannette Corneliusen was an excellent seamstress. *Courtesy Helen Heidlebaugh.*

116

A number of women worked as housekeepers for neighbors or as waitresses, cooks, and housekeepers in town during the winter. Gertrude Stevens did housework at nearby ranches. Several women worked during the threshing season in the cook cars, preparing meals for the harvesters.

Viola Stramblad and her mother owned a millinery store in Jamestown. They made hats for their own store and trimmed "pattern hats"—hats decorated with big cabbage roses, feathers, and so on—for a large wholesale house in Chicago. They would split a chiffon thread to make the roses so the stitches would not show. Mary Lien made 50 cents a day sewing shirts for bachelors in the Fordville area.

Lillie Tysver contested a claim near her brother's land. She won and moved to the claim. Income she earned from nursing and teaching paid for her legal expenses, materials for the shack, and seed for her fields.

Julia Pettingill and her daughter, Sadie, provided a variety of services for the Amanda community. Sadie's shack doubled as the Amanda Post Office as well as her home. She also taught school. Julia ran the Amanda store from her nearby two-room shack. She would drive a team of horses 62 miles into Minot to buy supplies.

Kaia Johnson and her cousin, Sena, drove their horse and buggy 20 miles to Balfour to pick up laundry from the railroad workers. They washed and mended the clothing before returning it.

Table 10 lists the occupations of the women in my sample. Only 31 percent of the women held no additional paying job while they were homesteading, and many of these "worked out" before taking a homestead. Almost all were traditional occupations considered acceptable for unmarried women. Most taught, kept house, and sewed. Six women worked in what could be classified as nontraditional occupations, such as journalists, postmasters, and mail carriers.

In many respects, the marital and occupational patterns of these women's lives look surprisingly like those of today's women. Many women postponed marriage, leading busy lives that required juggling many responsibilities.

Although a majority of homesteading women worked in paid labor as well as domestic work, they did not leave the management of

TABLE 10

Women Engaged in Other Occupations While Homesteading

Occupation	Percent[a]	Number
Teacher	25	59
Housekeeper	22	54
Seamstress/milliner	21	50
Midwife/nurse	8	19
Cook in cook car	6	15
Sales clerk	4	9
Waitress	2	5
Laundress	2	5
Post office clerk	-	2
Mail carrier	-	2
Postmaster	-	1
Baker (bread)	1	3
Piano teacher	-	2
Photographer	-	2
Stenographer	-	1
Secretary	-	1
Telephone operator	-	1
Journalist	-	1
No other occupations	31	75

[a]Percentages add up to more than 100 because some claimants had more than one occupation. Information was available in 241 cases.

TABLE 11

Those Who Managed The Homestead

Manager	Percent	Number
Woman herself	94	231
Other	6	16
	100	247 *

*Information was not available in all cases.

their land to someone else. In answer to the question, "Did you/she manage the land?", 94 percent of the respondents answered "yes." Only 6 percent left most matters pertaining to the land to someone else, usually a father, brother, or other relative. (See Table 11.)

Most of the women who took land assumed responsibility for managing it in addition to their other duties. The majority of women who took claims were responsible for three types of work: (1) paid labor,(2) basic domestic duties related to maintaining the household, and (3) management of the claim.

Pauline Shoemaker hired her neighbor, Bill Backfish, to break the sod on her claim along the Knife River. Courtesy Sheila Robinson.

While the types of work involved in the paid occupations and domestic work are easy to describe, the activities in which women involved themselves to manage the cultivation of their claims are more difficult to ascertain. Some women rented their land to family or neighbors, concerning themselves with financial arrangements and leaving other decisions to the renters. Others hired men to do some of the field work or traded domestic work for field work. And some, through circumstances or choice, did most of the work in the fields themselves.

Hiring others to do the field work was a practical solution for those who taught school or worked off their claims. Katie Gramling taught school while she homesteaded. She rented her land to two neighbors and kept no livestock except for a horse, which transported her back and forth from school. Almost all women took care of certain chores, though. They tended gardens, raised poultry, and milked

Betsy Aslakson. Chickens were an important source of income for many women. Courtesy Berglot Aslakson.

cows, and some cared for the horses that provided their transportation and draft power.

Lucy Goldthorpe combined teaching with homesteading. She mentions the differences in skills among women who homesteaded. While some women were proficient in outdoor activities, she found it more efficient to trade homemaking skills for farm work.

All the homesteaders that had remained on their land were feeling the confinement of the long winter days. I treasured the times when some young father would come and ask me to help out a few days due to the arrival of a new baby. Since everyone was struggling to live on their small savings until crops began to produce, payment for helping in this fashion was made in return help. Some of the homesteading women could drive a fence post or plow a cleared area as expertly as a man, but for me it meant swapping services and occasionally paying for heavy work done. Every time I "helped out" I was really putting in a new section of fence or getting some plowing done, besides enjoying the change of scene that came with the job.[3]

The circumstances of some women did not allow them to hire help or trade domestic work for their field work. They did much of it themselves, often sharing some of the heavier tasks with friends or neighbors. Kari Skredsvig, a widow, and her 10-year-old son labored to break her first 10 acres with a team of horses. The first breaking of land was especially difficult, however; and many men as well as women hired someone else to do it. Edith McGuire's uncle and father helped with the breaking, but she took her turn walking behind a breaking plow hitched to four horses.

Apparently Anne Furnberg did most of the farming of her 80 acres, at least for a time. When she heard that her sister and brother-in-law were coming to America she asked them to bring her nephew, Ole Furnberg, who was 11. Ole took care of Anne's small son, Christian, and cooked the meals while Anne did the farming.

Elizabeth Brumwell was characterized as "used to hard work." She, like many others, dug her first well by hand. Elise Linn was described as "capable of doing all sorts of heavy work and jobs believed suitable for men." And Christiane Anderson was "never afraid of hard work." She not only worked in the fields but took care of chores usually delegated to women, such as milking, gardening, and caring for poultry.

In a number of instances, women mentioned a preference for indoor or outdoor work. Luella Rodenbaugh took care of the household work, but her mother was an outdoor person: "My mother liked outside work. She herded cattle and I did the cooking and the housework." Christine Larson looked upon housework as the "hard" work compared to field work: "I worked outside so much. I know it isn't nearly as hard [as housework]. It is heavy, but it isn't nearly as much of a strain as it is to be in the house."

Ella Reetz's father and brothers did most of the outdoor work, but she sometimes helped with seeding, cutting and shocking grain, and rock picking. Nora Johnson's neighbors helped break the land, but she did the rock picking: "I'll never forget the sore muscles acquired when I dug and hauled all the rocks from my first ten acres by myself."

Christiane Oslie Anderson, shown here with her daughter, was "never afraid of hard work" and often worked in the fields. Courtesy Mrs. Carlott Andvik.

Many women mentioned helping to harvest grain, cutting, stacking, and shocking. Anna Nelson mentions how she liked to shock and stack grain and regretted losing her job to the combine.[4]

Nancy Smith broke and trained horses: "I never used a saddle with cinches pulled up tight. I always rode them bareback. No bridle, either. I'd just use a small whip and hang onto the mane. At the water trough I would slide my saddle onto a 'new' horse, then ride him until he was tired."[5] When the horses tired, she would take them to the corral to work with them, putting on a halter, tying them, mounting, and dismounting.

Isabel Peterson had to put up with bucking horses, too. She would ride them to the spring to water them. They scared her, but, she said, "bucking horses were cheap" so she learned to get along.

Women were known for raising poultry, but Pearl Robertson took this vocation further than most. An Ancona rooster she shipped to her homestead from Minnesota became the founder of a flock of registered Ancona chickens. Pearl raised these chickens for 45 years. In 1940, a prize rooster, Nodaway of Loraine, won first prize in the poultry division at the International Livestock Show in Chicago.

Often women did not assume responsibility for outdoor work until after they proved up and married. These tasks were usually seasonal work, which they added to their domestic tasks. Sena Amdahl Rendahl tells how she hauled wheat to market.

122

During one fall I helped haul wheat to Esmond, eighteen miles from our Girard Lake homestead. We started out at daybreak and I took our two-year old boy with me on the wagon seat. He didn't cause any trouble, and I didn't have to promise him anything to sit still either. We had good dinners at Mrs. Erickson's restaurant. We made the trip every other day, fifteen trips in all. After that I did not haul any more wheat, but I helped with the haying the first years.

Women often teamed up to help each other. Because Alta Davis Eberle's husband, Frank, was often away, she assumed the management of the farm, including much of the heavier work such as hauling coal and plowing. The following account tells how two families threshed together:

We threshed with the Sandeens. Barbara, about 14, and I had a team and rack. Helen and Maudie had a rack together; Wendell had one alone. Edgar, 12 and Freddie, 10 years old, manned the fourth rack. Frank and Gus ran the machine, hauled grain, and helped pitch bundles. Sadie, with 12 year old Margaret, cooked and cared for the four small children. . . . It was real cooperative farming, and worked to the benefit of both families.

Emma Bublitz Freitag described her life after marrying and moving to her husband's farm. "We raised cattle. We milked cows for a while. That put us on our feet. The most we ever milked was 11. We farmed with horses at that time. We finally got a tractor and you know a tractor doesn't get tired. We used to stay out until 8 o'clock and then we had those 11 cows to milk. Separate the milk, feed the cattle. We never got to bed before 12. I don't know, I didn't seem to get tired at that time."

arson rented out her homestead acres until she
ed to her husband's farm, where she took up field
cks, and cutting, raking, pitching, and stacking hay.
ed her to help even more. When they could not get
ne.. ir new combine, she learned how and ran it for three
years.

Some women remained almost completely within the boundaries of their domestic roles. Mary Belle Hanson married the day after
she filed on her land. She and her husband accumulated substantial
landholdings. Mary Belle's responsibilities were traditional, but
running her household required a high level of skill in management
and organization. Mary Belle was in charge of providing food,
housing, and clothing for five to eight men in the winter and for 15 to
45 men in the spring and fall. In addition, she cared for her seven
children and husband. She cooked, baked, churned butter, raised
turkeys and chickens, sewed, gardened, and cleaned their large home
and the bunkhouse.

Women who took claims could pattern their lives a variety of
ways. They undertook a multitude of duties and, depending on their
circumstances, opportunities, and interests, they managed to juggle
their roles to meet their responsibilities for paid and domestic work as
well as the affairs of their claims.

These women, while usually assuming the expected domestic
role, used their initiative at the same time to develop skills that
allowed them to provide an income for themselves as well as to
manage and acquire property. They showed independence, creativ-
ity, and competence, characteristics that often have been classified as
masculine.

Men, too, assumed roles of the opposite gender more than we
realize. Although it was not the purpose of this study to look at men's
role's, references made to men who assumed some of the domestic
tasks women traditionally do give some insight into the circumstances that prompted this action.

In a letter to her sister, Ida, Sophia Peterson tells how their
brother, Pete, cooked alone in a cook car for three weeks. He earned
$3.25 a day instead of $4 because he could not bake bread. On the other

hand, Bessie Schwartz's uncle was a skilled baker. Bessie explains, "My Uncle Hash Rigler taught me how to bake bread, but without any measurements. I made enough bread to last for many days, as he kept saying, 'Add more water. Add more flour.' The worst part of it, was to bake it in an oven that was attached to the smoking stove pipe. One should have received the first prize in baking bread there. And it was good too, in spite of everything."[6]

Eliza Crawford observed that one of her neighbors, a Mr. MC, was particularly interested in cooking. "His very fussiness is interesting. He tells about his graham gruel 'wadding up in little wads.' "[7]

Randi Garmann's husband wrote about his own disappointment when he found himself responsible for the household while his wife was out delivering a baby.

To the husband of course these regular excursions were more or less annoying although the many extra dollars came in quite handy, but there were a good many times he would have been glad to pay out money instead of getting it if he could have had his wife stay put. That however was unthinkable—she was needed and she went leaving whatever work she was busy with—washing clothes, churning, making supper—and the poor guy had to take over. It made quite a handy housekeeper and babytender out of him, but he was more than once a very disgusted one and especially if he after a long and cold trip to Tioga, having taken up a load of wheat, came home late in the night to a cold and empty house with a short note on the table from his wife telling she was again on the go and had deposited the progeny at some neighbor's place.

Randi Garmann was a well-known nurse-midwife. One of her own children was born minutes after she arrived home from a trip to help a patient. Courtesy Elsa Ferguson.

In spite of some crossover in the division of labor, women who took land were still in charge of the domestic sphere. In this respect, the difference between women who took land and those who did not was small. Regardless of whether or not they owned land, women usually saw to the routine domestic chores. If they chose to own land or "work out" or do field work, this merely extended their responsibilities.

The following passages from diaries and written recollections were selected because they provide a sense of the ebb and flow of the more mundane activities associated with life on a claim. Here we see chronicled the concerns of homesteaders, their relationships with each other, and the daily tasks necessary for survival.

Lucy Goldthrope (Williams County, 1905)

Lucy, a young, single schoolteacher, came from Iowa to live on a claim near Epping. She described to a reporter her routine, survival during the winter, and the cooperative efforts of neighbors, and contrasted her childhood fantasies with homestead reality.

A fine neighborliness existed among the settlers and people helped each other whenever possible. Before Epping was established the hike to either of the other two nearest towns was too great for personally toting any amount of supplies, so neighbors with teams would stop by and get a list of my needs, which they would drop off on their return trip. Later, when merchandise was available in Epping, I would take my little telescope suitcase and hike over the hills to get small, light-weight items. Heavy supplies like coal, flour and kerosene were still brought to me by passing neighbors.

The neighboring young men hauled barrels of water from a spring over a mile and a half away for their household use, and to water their stock. They suggested that I use water from their barrels rather than attempt to carry it from the spring, so I and the other homesteading girl carried pail after pail of water to our shacks.

The settlers were quite a mixture of young families and single people. For survival and progress it took the combined efforts of all. Sharing seemed to double the pleasure of the good times and helped ease the rough ones. . . .

That first summer and fall were gone before I realized it and winter was suddenly beating against my shack with a

Lucy Goldthorpe was confident of her success. "Caught up in the excitement of the moment, I had no doubt but what I could prove up on land as well as anyone else. I had a little money saved and no fears of the rural life ." Courtesy Vernon Vandeberg.

full amplement of ice, snow and wind. Christmas away from home that first winter could have been a lonely experience; my sister's school, closed for the coldest months, gave her an opportunity to go home and many of the homesteaders had left for the winter. The outlook was mighty bleak until Anna Kallak, a girl my age, homesteading two miles away, came to spend Christmas with me.

Hiring a livery rig, Anna drove over early and suddenly we were planning a gala day. Inviting the two boys that had claims near mine, gave the dinner an extra holiday note. In spite of the limited variety of food and the temperature hovering over thirty degrees below zero, the dinner was a great success. . . .

That winter of 1906-07 was the worst known up to that time in the Dakotas. From the middle of November it seems as if there was a blizzard about every other day until spring. Many buildings were covered completely by huge drifts, but my shack was up on a hill so that I was seldom snowed in. Livestock froze and people died for want of medical care. The temperature dipped to 40 degrees below many times and the night it went to 42 below was a bad one. Some believed it was 52 degrees below zero, and they couldn't be blamed for stretching it ten points, as it seemed even colder than that.

There were many long, cold days and nights in my little homestead shack that winter! The walls were only single board thickness, covered with tar paper on the outside. I'd spent money sparingly, because I didn't have much, but I had worked hard all during summer and fall in an effort to winterize the structure. Following the pattern used by many of the settlers, I covered the interior walls with a blue building paper. Everything was covered, including the ceiling, and the floor. To help seal out the cold I'd added layers of gunny sacks over the paper on the floor and then the homemade wool rugs I'd shipped from home.

Regardless of what I did the cold crept in through the thin walls. With no storm entry at the door and only single windows my little two-lid laundry stove with oven attached to the pipe had a real struggle to keep the place livable. Local lignite coal, used for both heating and cooking, was stored just outside the door, and snow had to be knocked off each piece before the day's supply could be brought in.

A neighbor family returning to their claim "from the outside" brought me fresh vegetables. They were such a prized addition to my meals that I put the bag in bed with me at night to keep them from freezing. Night after night I stored food and my little alarm clock in the stove pipe oven; that was the only way I could keep the clock running and be sure of a non-frozen breakfast.

Each day brought new, unexpected challenges and at times I wondered if I would be able to stay with it until the land was mine. Could any land be worth the lonely hours and hardships? The howling wind and driving snow, the mournful wail of coyotes searching the tormented land for food did nothing to make the winter any more pleasant. . . .

Alone in my homesteader's shack, thoughts of freezing to death didn't make my situation any better, so I would make an effort to recall the fun times when I was a youngster. The place we lived in when I was very small had a beautiful lilac bush by the gate, and the shade of the big maples, too, was a pleasant memory, along with the feel of cool water that ran in the trough made from a huge hollowed-out log. . . .

As a child I had enjoyed hearing my father tell of the hardships of the early days. They seemed so exciting to me as I listened in the warmth and security of our well built, fully winterized Iowa home. Like most youngsters I'd wished for the thrill of those other days. Little did I think that an opportunity for just that would come through homesteading alone, far out in the windswept, unsettled land. Believe me, it wasn't nearly as glamorous as the imagination would have it! . . .

The spring of 1907 with its freedom from the tyranny of freezing cold was most welcome and homestead life took on new hope and interest.[8]

Eliza Crawford (Adams County, 1906)

Eliza Crawford, a widow with two children, kept a diary during her nine months on a claim and some years later added some reflections on her experience. She brought her young son, Paul, with her to the claim but left a daughter, Ruth, behind so she could attend school. Her references to some navy beans given her on her departure reoccur throughout the diary, showing that even such a common commodity could be both of practical importance and an object of humor. It could be that thoughts of the friends who had given the beans were as rewarding as the nutrition the beans provided.

Our "Actual Residence" came all too soon and the first thing I knew it was time for us to be on our way, or some one might 'jump' our land. . . .

One of the funny things that happened about our packing, I had our trunk really full; and over came Ella and Millard with a lot of navy beans that they were going to give us—beans they had raised that summer so they were par excellent.

But where could I stick them in for everything was full. Millard said: "lets pour them right into the trunk" and, suiting the words to the action, and with no delay he grabbed the sack and shook the beans in, down among the clothes, clear to the bottom.

He took hold of first one end of the trunk and then the other—shaking it up and down to settle them down.

To add another laughable incident to the bean story, when we went to claim our trunk in the depot in Dickinson, as we walked along toward the express room, Paul said, "I guess we are on the right track for every now and then I see a bean." Yes the trunk was not bean tight, and a few had fallen out but not enough to make our supply short. Of course we did not claim our trunk till in the morning.

We stayed in Dickinson all night and of course in the morning I hunted up a livery. A man who would take us, our trunk and groceries down—to our new home, for quite a few months. And did I ever buy groceries! It was 70 miles down there and at that time 40 miles to New England, our nearest grocery store, so I did the best I could to be prepared.

I found a man who would take us to Mr. Wilson's, where I planned to go first. He, himself, had taken land not very far from us; and he and his good wife were already in their shanty. We stopped there just a few minutes got the key to our shack and were at last in our little home.

Our bill to our driver was $30. It took us the most of two days to go and of course I had to pay the hotel bill at New England for the driver both down and back also Paul and myself; as well as the keep for the horses too, both going down and also back. It all counted up to quite a bill. How wonderful it was that everything went the best ever and we were at last settled and starting to earn 160 acres of land by living on it.

December 23, 1906

We have been here just one month next Tuesday, have spent one very enjoyable holiday, Thanksgiving. We will never forget, will we Paul? Had such a lovely dinner and such a nice warm fire. Our stove has not come yet, we hope to get it the week of Xmas, and some beef too. My but we will live like Lords then. We have such lovely weather yet, only one two-day blizzard. We hope to get some mail when Mr. Omodt comes home from Dickinson. He will get it at New England, a letter for Xmas. I know nothing I would like better. Have only had 1 each from Ruth and Ella. We had bean soup for dinner today. We took a nice long walk since dinner. Our beans were so invigorating.

December 25, 1906

. . . I bro't a small laundry stove in Dickinson for we

really had to have something to cook on and warm us a little till our stove reaches us. Yesterday we went over to Mr. Bomonts and the King Ellingson's. I gave Mr. B. an order to get our cook stove, and at K. E. we bought a few groceries. They are putting in a stock of goods but they will of necessity be high, prunes 18 per lb, apricots 22, 'tinned' milk 15 cents per pint, and apples 3 for 10 cents. By the box, of course, they would be cheaper. But they did not have a box. As Paul says—Amen.

February 6, 1907

. . . We finally set our stove up January 18 and I baked some bread. Had the misfortune to break our lamp chimney and as we have no other and are unable to get another, we burn torches made of rags dipped in lard and wound into a round wick with thread.

February 13, 1907

The month is 1 half gone tomorrow. Today our sunshine did not come to stay. It is cloudy and the wind blows a gale. I was all ready to wash so I did. I wonder why I did not bring any clothespins out here. Think our brains act very carelessly sometimes. Of course I would need clothespins. How else could I keep the clothes on the line. I have tried common pins but the wind did not even notice that they were in the garments, it takes them off so quickly. I was disappointed Monday. I got no letter from home, I wish they would write more than once a month.

March 22, 1907

It certainly was a picnic yesterday. The wind blew a perfect hurricane. Our closet went over, so did Mr. Wilson's. And the little shack was blown as flat as a flitter and nothing but the stove is left standing. Mr. Rourke said his walls were just swaying back and forth and he came up and stayed with us. He was here for dinner. Arthin K. E. brought over a lot

132

Top: Wash day for Agnes and Viola Lamb. Courtesy Kathy Crary.

Left: Randi Garmann washing clothes. Courtesy Bergliot Schanche.

of mail for the neighbors today. None for us though. . . .

Oh yes, I almost forgot to tell you that we had beans for dinner. We have been making homestead potatoes. We like them so very much. What are they you ask!? I'll tell you. Take real dry bread. I always put some aside to get dry, have your spider [frying pan] hot with a little fat (we have only lard) in it, for frying. Cut the dry bread up in small pieces (not crumby), pour just water on them to moisten, but do not mash them up, and fry quickly, lift and toss in the spider very carefully, frying to a delicate brown....

When we first lived here as you have noticed by reading we carried every drop of water we had, from a spring 1 1/2 miles away. When the snow came we were glad and thankful, for then we could melt snow. And did we ever have great high banks of the valuable stuff, especially on one end of the shanty. But, when spring came we'd have to make some different plans. Rev. Shaw, our pastor in Cooperstown said in one of his sermons, that "for every need in this world there was a help close by if we could only see it."

The help was close by too and Mr. Powell pointed out to us. He runs a sheep ranch and in the spring it was hard to manage so many, until the grass is ready.

So he came over and made us this offer. If we would herd 50 of his sheep for one month he would dig us a well as soon as he could get at it, and were we ever glad to do this. He would bring them over as soon as the weather would permit, but as is often the case winter hangs on. Still it is not late. We can't expect spring to come in March.

Some days we think it is really here then when we get up some morning old man winter blusters at us as soon as we open the door and says: "You are not rid of me yet. I have quite a few days yet before Old Sol can drive me away. But Old Sol always does as God Plans he should and Spring will come.

It is wonderful after all how well we have gotten thru the winter.

April 7, 1907

... Holding down a claim is not what it is cracked up to be.

I wish I had not taken this one for I will have to go through so much before I can prove up. I am not feeling at all well and I am tired of everything connected with this homestead business. I especially hate the powers that be in the department of the interior. That sounds badly, I guess God will forgive me for I don't believe he has any too much love for the way they keep making it harder for the home-steaders.

April 13, 1907

My Saturday's work is all done. My cupboard is full of nice baking for Sunday. We have a jar of our blessed beans and some prunes.

Laying all joking aside, our beans have been a God send. I don't know what we would have done if we had not had them and if we had to buy them and pay 6 cents a pound as the rest have done, I think we would have noticed it a little.

April 17, 1907

... I think it would be nice if I explained how our mail gets to us, or near us I should say. Our address is as it is of every family who lives in this vicinity, New England, ND (of course) In care of Powell's Ranch as that is a well known place here. Of course the mail comes to New England from Dickinson by stage; and the mail got there this way. In a neighborhood adjacent to New England, & doubt-less quite a distance too, for it was 40 miles to Powell's Ranch. Someone who was situated so they could, would go to New England & take all the mail that went out that way to his place. Everyone who lived in that neighborhood would go to his place, look the mail over & get what belonged to them.

135

Some one in the next place, farther on would go to
that place & bring all the mail not claimed & that belonged
in the Powell Ranch bunch, on to his claim. I do not know
how many times it was carried on to a different place,
always toward Powell's Ranch, just thru the kindness of
different homesteaders.

Before it reached the Ranch & I think it was wonderful too that it did.

Later in the spring a stage or mail stage, at least, was
put thru, after the store was opened up at Wolf Butte, and
the mail all came there. Everyone was Kind tho & if they
went where it was, they always took their neighbors mail to
them. I mean if they went by their place. I think we did well
to get our mail at all.

April 24, 1907

The ground is all white with snow this morning. I am
baking beans and bread and I made a homemade pie and
some little tea cakes or whatever name they go by. I am
about ready to walk over to Wolf Butte to see if Nell is there,
or a letter & send one to Ruth.[9]

Grace Jacobsen (Grant County, 1912)

Unlike Lucy Goldthorpe and Eliza Crawford, who left family
and friends to embark on a homesteading adventure, Grace Jacobsen
was not troubled by isolation. When reading her diary, I was surprised at the number of her contacts with friends and relatives, with
whom she visited or worked daily. She obviously spent a great deal
of time in her parents' home, though she also stayed on her claim and
on her sister Carrie's claim.

Top: Grace Jacobsen in the yard in front of her shack.
Courtesy Marjorie Peterson.

Left: Grace Jacobsen's diary, 1912.

August 6, Tuesday
I sewed all day on Carrie's dress. An awful storm in the afternoon, walked over to Carrie's house in the evening, talk about wet feet.

August 10, Saturday
Pat & Auntie & John D. came over from Aunt Marthas in the afternoon. After supper we all went up to Almont to ice cream social. Had a very nice time. Came home about 2 P.X. [sic]

August 12, Monday
Got up at 8 bells and got ready to go to town with Thor. Went after a load of lumber for my house. . . .

August 13, Tuesday
Pa & Harry cut Crofoots Grain. Auntie & Ma went picking berries & Carrie & I washed clothes. I slept over to Carrie's house with her.

August 14, Wednesday
Carrie and I shocked Barley all forenoon. Oh, such a job. . . . I done some fancy target shooting. . . . I took some pictures. Ma and Auntie went down to Olof Olsons. I ironed all afternoon.

August 16, Friday
. . . Thor and I went down to my claim and layed the corner stone on my place and began building. After we came home, the whole family of us went up to Oscar's for supper had a Dandy supper. Then we made candy but it didn't get hard. We had to get the lantern to go home with as it was quite dark. Pa drove Carrie and I over to her place.

August 17, Saturday
Ma and Auntie went over to Aunt Martha's to pick

berries. Pa and Frank and Thor building on my shack. I took dinner down to them and it was a circus. Carrie and I done the house work then we took a bath. Lonie Larson came from Carson and stopped awhile with us and had coffee.

August 21, Wednesday

Papa and Frank, Pat, Richard and Harry all worked on my house. Auntie, Ma and I took dinner down to them and took some pictures. Then Carrie and I cleaned up and baked and Mama and Auntie went over to Carrie's place. In the evening the town bunch came out and surprised us with a barn dance in the barn. Swell music, swell floor, Dandy lunch, fine time. Everybody went home feeling good, about 40 people.

August 25, Sunday

In the morning Harry, Pa, Richard, and I moved my furniture down to my place. Pa and I stayed there until 2 P.X. and done carpenter work. Then we walked home. The rest of the folks went to S.S. [Sunday School] Pa and I stayed home and cleaned up. . . .

August 28, Wednesday

. . . After supper the six of us went over to Melia's shack to sleep and Oh such a time. No doors or windows. Laughed about all night.

August 29, Thursday

Got up quite early. After breakfast took some more pictures. Then went home, picked some choke cherries, lost my Kodak on the way home, went back and found it. Carrie and I shocked Grain after dinner. It began raining so we had to quit. We darned stockings and made Jelly, after supper developed pictures and they were good. Then walked over to Carrie's place.

September 29, Sunday

Got up real early and chopped wood and built a fire, then we both took our rifles and went after water and then had breakfast. After that we took some pictures again, then went out hunting. Met Ma on her way to church. We only saw 2 chickens and we walked for 2 hours. Awful tired when we got home. Had dinner then Christine and Carrie and I walked to S.S. and back. . . .

October 12, Saturday

. . . Carrie and Ma dug potatoes all day and we all helped to pick them until it was dark. We were very tired so we slept at home.[10]

Bess Cobb (Grant County, 1906)

Bess Cobb wrote a letter bubbling with optimism to a friend.

Suppose you girls are saying "Poor Bess" and feeling dreadfully sorry for me out here in the wild and wooly uncivilized regions of America. But really time just seems to fly. I haven't done half I had planned and I am afraid winter will be here before we are ready for it. I've sewed some, done a little fancy work and lots of darning and mending but most of my time has been spent out of doors digging in the garden and riding. . . . You can see a team miles away— up one valley we can see ten miles, up to the Cannon Ball river—so when any one starts to our shack, if we see them in time we can comb our hair, change our gowns and get a good meal in running order before they arrive. You see Dakota has some redeeming qualities. Wish you could come out, but I suppose you think I am too far away. I have the neatest little shack I've ever seen and "my crops" are tip top. I know you would enjoy our camp life for a short time.

I have a new bronco. He is white and has two brands (V.R. and S.P.) on him. He was surely a bucking bronco when we got him but now he is real dignified, except at times, then he lays back his ears, flips his head on one side and you have to dig in your heels and knees and hold on for dear life. However I think he will become civilized in due time by merely associating with me—ha! ha! Riding horse back in Viroqua isn't in it at all. Here you don't have to be bothered with fences and roads but just go any old way you wish. Twelve miles when you mail or get a letter isn't any ride at all. I rode 20 miles last Saturday and 20 Sunday and I try at least 10 every day.[11]

Thina Thingvold (Williams County, 1904)

Several of Thina Thingvold's brothers and sisters homesteaded, but her land did not adjoin their property. Since she was alone on her homestead before her marriage, her 8-year-old niece, Minnetta, stayed with her over the summer. Relatives recounted the stories they heard about Thina and Minnetta's experiences.

Thina and Minnetta lived in a one-room shack that leaked when it rained. They walked across the prairie and fields to a neighbor several miles away to get a ride to church. If weather permitted, the congregation brought lunch and socialized for the afternoon. Because Thina's neighbors lived on their homestead year around, she got fresh farm produce and chickens from them. Thina and Minnetta picked dried buffalo chips for firewood. They bathed and washed in a nearby slough, and also caught water in rain barrels by the shack when it rained. They were constantly on the watch for wolves and coyotes, which often followed them as they walked, and for protection carried heavy sticks, though they were never attacked.

At least once a day Thina and Minnetta ate cornmeal mush with butter and sugar on it. This was accompanied by Norwegian flat bread and a glass of sour milk or coffee. The extra cornmeal mush was put into a bread tin and cooled until firm. Later it was sliced thinly, fried in fat until crisp, and served slightly salted. They often had to sift bugs out of the cornmeal before they could cook it. Much of the time it came from the store with bugs in it. They also purchased salt pork, dried fruits, and other staples.

Thina spent her time knitting, sewing, crocheting, and doing needlework. She made beautiful lace collar-and-cuff sets to use on their dresses.

Clara Troska (Burke County, 1905)

Clara Troska, her sister, Mary, cousins, Helen and Christine Sonnek, and friend, Leona Taylor, all homesteaded near one another. Clara told her story in 1970.

Helen, Mary, Leona, Christine and I bought a horse and buggy. Leona built a lean to on her shack for the horse. We had hay out for the horse. We each dug a well 12 feet deep, cleaned 12 acres and hired the plowing of a fire break and planted a garden.

The coyotes and wolves would howl at night making me homesick. Stray horses would come by, maybe a skunk snooping around rattling a pail left outside. Cowboys would go through the herds of cattle going to market. We would gather pans and pails and milk the cows, in similar fashion to wild cow milking at a rodeo. We had cottage cheese, milk soup and pancakes. We all had a dirt cellar in which a large wooden bin was placed, and in these we stored our food . . . .

To pass time we would walk over the hills gathering buffalo chips, putting them in piles to burn and also gathered stones. We bought lignite coal at $2.00 a ton and $20.00 to haul a large wagon box full. This was surface coal. There were plenty of June berries to be had for the gathering for sauce and jelly.

Christine Larson (Divide County, 1913)

I lived there the first year and then the second year my younger brother came to live with me. He was about 9 years old. I got married before I proved up and we lived on the claim until 1917. . . . I had a little garden that I worked at. It was a mile away to get my drinking water. I went to get water everyday. During the first winter I went home to my folks, about 300 miles. I took the train from Wildrose. . . . I had an Uncle near me but they moved away so I was basically on my own. We could hear the coyotes in the night. They never bothered us but we could hear them howling at night. . . . I snared lots of gophers. We put a string around the hole. When it came up we could pull the string and get it. . . . I had to go with neighbors to get supplies from the town. I didn't have a buggy. We had to go 5-6 miles. Mostly in the afternoon we'd make it there and back. . . .

I got my mail from the Ella post office. That was north from where I lived, the opposite direction from town. We tried to go once a week. . . . It was a happy time. Well, it was just the going thing. We didn't require a lot of recreation or company. . . . Neighbors did get together. You never knew how many you'd have for dinner. People dropped in. They'd say, let's go to so and so today, and they'd come. And we always had something to eat. When I think back, I don't regret it. I enjoyed it.

Flora Whittemore (Mountrail County, 1907)

Flora Whittemore's parents lived with her while she was proving up; a brother was close by.

My father broke the land and he borrowed my brother's equipment, horses and the plow. . . . The next year we put it into flax. . . . I did most everything. I did some sewing and I remember painting my brother's office and I used to make candy for the school teachers to give to their pupils in the springtime and I did sewing and made hats. I made hats just like you'd make a dress. . . . After I proved up I worked in town. . . . I had a little shop and did dress making and dry cleaning. . . .

We had to build a fire break because we had so much trouble with prairie fires. The Great Northern ran through about a half mile from my claim and they [trains] used to set fires accidentally . . . we always had to keep a tub of water or broom and sacks to put the fire out. . . .

We charged most of our groceries. You were supposed to pay when you got your first crop. That's why it made it so hard for me because my first crop froze. You were not supposed to buy groceries that you didn't need. That was for sure, and I'll tell you, it was pretty slim picking. . . .

The only training I had for dressmaking was from books. I really was just shoved into it because that was the only way I could make a nickel when I was proving up. Somebody would want some little thing done, and I would be able to get 50 cents to a dollar for doing it. That looked awfully big. I think at that time I got about a dollar and a half for a blouse and 3 dollars was a pretty good price for a dress. I hated it like poison but I decided if I had to sew, I might as well like it. I really like to sew now.

144

Hulda Krueger (McLean County, 1916)

I was working in the post office in Ryder so I used to go out on the weekends . . . and I went out as much as I could in the summer. I'd take a little vacation and stay up there. I didn't have a car but I always had a ride with somebody. Mrs. Tibbs had a car. Sometimes we'd stay one night at her place and the next night at my place. She was two miles away at most.

Katie Gramling (Burleigh County, 1909)

I taught school around there while I proved up. It was 18 miles from home [parents]. Saturdays and Sundays I would go home with the horse and buggy. . . . Sometimes I had my sister with me. . . . We did go to town when necessary. About every two weeks we'd go to town. . . . I went back and forth to school everyday. It was about 4 miles. I wore a cotton or wool dress, overshoes and heavy stockings.

Theona Carkin (Hettinger County, 1906)

After borrowing money from her father, Theona Carkin traveled four hundred miles to her claim in western North Dakota. She lived in a shack close to a cousin who had the adjoining claim. Her cousin hauled water for her, and they did their cooking and eating in her quarters.

The nearest town to my homestead was 5 miles away—New England. . . . My supplies and mail came from there and it was possible to have a meal out in the town in a nice eating place "family style." I also taught two neighbor boys in the 6th and 7th grades and in exchange for this I received fresh milk and German lessons from their sister. . . . My mother came out to visit for six weeks in April of 1908 and rode a neighbor's horse on which she galloped all over the acreage and had a wonderful time.

I had a $10.00 borrowed sewing machine with me on the homestead and to match an outfit that I admired on a friend, I created, using no pattern, a pale tan riding habit. It consisted of a long, split skirt and a jacket. But the unique feature of this outfit was the pleated panel of material that I could button over the split, making a solid effect when I was not horseback riding. I always felt this was my most outstanding article of clothing while in residence on my "homestead."

Thea Thompson (Williams County, 1910)

I think I stayed about 18 to 20 months. . . . Flax was my first crop. My uncle put that in and farmed it. He broke only about 10 acres. . . . I did sewing and reading and then we visited. We were close enough to my Uncle's so we walked down there quite a bit and also to other close neighbors. My Uncle built the shack. It was just one room. I had a newcomer girl—a girl that had come from Norway a few months before and she didn't have any job so she came out here with me. . . .

Our mail was delivered about a mile from where I lived. . . . There was a blizzard now and then but most of the time we could read the weather so we would go down to my Uncle's place. . . . One of the bachelors got a new top buggy and we thought that was great. He would make the rounds and pick up the whole bunch for church or something. There was church once every two or three weeks at a different house.

The personal accounts included here seem to be representative of the lifestyle of the women who homesteaded on the North Dakota plains. Certain basic needs had to be met.

Shelter was the first and foremost concern. Accounts almost always include a description of the shack—its dimensions, construction materials, the contents, and the degree to which the woman participated in the building process.

The water supply was crucial. The source of water and the distance to that source were of primary significance, whether it was a river, a slough, or a hand-dug well. The distance to the nearest

Ina Marie Lee and her homestead shack, 1903. Courtesy R. Warren Pierson.

town determined the difficulty in replenishing food staples and supplies. For some, this distance was a mere half-mile, but more often a trip to town meant a considerable investment of time and effort. The distance to town commonly fell in a range of eight to twenty miles, but for some it meant going as far as 60 or 70 miles.

A source of fuel was also critical. Fuel was used for cooking the year round, but it was essential for heating during the winter months when the temperature dipped to far below zero. Accounts tell of collecting cow chips on the prairie, going to a mine for a load of coal, twisting hay to use for burning, gathering wood when it was available, and traveling some distance to purchase fuel.

Access to many of the basic necessities was gained through the establishment of a network of family and friends. Barter was practiced extensively. Eliza Crawford told how she herded sheep for a neigh-

Sara Isaacson's sister, Ingeborg, hauled water to the homestead with a stone boat. *Courtesy Sara Isaacson Ingle.*

Helga and Anna Tompte saw friends nearly everyday. *Courtesy Andrea Langeberg.*

bor who in return dug her well. Theona Carkin agreed to teach two boys and received fresh milk and German lessons for her efforts. Cooperation, then, was a common theme. Most accounts relate stories of mutual aid among neighbors. Lucy Goldthorpe spoke of "a fine neighborliness among the settlers."

Thina Thingvold's neighbors saw to it that she had fresh produce and rides to church.

Contacts among neighbors were frequent. Although women occasionally expressed feelings of loneliness, their accounts more likely tell of get-togethers or visits to and from family and friends. Many women met relatives or friends daily. Eliza Crawford, who came to her claim with only her young son, soon made friends with her neighbors. Lucy Goldthorpe came alone, too, but soon formed friendships with the single young women and men who had claims near hers.

But the account that most clearly shows the constant visiting among homesteaders is found in Grace Jacobsen's diary. The pages are filled with the comings and goings of family and friends. Her activities were an integral part of those of her immediate family (parents, brother and sister, uncle and aunt) and friends, the "town bunch." Daily tasks were accomplished together, whether it was harvesting grain, hunting, or planning a party.

Weather could be a formidable foe. Some abandoned their shacks during the winter for more substantial buildings, family homes, or residences in town, but many such as Lucy Goldthorpe withstood the rigors of winter.

The ingenuity of the women who homesteaded was reflected in many diverse situations. Food was protected from freezing by putting it in the bed at night. Josephine Thedin used this method to raise her bread. When skills were lacking, they were learned, by trial and error if necessary. Theona Carkin fashioned a riding habit without a pattern. Flora Whittemore "hated sewing" but learned to like it when she found it would provide her with needed additional income. Women with city upbringings had to learn the most basic of skills such as driving a horse and buggy or milking cows.

Settlers found great comfort in receiving mail. All anticipated letters from those who were left behind. Descriptions invariably included the way in which mail was delivered or the distance to the post office. Again the effort and time required to get to the post office differed. For some, like Lena Timboe, it was an invigorating walk (about five miles); for others, like Bertha Claude Breckenridge, the trip was 50 miles by horseback.

A number of women had someone come to live with them for at least part of the time they were proving up. This companion was sometimes a younger sibling or another relative: a sister, mother, friend, neighbor, or, in the case of Thea Thompson, a "newcomer girl." Mary Lien had two neighbor girls stay with her. Young widows such as Eliza Crawford often brought their own children with them. Pets, too, could be good companions. Annetta Erickson had "a large dog and a good horse that were her constant companions."

Transportation was another important concern. Standard modes of transportation included walking, horseback, horse and buggy, horses and wagon, and in the later years, cars. During the winter some, like Gertrude Stenehjem, used skis. She skied into Arnegard, about five miles away.

Top left: Esoline Matilda Evenson and her dog, Vixen, near her shack. Pets were important companions. Courtesy Evelyn Conger.

Top right: Viola Lamb and a favorite horse. Courtesy Kathy Crary.

Bottom left: Cora McCombs' land was near the Mouse River. A trip to Towner by horse and buggy was a 10-mile, all-day outing. Courtesy Vera Fairbrother.

Bottom right: To visit Fargo, Anna Helland would walk from Ruso to Velva to take the train. She carried her bags and walked barefoot some of the time to get around the sloughs. Courtesy May Bredeson.

*Right: Julia Lyngen
lived five miles south of
Reeder in 1908. Horseback
was her chief means of
transportation. Courtesy
Helen Cusher.*

*Bottom: In winter,
Gertrude Stenehjem skied
about five miles into
Arnegard from her claim.
Courtesy Sara Vuylsteke.*

Olga Olson rode her bicycle 35 miles to her parents' home. Courtesy Joy H. Kline and Herbert Thompson.

The bicycle was popular and useful even for traveling long distances. Olga Olson lived about a mile and a half from town. She rode her bicycle when she went to get mail and supplies and on longer trips to see her parents, who lived 35 miles away.

Rosa Kateley often taught school away from her shack. She would ride her bicycle to get home on weekends (about fifteen miles) until the snow got too deep. Then she would walk home on Saturday. Arriving home tired, wet, and cold, she would have to build a fire to warm herself. The next noon she would start walking back to her school. Rosa Kateley's daughter tells of a trip Rosa took from her claim to Washburn to write a state teachers exam:

Rosa Kateley bicycled 75 miles to take a teaching exam in Washburn. Courtesy Olive Sprague.

On a cold March day (1901) she borrowed a fur coat and started out alone on her bicycle to go about 75 miles across the prairies. No map or roads only wagon trails, she found a ranchers home where she stayed one nite. Arriving

152

in Washburn in time to write her tests and immediately got
on her bike and started home, stopping in a deserted ranch
house one night and then riding until after 10 P.M. to get
home. . . . She had to get home that nite because early the
next morning she started to teach a new school!

Ruth Abbott rode only a mile and a half to the school where she
taught. She was often seen on her bicycle, carrying her lunch pail, a
broom, and a .22 rifle. At the end of one term, she made a long,
unexpected trip to collect her salary.

W hen the term was over the job of collecting her
salary of $30.00 per month for four months making $120 for
her summer's work had to be assumed as Ruth was going
back to Grand Forks County to teach a winter and fall term
beginning in September.

The officers in the "Great River District" lived far
apart. The clerk Mr. Geo. Summers lived about 20 miles
north of her homestead so one day she started on her bicycle
to find him. She found his home but his niece who was his
housekeeper said he was not home and she did not know
when he would come so poor Ruth had to go back disappointed.

She started back in a few days and again found him
away but she told the niece "I am going to stay right here
until he comes home, even if I camp on this doorstep all
night." The young lady laughed and after supper took me to
a nearby shack, for which she had the key. . . . she [Ruth]
was tired and slept wonderfully and when she went over to
Mr. Sommers' house for breakfast she found him at home
and laughing heartily at her.

After he had written out her school order she
mounted her wheel and started eastward to find the presi-

dent of the school board. His name was B. R. Corey and he lived near Deep River post office which was in a store kept by the Bucholz family. . . . It was evening and the Bucholz family knew that Mr. Corey was not at home. Firm in her determination not to give up in locating the necessary men to sign the papers to collect her salary, she got the people at the post office to give her supper and nights lodging which they did with great hospitality.

Next morning she rode a short distance and found Mr. Corey at home. . . . He soon signed the school "order" and she rode off to find the school treasurer, John Ebersole . . . . The Ebersoles were a charming couple and invited her to have dinner with them. . . . Thankfully with her task accomplished, she turned her bicycle toward the southwest to the neighborhood of her homestead. There were no roads as we now know them. Only an occasional "track" made by lumber wagons on the prairie but Ruth generally managed to keep her "wheel" going. She found no mud but in some places the sand was so soft and deep that she had to dismount and walk pushing her wheel.

This was hard work as the day had grown hot. She came to a little farm and turned in to ask for a drink. Here she found friends. . . . They coaxed her to rest and have some refreshments and they all had a nice visit. As the sun was far in the west she had to be on her way and before dark she was in her own township again.

She found some neighbors who asked her to stay over night with them and as she was very tired she slept there. She had ridden over one hundred miles and slept three nights away from home but had collected her $120 for her summer's wages.

Human beings were not the only residents of the plains. Many accounts mentioned the ever-present coyote. Josephine Thedin heard their mournful howls her first night on the claim. Others mentioned being startled by the sudden appearance of coyotes, who followed their movements as they walked across the prairie. Lucy Goldthorpe talks about "the mournful wail of coyotes searching the tormented land for food." It seems fitting that this animal, so much a part of the wild, would be in the background watching as women and men transformed the plains from the natural and the wild to the cultivated and the domesticated.

5

Fear, Frustration, Fun

Yes, we had rattlesnakes. We usually killed them if we had something to kill them with. Sure, I killed them by myself. It didn't take much to kill a rattlesnake.

— Sara Isaacson Ingle

I remember once we were down to the last quarter and I went to town and got the mail and in the mail was 50 cents. I had paid that much too much at the land office and they sent it back and that came in so handy. I remember I bought kerosene with it.

—Flora Whittemore Walter

[In] wintertime several of us would get together and ride in bobsleds with lots of straw in the bottom to keep warm. In summertime we rode with horse and buggy. There were barn dances as well as [dances] in the community halls and homes. In the homes rugs and furniture were removed and we danced and had a real good time. Music was furnished by neighbors who played violins and guitars. I enjoyed every minute of my three years of homesteading.

— Hilda Paulson Oakland

The previous chapter focused on the daily routine of women who took homesteads. There were many variations, depending on the range of responsibilities assumed by individual women, but all shared the need to provide for the daily necessities of life. Mixed in with the routine, however, were events that disturbed the regular pattern of life.

The tendency is to view the lives of pioneer women in terms of tragedy and fear. When introduced to the idea that women, too, homesteaded, many people remark, "I don't see how they did it" or "They must have been so lonely and frightened." Although tragedy and fear were part of pioneer life, they must be viewed in the proper perspective, that is, as a part of life but not as overpowering forces.

I no longer think first of the difficulties of homesteading but rather of its advantages and the fun and enjoyment that were part of pioneer life. The responses of the women I interviewed and the recollections of friends and relatives of homesteading women were impressive. While all the women experienced some degree of difficulty and hardship, they remembered and treasured the "good times." This phenomenon can in part be attributed to our tendency to dwell on positive events, particularly in later life. In light of the evidence, the good times were more common than we sometimes think. This notion was aptly expressed by the son of Ella Reetz, Arnold Erbstoesser, who remarked, "There were many stories my mother told me of her earlier days. . . . She didn't tell too much about the hardships because it seemed to be taken for granted. . . . My mother just wasn't one to tell how severe it was year after year, or tell stories about hard times. Rather, what I most remember are the fun times."

To present both perspectives, I have divided this chapter into two parts, "The Difficult Times," which includes a discussion of tragedy, frustrations, and fear, with a special section about fear of men, and "The Good Times," which tells about fun, socialization, and courtship, with some mention of the arts.

THE DIFFICULT TIMES

When asked about being afraid, the women interviewed gave similar responses: "No, I wasn't afraid," "I wasn't afraid at all," or "I guess I never thought of being afraid." Despite this initial response, upon reflection, informants did recount particular incidents that were frightening and many more events that were frustrating. These incidents were isolated cases rather than part of the daily routine. As Anna Nelson commented,

> I was only scared once, and I know what the meaning was when they say they "get scared stiff." One night I woke up, and it sounded like someone was trying to get in. I could hear the doorknob rattling and not any other sound. After awhile, it quit at the door, but started at the window, so I was sure someone was trying to break in. After a while everything was quiet, so I went back to bed, but I did not go to sleep. I was too much of a coward to look outside. In the morning, I drew the curtain and looked out. I saw a lot of cows, so I dressed and went outside. I counted 40 Hereford cows, they had come there to get shelter from the storm. I did not know about the storm, as I could not hear the wind in the sod house. It was warm and cozy inside.[1]

Cattle and horses rubbing against the shack was a common occurrence, usually more frustrating than frightening. Animals not confined by fences used the shacks as shelter and scratching posts. Lena Timboe was often awakened when oxen rubbed themselves on the corners of her shack, rocking the whole building. Ann Hewson and her sister, Libby, had occasional run-ins with cattle. Once some bulls broke down the door. The animals did not come into the shack, but the two women spent the night up on the rafters just in case.

Another time, the two women were out walking. A small herd of cattle wandered so close that Ann and Libby decided to climb a tree. The tree branch broke, tumbling the women to the ground. Luckily the commotion scared the cattle away.

Martha Ann Smith remembered a time when "the big bulls came and rubbed their shoulders on the corners of the shack rocking it off the flat limestone corner stones. She was out of water but dared not go to the spring one-half mile to the north. After two days, the herd moved on leaving behind a good supply of 'buffalo chips' which was a more lasting fuel than the twisted bunches of grass she used to heat tea water."

Anna Underdahl fenced in her shack during the winter to keep the horses from breaking windows when they licked the frosted panes. Janie Brew encountered a "cattle problem" while she was visiting her father's homestead. A large herd of long-horned steers came to drink out of the spring near the shack. Janie was alone and "did not want them to trample the spring, so she rushed out toward them, waving her apron and hollering. . . . they all stopped, raised their heads, stared at her, then they turned tail and took off with a loud clatter of hooves."

The plains did offer more serious hazards, ones that could be life threatening. During the summer and fall, prairie fires were always a concern. Emma Bublitz recalled,

I was watching those red flames coming closer and closer. I could have done nothing to get away. . . . it was a little scary. My brother never got home with his wagon and four horses until 10 o'clock at night. He saw that fire and put his horses in the sod barn. And he went to help fight. He said, "If the fire comes down this way, then turn the horses loose. But he didn't tell me what I should do with myself. He was too excited. . . . And that 10 acres of flax saved it coming our way. It was green, and that didn't burn.

Blizzards and severe weather were the subject of many stories. Annie Deming recalled waiting out a storm: "I got up, put in the window, dressed and sat up all nite awaiting the end of the storm." Freezing temperatures were always a threat, but the tale of Helma Nelson has a surprising twist. Helma had a claim about 13 miles northwest of Velva. On March 24, 1902, a dispatch from Lisbon, North Dakota, reported, "Helma Nelson, daughter of Andrew Nelson, a farmer living near Lisbon, was found frozen to death in a cabin on her claim near Velva." Several newspapers carried the story, including the *Minneapolis Journal.* Helma, very much alive, was shocked to read this report of her death and responded to the *Journal's* account:

Annie Deming sat up all night waiting out a storm. Courtesy Vera Fairbrother

To the Editor of the Journal:

Valley City, N.D., April 2.—The other day while reading your paper, I found an item which surprised me very much. It was my own death announcement. . . . The item is correct in every detail except that I was not frozen to death and wish you would correct it.

I am at present at Valley City and have been here since my return from Velva. I do not understand how anything so unfounded as this could get out, but perhaps the following will explain.

I have a claim thirteen miles northwest of Velva and had gone there to live upon it for some time. My "shanty" is not of the warmest kind and I was caught there in the big blizzard of March 14, 15, and 16. I had only a limited supply of fuel and had not reckoned on a storm like that. When my fuel was gone, I broke up my table, bed and everything I had and burned it. After that I appropriated the bedstead and floor for fuel out of a claim shanty about twenty feet away belonging to Miss Hannah Sollin.

George Selvig, of Norwich P.O., N.D., a neighbor, and Mr. Sawdey, of Tilton, Iowa, deserve credit in their effort to come to my rescue. On Saturday, the second day of the storm, they, with great difficulty, found their way to my place, about two miles from theirs. They thought it best if I could stand it, to go with them to Mr. Selvig's and off we started, Mr. Selvig taking the lead. I will admit I did not have bright hopes of ever seeing or finding any house or place of refuge when we left my shanty, but after wading through the snow and facing the wind which was freezing one side of our faces, we spied Mr. Selvig's house when about two rods from it. . . . I think we were very fortunate, indeed.

The newspapers wrote retractions stating, "She is out on her claim again and expects to have a bumper crop this fall."[2]

Nora Pfundheller. Fancy-work was a common pastime during the winter months. Courtesy Nora Pfundheller King Lenertz.

For most settlers, the snow and sub-zero temperatures were more confining than life threatening. Anna Marie Bergan spent her first winter in a dugout. The door was constructed so that it swung outward. When a blizzard piled up drifts of snow against the door, Anna could not open it for about a month. During such periods, Anna spun yarn, knitted, and did fancy work. She reported one winter that she had made a pair of leggings for herself from wool and the long, silky hair of a collie; they were serviceable for 20 years.[3] Many years later, her daughter still had a large pile of doilies that her mother had made while on the claim.

Doctors were scarce and medical facilities few. When Barbara
Stracker became desperately ill she hung out a white cloth as a signal
for help. The mail carrier saw the cloth and summoned assistance.
Barbara was taken to a hospital in Miles City, Montana, where it was
discovered that her appendix had ruptured seven days earlier. She
made a miraculous recovery. Others, however, were not so fortunate.
Grave situations involved the help of the untrained. Bertha Haug
found herself helping an old country doctor amputate Peter Kulberg's
leg after he developed gangrene.

Rattlesnakes, particularly in the southwestern part of the state,
posed a hazard, but most settlers took them in stride. Romaine Clouse
described an incident she observed when she was a small child
homesteading with her mother, Margaret Madson Shaski.

Mother always kept a long green diamond willow
by the door, for snakes. One day when she was carrying
wash water out to empty it a rattler crawled in the house
and behind a curtain that hung down on the corner wash
stand. I saw it and hollered a warning to her. With the
"snake stick" she managed to lift the curtain up on top of the
stand. It took some doing to get the snake out on the floor
where she could "stun" him. We could hear him striking a
glass jug that held kerosene. He was finally stunned so she
got him on the end of the stick and outdoors where she "finished" him.

Hilda Paulson's cat tangled with a rattlesnake. "One day I
heard a rattle all over the house. . . . I opened the door and here was
a rattlesnake just in front, you know, and the cat was jumping at the
snake. Boy, I killed that rattlesnake, but I had an awful time. That
rattler had ten rattles on it." Then there was Eva Popp, for whom
snakes were not much of a problem. Eva, known for her skill with a
rifle, "could pick the head off a rattler at 100 feet."

Accidents involving horses were another hazard. Andrea
Farland broke her wrist when she fell out of a buggy. Nell Elliott left

Eva Popp could "pick the head off a rattler at 100 feet." Courtesy L. A. Joyce.

Rhame in southwestern North Dakota on horseback, planning to spend the night with a friend. A storm came up, "it was dark, raining hard and coyotes were howling. In a coulee the horse stumbled and Nell fell off, but she heard him snort and was able to reach him and remount. Entirely confused by this time, she gave him the rein; and he led the way out of the coulee and stopped at her friend's door."[4]

One day when Maude Ellis was mowing, her horses bolted. She crawled under a wagon where she would be safe from the mower sickle. Marie Burns had an experience with runaway horses.

One time I remember it was terrible windy and I was going up over the hills. Had to open the gate so I wound the lines through the whip stock of the buggy [and got out]. . . . I had trouble getting the gate shut and the lines were taut so the horses thought I had gotten back into the buggy. They took off and I couldn't catch them. I thought they would stop, but they didn't. Fatty was for stopping, but Lizzie wanted to go on. And so I kept running. . . . The horses went through the creek so I had to wade the creek. Finally I got to them, and I just fell around Fatty's neck, I didn't dare to take Lizzie's neck. She would have kicked me in the face. It must have been a mile and a half we were at this. . . . I can still see the horse. She was so surprised.

Some incidents ended in tragedy. Bernice Deming was killed when her horse was frightened by a car and ran across a rut, throwing her out of the buggy.

Ordinary work necessary to improve the claim could turn to disaster. A neighbor was digging a well for Bertha Breckenridge.

When he reached a depth of about 20 feet, he was overcome by gas and collapsed. Bertha rode her horse a mile to another neighbor for help; but when they returned, the well-digger was dead.

Flooding and high water were a concern. Christiane Anderson returned from town to her claim with her son and two daughters. It had been raining hard, and the water in the creek was high. The four were on horseback and barely made it across safely.

Simply getting lost could pose a problem. Anna and Mary Olson walked the five miles into Bonetrail one afternoon. They stayed late, and it got dark on the way home. Losing their bearings, they finally had to sit down and wait for daylight.

Lillie Tysver told of unexplained noises in the night. She always investigated the source by going out and would chuckle when she found it was just an owl, a coyote, or a sudden rustle of the wind. Then she could sleep the rest of the night.

Financial matters could be embarrassing and frustrating. For Rosa Kateley, food was scarce many times.

But her "hungryist" experience was when her brother took her teacher's paycheck ($30) and her shopping list to Anamoose and promised to come back home the same day. One day went by, two days, a week, and her food was all gone; she was too ashamed to go to neighbors and ask for food. She hunted thro all her possessions trying to find some money—finally in a little ribbon box she found a dime. She walked four miles to a rancher's house that had the Post office and a few staple groceries, with her dime she bought a box of crackers—she hurried away and sat down behind a clump of bushes and ate her crackers—She often said that those crackers were the best tasting food she ever ate.

Karen Kittelson Olsen told of writing a letter to a friend in Minnesota and having to wait for six weeks until she had the two cents to buy the stamp to mail it.

165

Karen Kittelson Olsen waited six weeks until she had the two cents necessary to mail a letter.
Courtesy Edmond Strand.

Kari Skredsvig learned indirectly about the status of widows in her community. It seems that it was considered proper to pay her children less for doing odd chores because they "were the widow's kids."

The clothing styles of the day caused some problems. Kirsten Knudsen encountered snow enroute to her claim. She was traveling by train with two other women; and when the train stopped in a small town, they got off and went to the nearest store to buy some food. As they were returning to the train, it pulled out of the station. The women ran to catch it, but large snowdrifts, coupled with their long skirts and high-heeled boots, spelled disaster. One woman fell, and the train was gone. All three sat in the snowdrifts and laughed! On one occasion, when Karoline Holen was fighting a prairie blaze, her long skirts caught on fire. Ole, her son, stamped out the flames.

For those who had grown up on their parents' farms, the skills needed for living on their own claims came as second nature, but young women from the city had a lot to learn. Tyra Mattson Schanche, Randi Garmann, and Kirsten Knudsen were immigrants, well educated, and from well-to-do urban families. They came ill equipped to face the hardships of a homestead; but with courage and determination, they mastered the necessary skills, learning to milk, harness a horse, clean the barn, and do whatever else needed doing.

Anna Erickson remembers learning to ride a horse: "Rode over to Liberty (three miles, you know) on horse-back and was so stiff when I got back Mabel had to get me a cane to use. I thought I would have to be helped out of bed this morning, but was surprised to find myself all in good shape and ready for some more riding. I can't 'lope' much yet, have to learn by degrees, I guess."[5]

Marie Burns had to learn to ride horseback. "My brother-in-law said I looked like a bean bag tied in the middle. I had quite a time." When she drove the team to her claim for a day or two, she left the

Tyra Schanche spent some time in Paris studying painting before her marriage. After her husband's death, she learned the skills necessary for running a homestead. Courtesy Bergliot Schanche.

horses in the harness. "It was quite difficult for me to harness a horse. I was so short. When I went to my homestead I didn't take the harness off the horses . . . but I did unhitch them from the buggy and get them into the barn."

There were a variety of simple frustrations. Ida Peterson found her fuel supply rendered useless one spring. During a thaw, the snow had melted and run into the cellar, drenching the coal that was stored there. Another time, a weasel killed her chickens. Lizzie Taipe had some trouble getting her apples home from the store. When her horse became frightened and started to run, "she couldn't hold on to the reins and the bag of apples at the same time so the bag fell to the bottom of the buggy, came open and apples were strewn along the road for quite a distance."

Lizzie had trouble with another animal. "She had no cow, but neighbors sometimes brought her milk and cream. . . . Having received a gift of cream, she was anticipating having some freshly made butter. It was spring and she had the heater in her house taken down. The stovepipes lay out beside the house. Looking outside she thought she saw something move into one of the pipes. She went out and hit the pipe with a stick. In so doing she disturbed a skunk, which so contaminated the atmosphere that she could not use the cream."

Caroline Budke cooked some prunes one day and set them outside the shack to cool on a wooden box . When she came to get them, they were gone. It seems her cow had enjoyed the fruit and later came back for more.

Insects had to be dealt with. Rebecca Heide told of "flies so thick you had to burn them off the ceiling at night when they didn't move. Whenever butter or cream was put on the table, the flies got into it." She also described techniques for getting rid of bedbugs. Some women took the bedsprings out of the house and poured boiling water over them to destroy the eggs. A more drastic measure was to drench the bedsprings in kerosene and set them on fire.

Rebecca Heide told of "flies so thick you had to burn them off the ceiling." Courtesy Agnes Veeder.

Even though loneliness did not seem as pervasive as sometimes portrayed, women were lonely at times. These times, however, were momentary and usually were dispelled by a visit to a neighbor, a visit from someone, or other activities. Luella Rodenbaugh said, "I did get lonesome and homesick but I read a lot." Gertrude Sheidamantel started her homesteading venture with her brother; but after his untimely death, she managed alone, making good friends with her neighbors, the Murrays.

Ethnicity was sometimes more isolating than remoteness. Christine Larson said that while she herself was never lonely, her married neighbor often was and implored Christine to visit whenever possible. "I did visit a neighbor a lot. . . . She was so lonesome. She was married and had one baby. She was German but the people around were all Norwegian. . . . She was so glad I could speak English. . . . She could speak English. I visited her almost every other day."

Some women devised ways to let others know when they wanted company. If Gertrude Stenehjem needed help or wanted someone to stop by, she hung a dish towel on the line.

Some women sought a claim that provided relative isolation. Gunhild Berge said that being alone was a joy to her. Others mentioned getting away from relatives who were difficult to live with. They appreciated the privacy and freedom of their own shacks.

An account by Bessie Schwartz shows that some women were not satisfied with life on the land. Bessie was born in Romania and came to the United States with her parents via Montreal and Quebec, finally reaching Minneapolis where the family made its home. She later came to North Dakota with a group of relatives who sought homesteads.

So half dozen of our two families ventured out to southwestern North Dakota, to a miserable area of land—six pieces of land, one hundred and sixty acres for each one. . . . The land had no water, was covered with stones, debris from the strong winds and storms; no towns nearby. . . .

It was a very hard trip for me to venture out, but still I wished to do it. The country was wild, bare, coyotes all over like little wolves . . . each one [of us] had a one room house built on his claim. The interior was of lumber, the exterior for warmth, was of sod. It was nice and warm. The furniture consisted of a bed, stove, trunk, shelves on the wall. I myself dug out a two foot cellar, to keep milk and butter cold, in a pail of water. . . .

My Aunt Rose and Uncle Osias had their homestead within a half mile from mine; so they had a grocery store just for neighbors around there. They had a horse and buggy. One day I decided to borrow that horse and buggy for an errand, and not knowing that the horse had to have a bridle in his mouth, the moment I took reins, and no bridle in the mouth, the horse began to run, and me in the buggy—me yelling and yelling for help. Fortunately, several customers were going toward the store at that time, but the horse made up his mind to get rid of me, and run back to the barn. So he did that—threw me out, one foot away from a forty-foot open well—lucky me, I came out all right. . . .

Time went on—soon it would be time to prove up the

land and return to Minnesota. I was sick and homesick. . . .
I was the first Jewish girl to try something like this. . . .
    We proved up in Bowman, North Dakota and a
railroad was built during our stay, six miles from our land. I
was the first one to go home. Not only was I glad to go, all
were glad to see me go—sick and homesick.[6]

Bessie had stayed on her claim in Bowman County only long
enough to prove up (nine months). Yet after her marriage in Minneapolis, she and her husband returned to western North Dakota to the
town of Belfield to operate a small business.

The negative experiences of women holding claims ranged
from simple frustrations to life-threatening events. In general, the
more serious incidents were infrequent. Everyone living on the
plains, not just those who filed on claims, had to contend with the
"difficult times." The weather, prairie fires, accidents, animals,
insects, illnesses, and financial insecurity, as well as more minor
frustrations, presented the homesteaders with continuing challenges.
    Incidents of rape, abuse, and assault rarely were recorded or
talked about in public. Yet when one reads carefully, there are hints
and suggestions along with short descriptions that reveal an awareness of these realities. Pioneer women were not foolhardy. They
understood their vulnerability and took precautions to protect themselves.
    There was reason for concern. A headline in the *Williston World*
on October 4, 1906, read, "Young Lady Assaulted." The article
continued:

Last Saturday noon a tramp of the lowest type
appeared at the home of a young lady, who is holding down
her claim, some few miles south of here and demanded
something to eat. After finishing his meal, he immediately

made an unsuccessful attempt to rape her. The young lady fought herself free from the brute and escaped to the home of a neighbor, who immediately came to town. A crowd of citizens at once started for the scene, and after some little searching, the fellow was located hiding in a hay slough. He was taken back and identified by the girl.

C. R. Hamilton and E. A. Hill took him to Crosby where he was turned over to the authorities at that place.

At the hearing Monday he was bound over to the district court with bail fixed at $500. Being unable to furnish that sum, he was taken to Williston Tuesday and placed in jail.

When one woman's brother was unable to meet her at the train station and take her out to her claim, she got a ride with a fellow who promised to take her there. Instead he took her to his claim. He wanted her to sleep with him and took her shoes; but she escaped, spent part of the night outside behind a plow, and in the early morning found another shack close by where she got help.

The only account in the case studies that openly expressed exasperation at having to be wary of men's intentions was found in the diary of Eliza Crawford; and even here, one has to read carefully to pick up her message. Eliza reported:

Mr. Powell's sheep herder came by & stopped. I do not like him. He stayed too long. I wondered why he did not go. I was polite but not talkative. . . .

I hope I shall never have anything to do with a R.R. camp again. Most of the men were perfect gentlemen, and O.K. as far as I know but one or two were far from it. . . .

I have kept my eyes open all the morning for the butcher. I thought if I saw him coming I would not be at home. Paul is not here with me or I would not do that. A child is a great protection. Isn't it horrid to be obliged to sort of protect yourself from the men? I don't know as I am so afraid of what he might do, I'd see to that, but of what he might say![7]

A few women told about assaults or attempted assaults. Years after the incident, one women revealed to her 10-year-old daughter a frightening night on the claim when her sister's hired man forced his way into her shack, blew out the lamp and attacked her. She struggled and he left, only to return later with a hatchet. By this time she had relit the lamp; and before he could blow it out, she recognized him. She told him she knew who he was and that he could kill her, but someone would know. She said, "God knows." The man dropped the hatchet and made her promise not to tell he had been there. She promised and he left. She stayed up all night hoping he would not return. The next morning she walked to her nearest neighbor. Though she was obviously upset, when the neighbor questioned her she responded, "Oh, I guess it was just a mouse." When the men left to do chores, however, she told the woman about the incident. Her brother finally convinced her to tell who the culprit was; but since she would not bring charges, they were able to do nothing but see that the man left the area.

Another woman mentioned turning down a teaching position when she heard a man brag that he slept with all the teachers.

Although most women reported that there was little prejudice against women taking claims, some incidents indicate disgruntled men apparently felt women were overstepping their bounds. When Gertrude Sheidamantel returned from a winter in St. Cloud, she found her shack door full of bullet holes. She suspected a man who had contested her claim. Olga Trygstad was harassed one evening when someone came and made a commotion outside her shack. She borrowed a .22 rifle; and the next time it happened, she opened the door and fired two or three shots into the air. She had no more visitors.

Several accounts described safety precautions. Relatives often looked out for each other. During the time the railroad was being laid

across Anna Hel-
land's land, her
brother, Pete, who
was on an adjoining
claim, would spend
the night with her or
she with him. "On
one occasion three
men came to her door
at night and Pete
went to the door. . . .
Pete, being a robust,
huge man, scared off
the intruders, never
to return again."

Anna Helland and her brother, Pete, who stayed with Anna while the railroad was being laid across her land. Courtesy May Bredeson.

Mary Jennings remembered
her mother, Margaret, kept a loaded
revolver under her apron when men
came to the door asking for direc-
tions. A man came to the door of
Hattie Jones late at night and wanted
in. She told him to leave or she
would shoot through the door. She
had a small colt revolver. He would
not leave, so she shot. "The next
morning there was no one there so he
must have left." Many women were
proficient with guns. Their targets
were usually gophers or snakes, but
skills developed through hunting
could also be used for defense. Eva
Popp could have used her skill with a
rifle against a human rather than a
rattlesnake.

Grace Jacobsen, like many women, was proficient with fire arms. Courtesy Marjorie Peterson.

Gunda Ryen had only a small hook on her door, but she kept a box of lye sitting on a small shelf nearby. While she was visiting her father, a neighbor stole some of her possessions. "She had just returned from her father's home, when she heard a rock hitting the wall after dark. She got up from a sound sleep, lit the lamp and stood ready with the lye can to aim the contents in the intruder's eyes. When he saw she had returned, he returned to his home."

Cecil Nickelson did not own a gun. One night, very late, her dog's barking awakened her. Horseback riders were shooting and yelling in the distance, no doubt on a "drunken spree." Since her cabin was dark, she hoped not to attract attention. She let the dog out and crawled under the bed. As the riders passed, shots rang out, and the riders came so close she could hear the horses brushing against the tar-paper shack. They went on by, and she waited some time before coming out from under the bed. She was afraid the dog had been killed, but toward morning he was scratching on the door.

Anna Koppergard also told of her fear of unidentified riders. "Once while my cousin and I were staying on our homestead, we spotted three riders in the distance, but coming our way. We became frightened and as they came closer . . . we slipped into the cellar of my shack and remained very quiet. As they neared we could hear them talk and then it grew quiet. Finally we dared emerge and happily found them gone."

Thea Thompson stated, "The only time I was frightened was when two strange fellows stopped by. They had tried to take a shortcut to wherever they were going and got lost. I felt very vulnerable, but they were nice fellows. Their horses were tired and they were just looking for a place to spend the night so I directed them to the nearest place with a barn."

Josephine Thedin tried to use humor to get rid of an unwanted guest, but she ended up having to sit up all night.

It was a nice late evening and I had the door open.
And a man came by and sat down on a chair and didn't
speak to me or anything. I sat down on another chair . . . .

174

he talked about the weather and wind and about the living on a claim. So at 10 o'clock in the evening then I said, "Well, there is the door the carpenter made and that's as long as I keep company." But he did not move. He sat there until in the morning the next day. And I sat down on the same chair all night and I thought, well, he was not bad company at all. But then, they told me he was a drifter. He'd go from home to home and visit and then drift around. But I didn't see him anymore.

Although women were sometimes fearful, fear did not dominate their lives. Danger was a part of life, no more so for women who took land than for other men or women.

Unfortunate encounters with men usually went unreported, but there is enough evidence to indicate that such incidents did take place. Pioneer women, though they seldom spoke of these events, were aware of such dangers and took precautions. Men, too, were aware of the dangers that could befall women, and in some instances, showed an unusual sensitivity to their situation.

One day when Anna Enstulen was at home in her shack, she heard light taps on the door. Outside stood Henry Green, the first black man she had ever seen. Henry was working as a sheep herder for the rancher, George Nohley. Knowing that his appearance might frighten Anna, especially since he was black, Henry stood a few feet away and threw small rocks against the door to get Anna's attention. Once she had the chance to see he meant no harm, he inquired if he could come and get a drink of water from her rain barrel.

THE GOOD TIMES

The tragedies, fears, and frustrations of homesteading were offset by the good times, which were just as much a part of life on the plains. Homesteaders knew how to have fun.

175

*Susie Wells played the
piano and sang.
Courtesy Leora Conn.*

"They were happy times and if I were young and had the opportunity I would do it again," reflected Emily Johnson-Bakke as she thought about her homesteading days. This was a typical response from the women interviewed. Of the 15 women I personally interviewed, only two said they thought they would choose not to homestead if they had it to do over again. Many women homesteaded when they were young and single. They were free of family responsibilities and enjoyed the adventures of youth. But even for widows or married women, there was time to make merry.

Get-togethers for dancing, card playing, baseball, picnics, and visiting were common means of enjoyment. Parlor games could help to pass the time during bad weather. Leone Thompson played cards in her cellar while waiting for a storm to pass. Music and dancing seemed to be a part of almost everyone's life. Anna Zimmerman recalled there were too few women:

We visited neighbors, danced at house parties, and played cards. At house parties our musicians were Goob Saunders on the violin, Hube Dehlinger and Chris Sperber playing the mandolin and violin. We went as far as 25 miles horseback to dances, danced all night, and then rode home. Later my brother John and I were called on to play at dances. We played accordion, violin and guitar. We packed our instruments on horses. With the shortage of girls, I often played the harmonica and danced at the same time. It shore was fun![8]

❦

176

Isabel Peterson promised six bachelors a party if they would build her shack. Three married couples were also included. In the one 12-by-14 shack, there was space for one dancing square. Her brother, Pete, played his violin.

In a letter to her cousin, written on January 9, 1906, Effie Vivian Smith describes a "shack party" and several other winter activities.

I never enjoyed myself better in my life than I have this winter. We go some place or some one is here from 1 to 4 times a week. A week ago last Fri. a load of 7 drove out to my claim. Cliff, Clara, David, and I had gone out the Wed. before and such a time as we had. My shack is 10 x 16 and I have only 2 chairs and a long bench for seats, a table large enough for 6, a single bed, and only 3 knives so 2 of them ate with paring knives & 1 with the butcher

Effie Vivian Smith (front row left) with some of her friends, celebrating the Fourth of July. Courtesy Madge Hoppie.

knife. We had two of them sit on the bed and moved the table up to them. They got there at about 5 p.m. Fri. & stayed until 12:30 p.m. Sat. We played all the games we could think of both quiet and noisy and once all but Clara went out & snowballed. They brought a bu. of apples, & a lot of nuts, candy, & gum & we ate all night. We stayed up until 5:30 a.m. & we all got so sleepy we decided to go to bed. I have a curtain up in front of the bed & we girls of course had the "bed chamber." Four of us, including

Clara, 2 other girls & myself, slept crossways on the bed, & Avis & the school ma'am slept on a straw tick on the floor at the foot of the bed. The four boys took all the extra quilts, robes, fur coats, & horse blankets and made themselves a bed on the floor outside the curtain. We slept until 7:30 and we girls woke up first & and lifted up the curtain & looked to see how the boys were. I never saw anything more comical in my life. They reached clear from one side of the shack to the other. They got up picked up their bed and such a sight the floor was. Just covered with nut shells. We had to dig out before we could do anything . . . . We got all nicely loaded in & started for home [parents] when one of the sleds broke & we all had to pile out but we had a lot of hot stones & plenty of wraps so we didn't mind it. We had 18 miles to go & all the rest had to go beyond our place. . . .

We have just started a literary society in our neighborhood. Had our first debate last Fri. The question was Resolved that city life is better than country life. All the judges decided in the negative. I was on and was so scared I didn't know what to do. Next Fri. I am on again & the question is: Is marriage a failure? I can't think of a thing to say. . . . Tomorrow our crowd is going to a literary 6 or 7 miles from here, and the next night to a dance at the home of one of our bachelor boys. We always all go in our sleigh. I am learning to dance this winter but don't attend any except the ones we get up ourselves and they are just as nice & just as respectable as the parties we used to have at Ruthven [Iowa]. I just love to dance. Can two-step pretty fair & am just learning to waltz a very little. We danced a square dance over in my shack & Clara and another girl sang for music. Pete Adamson came over one night about a month & a half ago & took Avis & me to a dance across the road from their place & we had just a fine time. Didn't get to bed until 6 o'clock.

🌹

178

Special days or events were a time for merrymaking. Women were not immune from the Halloween prankster. Carrie Doolittle chuckled when she told of a Halloween joker's printing "Doolittle and sit much" in chalk on the side of her shack.[9] Amanda and Mabel Farland, whose mother homesteaded when they were children, recalled holiday festivities. "We'd have a sleigh with a team of horses and at Christmas time we would go to all the Christmas programs far and near. We'd go for many miles, a bobsled of young people."

Hulda Krueger described celebrations at Elbow Woods, "We had a lot of good times. We had parties and dances and everything like

Anna Underdahl (center right) and her sister Sina (center left) enjoy a picnic at Rice Lake with Eva Prouse and Clara Drady. The men are in traditional dress; Native American dances may have been part of the activities.
Courtesy Odd and Dorothy Osteroos.

that. Elbow Woods was quite a drawing card. All kinds of entertainment. We'd go down there a lot of times."

Often mentioned were the festivities at Rice Lake, especially on the Fourth of July. After 1910, Rice Lake became a resort area with various special activities every Sunday. Annie Andin attended baseball games, rodeos, the Barnum and Bailey circus, and political debates there. Many small towns established regular celebrations, such as Gopher Day in Epping.

With the many opportunities for young people to gather for fun and socialization, the environment obviously was right for courtship. Many homesteaders, male and female, met their future spouses during their homesteading days. Grace Jacobsen married one of the "town bunch," a group of young folks who regularly came to her shack to hunt, pick berries and have parties. Bessie Hanson, a young widow, walked four miles to the post office to get her mail. The postmaster became her second husband. Hildur Erickson met her husband as she crossed his land to reach her brother's place. Lucy Goldthorpe's claim was adjacent to the young bachelor who became her husband.

Although some young people met each other because they had adjacent or nearby claims, others were introduced at special events. Pauline Shoemaker met her husband, Matt Crowley, at a dance held for all the neighbors. Jennie Naismith met James

Grace Jacobsen married one of the "town bunch." This group of friends met at Grace's shack to hunt, pick berries and have parties. Courtesy Marjorie Peterson.

Olive Murray, second from right, and friends enjoy a picnic. Courtesy Mr. and Mrs. Allen Murray.

180

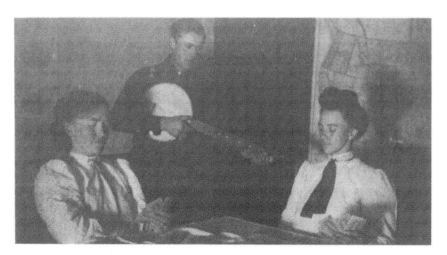

Top: Isabel Peterson homesteaded with her sisters, Ida and Sophia. In 1912, she attended this Howard picnic. Courtesy Harriet Graupe.

Bottom: Johanna Kuhn (right) and her sister, Mary, play cards to the accompaniment of a neighbor's banjo. Courtesy Lena Nelson.

*Top left: Matilda Esoline
Evenson used her gun for
recreation as well as defense.
Courtesy Evelyn Conger.*

*Top right: Annetta Erickson
after a successful hunting trip.
Courtesy John and Lila
Erickson.*

*Left: Matilda Esoline Evenson
"courting." Courtesy Evelyn
Conger.*

182

Top: Relatives of Cornelia Honens playing croquet. Courtesy Ralph Beeson.

Bottom: Anna Chermak "courting." Courtesy Ruth Hinkley.

MacLean at the Scottish Ball in Langdon.

In addition to all the parties and social events, many women pursued an interest in the arts. This merits some attention because it is a reminder that the arts were not left behind when women entered their humble homesteading shacks. Perhaps the arts did not flourish under these conditions, but their presence cannot be denied.

Folk art was a common means of expression. Many women were highly skilled at handwork such as knitting and crocheting. The beauty of their complex quilt designs is well known. Various ethnic groups passed down from mothers to daughters techniques unique to their particular heritage. But the fine arts of painting, sketching, music, and poetry were not forgotten. Some women worked to develop their talents in spite of the lack of resources. Annie Deming "wrote a very good hand, and did pencil drawings." Gelina Lyngen was proficient at drawing and painting. Matilda Esoline Evenson and Tyra Schanche painted in oil.

Dances demanded the skill of those playing the guitar and violin or fiddle as well as the accordion, piano, autoharp, and even the harmonica. Sometimes brass instruments were included. Maria Jane McElwain played the cornet. Many women played musical instruments for their own enjoyment and contributed to community functions.

Bertha Claude Breckenridge was a concert violinist when she

came to Adams County. She had played the instrument from an early age, participating in her high school orchestra; but her most serious and concentrated training took place during her college years at Lawrence

Bertha Claude Breckenridge was a concert violinist when she came to Adams County to homestead. Courtesy Don Walch.

University in Appleton, Wisconsin. She continued her musical interests throughout her life, playing at home and performing solos in
church. She regularly participated in the Saturday night concerts held
in Reeder every summer.

Singing was also a part of many recreational activities. Grace
Jacobsen frequently mentioned in her diary singing and playing with
friends and neighbors. "Mrs. Mann and the Crofoots drove over . . .
[and] we had music all evening."

Even opera found an indirect route to the North Dakota
plains! Kirsten Alida Knudsen sang and played both the guitar and
the violin. She loved the theater, and her brief background as a
chorus girl in the National Theater in Oslo later provided her
children with a special advantage. Her daughter remembered that
her mother:

Climbed up above the curtain in the theater to a spot
where she could look down on the performers. Here she
learned the entire score of many operas such as La Traviata,
Camille, Aida, and several others less well known but
popular in the early 1900's. She would sing all the parts for
us—making her voice low and gruff when singing a man's
part—and telling us the whole story as she went. Some
times her 'shows' would include dancing—which she loved
also—and we saw the cake-walk and Can-can performed in
her own inimitable style.

Many women played the organ and the piano, often for Sunday
School, church services, and other community affairs. Annetta Erickson
led community choirs for 45 years and, during that time, wrote two
books of songs.

Other less common art forms also survived on the prairies.
Mina Roneberg, a woodcarver, had brought her tools from Norway
when she immigrated to the United States.

Edith Divet wrote music, poems and stories and played the piano, mandolin and violin for dances in sod houses. Courtesy Fanchon Lien.

For many, aesthetic pleasure may have come from appreciating a beautiful garden or prairie wild flowers.

No doubt the arts added an essential dimension to pioneer lives, but the sacrifices necessary to maintain and develop these interests are apparent. Josephine Deming had to go to great lengths to ship her piano to North Dakota from Iowa. It was hauled to the homestead in a farm wagon. Ella Reetz rode on horseback nine miles to take piano lessons.

Ohers felt the inadequacies of what a plains environment could offer. Bessie Hanson was a pianist. Her daughter wrote, "I have often thought my Mother was very lonely at times.... She enjoyed good music, concerts and the social functions of a city.... She never complained but as I grew older I could sense her feeling of loss."

In 1901, Margaret Madsen Fjelde made entry on a homestead claim in Burleigh County. Her four children, Margaret, Astrid, Katherine, and Paul, accompanied her from Minneapolis, a rich cultural setting compared to rural North Dakota. Her late husband, Jacob Fjelde, had been an eminent sculptor in Norway and was just gaining recognition in the United States at the time of his death. Financially strapped, Margaret looked to homesteading to provide for her family. She may have been concerned about taking her talented children to the Dakota plains, but her options were limited. It was her son, Paul, who seemed to have regretted the move most. He wrote bitterly in 1973:

> My mother was induced, much against her will, to homestead, with disastrous effect on the Jacob Fjelde children. While "proving up" this barren piece of land, worth very little, we lived for most of five years in a 12' x 14' tar-paper pine board shack and had poor schooling and little

186

Margaret Madsen Fjelde (center left) and three of her children, Margaret (left), Katherine (center right) and Astrid (right). Courtesy Margaret Pratt.

of that! It was all a ghastly, blundering waste, imposed on the Jacob Fjelde widow and children.

Later in the letter, he acknowledged that he and his sisters did, in fact, almost reach the "top" anyway, and he credited one of his teachers at Valley City Normal School with encouraging the children to pursue their creative talents. "It was Mary J. Deem, art supervisor in Valley City, who opened the wonderful doors of opportunity for our talents. Otherwise we would have been a dead loss."

Paul's regrets about his early years in North Dakota show frustration with the lack of resources, but his experience shows that some people in North Dakota recognized superior talent and encouraged it.

The above descriptions illustrate the ways in which the arts were incorporated into the fabric of everyday pioneer life. Music, dancing, and the graphic arts were a part of the daily experience. Even though the resources of urban areas were lacking, every now and then someone with special talent could be found, a Kristen Knudsen singing Aida or a budding artist like Paul Feldje.

187

6

Returns on the Investment

I always used to say that the claim was the first thing I ever earned in my life so I wanted to keep it. . . . I never borrowed a cent against it . . . . I still own it.

— Hulda Krueger Olsen

She was so enthusiastic about this period of her life. She was so happy about having something of her own. Her dream was being fulfilled.

—Mathilde Haga,
daughter of Gunda Ryen Haga

FINANCIAL BENEFITS

Whatever other goals a settler may have had, a primary objective was to make his or her claim a financial success. The talk of "free" land was, in many respects, misleading. Establishing residency and turning the virgin prairie into cultivated acres entailed considerable expense. Initial costs included traveling to the area where land was available, hiring a locator to find suitable land, and lodging while land was found or the shack was being built. Money was needed to buy building supplies for the shack or to purchase a secondhand shack and furnish it.

Those who did not have friends or family with whom to share the work had to bear some costs for hired labor. Breaking the sod was a tough job, and many men as well as women hired others to do this task. Beyond these costs were those connected with purchasing seed and putting in the first crop, usually flax, and providing for transportation. Most women did not invest in a team of oxen or horses, but many purchased a riding horse or a horse and buggy. The homesteaders had to find the resources to buy household provisions and fuel for heating and cooking. Settlers who took preemptions or decided to commute their homesteads had to find the $1.25 or $2.50 per acre to complete the transaction. Those obtaining their claim through a relinquishment had to pay the asking price of the original settler.

Olive Murray bought a relinquishment from Jack Smith, a mail carrier from New York, for $250. She was fortunate to sell 11 acres to the railroad for a right-of-way. This paid off the relinquishment even though the railroad never built on the land.

Cora Barnfather hired a man who owned a nearby sawmill to break up five acres and plant flax. He harvested the first crop for his pay. After living on the claim for 14 months, Cora borrowed the money to commute her homestead, paying $1.25 an acre.

Olive Murray bought a relinquishment and paid it off by selling 11 acres to the railroad. Courtesy Mr. and Mrs. Allen Murray.

Setting up a homestead usually required an initial outlay of several hundred dollars and some continued investment thereafter. Financial arrangements could be difficult, and family could not always provide assistance. Clara Rowe's granddaughter commented, "Times were rough. Many letters were written to family in New York. Much sympathy was given but no money."

The women in my sample did enjoy some measure of success in their homestead ventures. They were among those who proved up and received title to land. The effort, fortitude, and financial investment of these women paid off in a variety of ways.

The land itself provided a home, at least during proving up. This length of time varied with the individual, which government policies were in effect, and the method chosen to prove up. Table 12 gives a general idea of how long the women lived on their claims. Sixty percent stayed little longer than the time required to meet the residency requirements; but 18 percent were on the land from six to 24 years, and 22 percent remained on their land from 25 years to most of their lifetimes. Including the 13 women who continued ownership but not residency with those who stayed on the land over 25 years, 27 percent of the sample owned the land for over 25 years.

	TABLE 12	
	Length of Time Lived on the Claim	
	Percent	Number[a]
Up to 5 years	60	143
6 to 24 years	18	42
25 years to most of life	22	52
	100	237*

[a]At least 13 women of the 237 retained ownership all their lives but did not continue to live on the land after proving up. They are included in one of the first two categories depending on length of residence on the claim.

*Information not available in all cases.

Enough information was available to give a general picture of what happened to the land after the initial period of proving up. Table 13 (page 193) shows whether the claim eventually became a part of a husband's or another relative's acreage. After marriage, 32 percent of the women consolidated their land into one operation with that of their husband. Many of these couples bought additional land, some of them accumulating extensive holdings.

Only 6 percent of the claims were sold to, or operated by, a father and 5 percent to a brother. A few bought or received land from

191

Anne Anderson and her husband, Olaf Hovde, consolidated their homesteads when they married in 1912. Courtesy Agnes Hovde.

Louisa Oberg Larson rented her land to her son and later sold it to him. Courtesy Alene and Abner Larson.

their fathers, brothers, and in some cases, sisters and other relatives. Marie Gjellstad and her husband built a new home on an 80-acre parcel she received from her father. The additional land adjoined the southern border of her own homestead. In 1900, Carrie Doolittle, her two sisters, Phoebe and May, and a cousin, Laura Bolles, of Cresco, Iowa, arrived at Berthold. Soon they all filed on adjoining claims about three miles south of town. After proving up, the other three turned their land over to Carrie, who moved into Berthold. She retained her ownership, buying an additional nearby quarter section. Marie Zirbes built an enterprise of 800 acres, which became known as the Ash Grove Stock Farm, from the nucleus of her original homestead.[1]

In a few cases, a settler traded an original claim for land closer to his or her spouse. Eight percent of the couples made the woman's claim the nucleus of the operation. In these situations, the husband either had no claim or the couple decided her land was the most productive.

Those women who consolidated their acres with a spouse or a close relative made a significant economic contribution to the farming or ranching operation. Not only did the acreage provide more cropland or pasture, but it increased the assets that could be used for mortgages. This allowed further investment and expansion. Mary Belle Hanson and her husband used their homesteads as the foundation of an operation that eventually included several sections of land.

192

TABLE 13

**Percentage of Women Who Consolidated
Their Homestead with a Husband's or Relative's Land**

	Percent	Number
Consolidated with husband's land	32	56
Sold to or operated by father	6	10
Sold to or operated by brother	5	8
Traded or sold land for land closer to husband's land	3	5
Husband bought or traded for land closer to her homestead	2	4
Couple made home on her land	8	15
Land sold to non-relative	44	78
	100	176*

*Information not available in all cases.

Some women moved off their claims shortly after proving up but kept ownership throughout their lives. The rent from these acres provided an additional source of income. Eliza Crawford, a widow who filed on her claim in 1906, reflected many years later on the wisdom of keeping her land.

And now after all these years, "The Claim" is really coming to the front. However, there never was a time in all these years, since proving up, that it has not paid its taxes. But for the last two years, "42 and 43" when the crops have been good, most everywhere, the check I received for my share amounted to $350.

I have a wonderful renter, Mr. Leslie Horal, one of the finest most conscientious men, and certainly an honest renter. . . .

The Fall of 1944 and here I stand—still bewildered and nearly overcome by the best news yet. I can scarcely believe it! It is too good to be true. The check from Mr. Beaumont for my share of the wheat from the dear old claim (Yes I can call it that now) was $945 (some cents).

Did it pay to go out there & stay till we could prove up? Yes, a thousand times Yes.[2]

Hulda Krueger and her husband operated a grocery store and the post office at Roseglen for 30 years. She kept her original homestead, which she filed on in 1916, and soon bought another piece of land in 1919, renting both quarter sections to neighbors. The land was still providing her with a steady income when I visited her in 1987.

Annie Elizabeth Koehmstedt's husband traded land with his brother to secure 80 acres adjoining Annie's homestead. Courtesy Clara Cox.

A 160-acre homestead was just the beginning of land investment for Lydia Lavalle. This asset enabled her to help her sister, Minnie, who had homesteaded an adjoining claim. Minnie relinquished her claim before proving up, married Albert Shipton, and moved to her husband's farm. The Shiptons needed additional land. Casting about for the means to buy it, they turned to Lydia, whose assets allowed her to invest further in land, which she rented to her sister and brother-in-law.[3]

While most of the women in my sample were successful in proving up, some lost their land in later years. Thora Johanson and her husband lived on her land for six years, but it did not produce: "We were there six years and we were hailed out every year." Given the opportunity to farm her husband's parents' land, the couple moved and let her homestead go for taxes.

Others, such as Mary Dooley, hung onto their land until the thirties. During these lean years, drought and debt finally forced some women to forfeit their land for taxes. Katie Gramling mortgaged her land to pay her mother's medical bills. She was unable to repay the loan and lost the land to the bank.

The claim provided a permanent home for the women who married and remained on the land, for some of the women who remained single, and for widows with children. While some single women returned to their parents' homes after proving up, others maintained separate households. Leone Sisco moved back to her parents' household, but the Olimb sisters, Caren and Petra, maintained their homes on their homesteads. Caren lived on her land for many years and later moved into Balfour, renting the land to neighbors. Petra remained on her land: "She managed the homestead throughout her lifetime and enjoyed her cattle and horses and all the activities on the farm."

Kari Skredsvig made a home for her seven young children and remained on the land until her death. Clara Rowe and her two sons, about 10 and 15 years old, proved up on a claim after Clara's husband was drowned. She lived there the remainder of her life. Anna Hensel was 68 when she filed on her claim. She lived on the land with her daughter and son-in-law for about 11 years.

Marie Holen's husband, Adolph Nelson, moved to her homestead and bought adjoining quarter sections of land. Courtesy Mabel McLellan.

Grethe Loraas lived on her homestead about 20 years. Courtesy Mr. and Mrs. Arthur Loraas.

Kari Skredsvig lived on her land until her death, about 42 years. Courtesy Margaret Lien.

Petra Olimb managed her homestead for over 50 years. Courtesy Olga Olimb.

A tree claim was home to Karen Ronning for 45 years. Courtesy Berta Soper.

For some women, the claim became an asset to fall back on. Sometime after proving up, Nell Sheridan married and left the area. Later, after her divorce, she returned to the farm. Anna Nelson proved up in 1912. She married in 1914 and lived with her husband in Bowman where he worked for the Home Lumber Company. In 1916, they moved back to her homestead to farm.[4] Julia Moen married shortly after filing on her homestead but was later divorced. Though she and her young daughter, Esther, left the claim soon after her divorce, she retained ownership. The income from her land enabled her to attend Aakers Business College in Grand Forks for a year.

Julia Moen used income from her homestead to attend business college in Grand Forks. Courtesy Esther Johnson.

A number of women set up a farming or ranching operation with their husbands and found themselves in sole charge after they were widowed. Janie Brew Scott and her husband bought land around her original homestead, accumulating about a thousand acres. Her son, Bill, remembers his mother as a person who "had a strong will to make things go in spite of the odds. She worked very hard all her life and after her husband died in 1931 leaving her with four children during a drought and a depression, she kept the land clear

. . . .She would not accept any government aid. Her motto was sink or swim. She and her sons milked 16 cows by hand to keep afloat."

Ordinarily, income from a claim was reinvested into the land or used to meet everyday expenses. But some stories reveal dreams that were fulfilled with the extra cash from a claim. Ella Reetz told of being allowed to go to school only every other year until she completed third grade. She alternated with her twin sister so that one of them would always be home to help with the younger children. After third grade, there was no more school.

Ella Reetz used several years' income from her homestead to buy a piano she had long wanted. Courtesy Arnold Erbstoesser.

In her late teens, she found odd jobs at ranches as a domestic; and with this money, she rode nine miles by horse to Hebron about twice a month to take piano lessons. In 1910, she filed on a claim. After proving up and marrying she rented the claim to her brother, Leo. Several years later, she used the money accumulated from her homestead income to buy the piano, which she had wanted for so many years.

Many women sold out shortly after they proved up. The following accounts illustrate some of the opportunities made available by cash sales of homesteads.

Land prices were determined by demand and the quality of the soil. A neighbor paid Cora McCombs $800 for her land. Kaja Kurz homesteaded with the idea it would be a profitable investment. After proving up, she sold the land for about $1,000. Some women sold land to family members. On the official records, Anna Matilda Jensen sold to her father for only $1. It seems likely, though, that Anna received additional compensation. Her father probably paid off a $250 mortgage, which Anna took out to finance her millinery shop. Gurina Espeseth sold her land to her father for $1,000, and Matilda Esoline Evenson sold hers in 1909—the same year she proved up—to a John Grant of Vienna, South Dakota, for $2,800.

Gina Brorby received $1,900 for her homestead in 1900. Courtesy Ida Hillestad.

Top: Matilda Esoline Evenson sold her homestead in 1909 for $2,800. Courtesy Evelyn Conger.

Bottom: Anna Matilda Jensen (right) sold her land to her father. Courtesy Anna Matilda Jensen Warke.

Ida Popp put the proceeds from her homestead into a farm she and her husband purchased. Courtesy L.A. Joyce.

199

Top: Anna Mathilda Berg traded her homestead for a large house in Warwick which she ran as a boarding house for teachers. Courtesy Mae and Floyd Jensen.

Bottom: Maggie O'Connor (Sister Anita) sold her land to a relative and contributed the proceeds to the Sisters of St. Joseph of Carondelet in St. Paul. Courtesy Patricia O'Connor.

Top: Dora Burud sold her claim soon after she married. Courtesy Linda Christensen.

Bottom: Income from a good crop on her homestead made it possible for Sarah Knutson to purchase a home in Velva. Courtesy Olga Gryde.

A number of women, such as Ida Popp, sold their land and used the proceeds to buy either land near their husbands' homesteads or needed supplies and equipment for their joint operations. Gina Brorby sold her homestead in 1900 for $1,900. She used the proceeds to buy another quarter section that adjoined her husband's land.

For anyone who did not want to expand a farming or ranching venture, the assets from the homestead provided investment for another business. Some years after she proved up, Lucy Gorecki traded her 160 acres for a business building in Fordville. Anna Thingvold and her sister, Emma, stayed on their claims only long enough to prove up; but they rented out their land and used the income to finance a millinery and dressmaking shop in Willow City, which was about 10 miles from the claims.

Anna Lee filed her claim in 1908. In 1912, she became a telephone operator for the Lunds Valley Farmers Telephone Company. After proving up, she sold her land and bought the Lamb Building where the telephone office and switchboard were located. She also opened a lunch counter, a confectionery, and millinery shop in the same building.[5]

Anna Mathilda Berg took a homestead beside the Sheyenne River near Warwick. After proving up, she traded her land for a large square house on the main street of Warwick. This home, with its four bedrooms and fine furnishings, provided her with a livelihood; she ran it as a boarding house, usually renting to teachers. Anna served meals on a padded, linen-covered table with linen napkins. "Everyone called her 'Tillie.' She brewed the best cup of coffee which she was always ready to serve and Oh!, her bread—Super good and beautiful finger rolls, perfect! She would take her turn serving Ladies Aid a monthly dinner and always had the biggest crowd and, of course, so the collection."

Maggie O'Connor (Sister Anita) came to the United States from County Cork in the early 1880s. She filed on a claim in 1891, returning there often enough to comply with the residency requirements. She proved up the land, sold it "And Sister joyfully gave the money as a gift to her community [Sisters of St. Joseph of Carondelet in St. Paul]."

Cash from the sale of her homestead helped Theona Carkin finance a university degree.

Life in general was dotted with hardships but there were many good times also. I have always felt that my efforts on my homestead were very worthwhile and very rewarding, and I have always been proud of myself for doing it all.

By teaching off and on from 1906 through early 1909, and upon selling the homestead, I was able to pay all my own college expenses. I attended the University of North Dakota at Grand Forks and graduated in June 1911. Grand Forks was about 40 miles north of our farm and it cost $1 on the train, a trip we took about every six weeks.[6]

Although the sale of homesteads provided some women with cash or assets to invest in other ventures, those who chose to keep their land passed down a legacy to their descendants, which, in many cases, had far-reaching and, in some cases, surprising consequences. A poignant account of the long-term impact of such a legacy was provided by Vivian Broberg, a granddaughter of Miriam Coburn West.

I wanted more training—to be able to teach in a "town school." To do that I needed a "standard certificate" and that meant one more year at a teachers college. But I hadn't been able to save enough money in a seven months term at $70.00 a month. But there was a way. Granny had homesteaded a quarter section of land in Dakota. Using that as collateral I borrowed enough to attend St. Cloud Teachers College. And so it was—with the $500 I was able to complete the next year and thus qualify for the coveted Standard Certificate....

202

In the fall, I was lucky enough to get a job—upper grades in a two room town school with a salary of $105 a month for a nine months term—a fair salary in those days. My first year I needed a car so I was able to make only a small payment on my debt. The next year the depression hit—and the bottom dropped out of the economy. Salaries took a nose dive and mine dropped to $85 a month.

By this time my sister's turn came to go to school. My commitment was to help her. There wasn't enough money left to even pay the interest on my debt that year. The next year was worse and still no payment on the debt and my conscience bothered me. Then came the drought on top of the depression. Nobody had much. We were lucky to save the home farm because I could help out with the taxes. But that didn't help my debt.

Another year and still hard times. By this time it was becoming evident I couldn't make it financially. There wasn't enough money to buy clothes. I wore the same brown wool skirt and orange sweater to school every day and washed them out on Saturday. My roommate's mother knitted me some mittens out of wool she had spun from the sheep they had raised. I couldn't afford to buy a new pair and the old ones were full of holes and the thumbs were all gone from wear.

In desperation and with my consent, Dad made an agreement with the man who held the mortgage to take legal action and foreclose on the land. So it was—my grandmother's homestead in reality paid not only for my college education but my sister's also—who in turn helped our brother with his education. In actuality then, Granny's homestead helped all her grandchildren to get an education and during a time when it would not have been possible any other way.

Miriam West's efforts to prove up her claim helped to finance the education of her grandchildren, even though the land was lost in the process. Undoubtedly there were many others who, like Vivian, benefited indirectly from the efforts of homesteading relatives.

For many, these benefits came in the form of access to land. Some inherited land from those women who held their homesteads until death; many other relatives bought land from homesteading women and in turn passed it on to their kin. For 174 of the case studies, I was able to determine if descendants still held title to the land. Fifty-four percent, or 94, of the 174 homesteads were still owned by a descendant of the woman who first filed on the land.

When she entered the convent, Maggie O'Connor sold her homestead to her brother, Tim. This land has changed ownership several times but has remained in the hands of a relative of Maggie to the present day.

Ella Fedje, her sister, Rannie, and several other sisters and brothers migrated with their parents from Norway to Minnesota. In the early 1900s, Ella, along with her sister and brother-in-law, came to North Dakota and filed on land. Ella actually lived on her homestead in a two-room house with a front porch only a few years. When she left the land, she had her house moved to Minot and added another bedroom and a second porch. There she rented the rooms to college students, providing their breakfast and evening meals as well as lodging.

Ella never married and remained in Minot the rest of her life. She was remembered as a mild-mannered, kind, and gentle woman who smoked a pipe. Odin Fedje, a nephew of Ella Fedje, now owns her homestead, and there may be a surprising and financially rewarding turn of events in store for him. A wildcat oil well has been drilled on her land, and the prospects look promising. As her grandniece, Rose Morgan, remarked, "Aunt Ella would be surprised, wouldn't she?"

BOUND TO THE LAND

Financial or material rewards were only part of the homestead bargain. Settlers felt personal pride and a sense of accomplishment in managing to prove up.

Land. One's own land. For many women, proving up was accompanied by the development of a strong bond with the homestead acres as well a certain reverence for land. Some readers may find this statement surprising, since the relationship to the land is usually seen in terms of men. Although women have been associated with nature, their activities have been envisioned primarily in terms of an interest in gardens or prairie flowers. Women usually are not characterized as having strong ties to productive, cultivated soil.

Mary Belle Hanson and her husband acquired several sections of land, but she kept her original homestead in her own name until she died. Courtesy R. Warren Pierson.

My interviews with women who homesteaded left no doubt that the women were firmly "bound to the land." The pride with which they expressed their sense of accomplishment in acquiring property was more than sentimentality about land. It was an intense and enduring bond to the soil. This commitment to the land was also apparent in many of the accounts in the case study files. Although Mary Belle Hanson and her husband accumulated a great deal of additional land after their marriage, she kept her homestead acres under her own name until she died.

Even women such as Minnie Lavalle, who relinquished their homesteads, did not forsake their attachment to the land. The initial experience left them with lingering thoughts of their near ownership. Minnie Lavalle's daughter described the desire of her mother, in later years, to see her homestead again. Even though Minnie had not proved up, "it had been Ma's dream for a long time to visit the Slatterys at Newbury, and look again upon the homestead that had almost been hers. Preparations were made for the journey, a distance of some seventy miles by the circuitous routes then available .... Happiness and excitement shone on our mother's face so we knew the trip was most worthwhile."[7]

Caroline Tolsby stayed on her homestead only long enough to prove up, but her daughter recalled that her mother always used the word land reverently. Anne Gjellstad left the state, but, as her niece recalled, "her heart was always in the Mouse River Valley." Martha Smith followed her husband to Oregon, her daughter remembers, "but my Mother's heart remained on the homestead and every summer my sister and she returned." After her husband's death, Martha returned to North Dakota for good.

Though the plains could be cruel at times, they could be captivating; and they claimed their share of allegiance. Addie Lindsley grew up in Jackson, Minnesota, and returned there after her homesteading venture, but not for long. She wrote of her feelings: "But the prairies had got such a hold on me that I had to come back when I had been gone but a year. While I was gone I thought only of the prairie with its unadulterated sunshine, its endless green and wonderful sunsets."[8]

Sarah Elizabeth Taipe found comfort in the landscape. When her parents returned to Providence, Rhode Island, Sarah stayed in North Dakota. When asked why, she replied, "I loved the rolling prairies and the waving grass reminded me of the ocean."

It was not just men, then, who stuck to the land. Caroline Gunvaldson married and lived on her homestead for the rest of her life, though two of her brothers who homesteaded left the state.

Some women went to great lengths to keep their land in their families. When Ella Curry could not repay a bank loan on her homestead, she arranged to have her brother pay it so the land would remain "Curry" land. Janie Brew's son remembered how much his mother valued her homestead; she taught this value to her children. Josephine Delong expressed her desire to keep her land in the family name. Women who failed to keep their land, such as Katie Gramling and Mary Dooley, expressed continued regret at the loss.

Rachel Taylor's description of her reaction to the cultivation of virgin prairie shows an early awareness of the environmental costs that came with the plow. "That first summer there I grew to love the prairie in its natural wild, untamed state and I felt a bit sad that now it would be cut up, plowed up, fenced up, used and trampled over by the feet of men, many caring only for the money it would bring."[9]

Not all women who homesteaded developed this reverence for the land. Undoubtedly some were glad to prove up and move on to another life. But the frequency with which strong positive attachments were expressed showed that many women as well as men felt very much a part of the land they helped to develop.

Some of these acres were named after their original owners. Gina Brorby's quarter was called "the Gina Land." Ingeborg Knudson's land was referred to as "Ingeborg land" even after her brother purchased it. Emma Anderson's land is still known as "the Emma Land."

Ingeborg Knudson's homestead was referred to as "Ingeborg Land." Courtesy Olga Gryde.

7

The Gender Factor

Uncle helped us a lot, but we helped him too. I couldn't handle the actual breaking of sod or some of the other field operations. I did, however, drive 4 horses on the binder and I have milked my share of cows. I found it restful and enjoyed doing it.

—Anna Koppergard Strand

Now my brothers when they were around, well, they couldn't boil water.... They were brought up in Norway. But Oscar was real handy in the kitchen because he was the oldest of four children, and Grandma Olson was poorly a lot times and needed a helper.... He could fix coffee ....When Agnes was born we needed diapers washed after mother had gone home.... Well, he said, I'll do that, I can wash diapers.... I washed diapers for all my brothers.

—Thora Johanson Olson

When skeptics are told that thousands of women took land in North Dakota, their reactions reflect longstanding notions about gender roles in which women and women's work are relegated to a subsidiary status. Women's place, they say, lies within the private domestic sphere while men are in charge of public affairs or the

worldly sphere. Because the domestic sphere is considered secondary, women themselves are characterized as inferior. They are seen
as weak and dependent creatures relying on men for both emotional
and financial support.

The idea that women are not as capable as men, particularly in
the worldly sphere, has been a persistent one. The existence of this
idea, even today, has been responsible for much of the distortion that
surrounds the description of female roles on the frontier.

Images perpetuating the distortion of female roles focus on
three themes, which make up what I refer to as the marriage, madness,
and marginality syndrome. Women are portrayed as depending on
marriage for fulfillment, as unable to cope with severe adversity, and
as marginal or secondary contributors to the important business of
society.

The following news article, which appeared in the *Williston
World* on September 25, 1906, illustrates all three themes as it describes
the misfortune of a young woman.

MAMIE WON HOMESTAD, BUT LOST LOVER

Heartbroken when she found that the man who she
had expected to marry this fall had married during her
absence on a claim near Columbus, N. Dak., pretty Mamie
Barnes threatened to take her own life last week and but for
the intervention of the police would probably have carried
out her threat.

It was about 10 o'clock last night when the police
were first informed of the affair. Howard Pickering, a
Moorhead butcher, who Mamie Barnes claims she was to
have married this fall and who had already taken a partner
in life, rushed into the police station and asked Captain
Dahlgren to take care of the girl.

"She is out of her head," said Pickering, "and I am
afraid she will make good her threat to end her life." Captain Dahlgren, a member of the fire department and Picker-

ing at once set out to find the young woman. The captain finally located her on Broadway and escorted her to the police station. She wept pitifully but without hesitation told her story, and in a rational manner. . . .

With vows of faith in each other the couple separated, the young man to accept a position in a Moorhead butcher shop and the young woman to her claim in this state. The monotony of the weary months on the homestead was relieved by the thoughts of her approaching marriage and it was with feelings of great joy that the time finally came when Uncle Sam's requirements had been sufficiently ful-filled so that she could take a trip without fear of losing her rights to her claim.

It was not long after her arrival here that she dis-covered that her lover had not remained true to his vows. He had married a pretty Moorhead girl. . . .

While the young woman displayed marked indica-tions of losing her mind, she was reported to be much better the next day and left for her homestead near Columbus that evening.

The report of this incident serves to trivialize women's contri-butions to settlement. Mamie's existence is seen as revolving around her pending marriage. The article infers it was her anticipation of marriage that enabled her to endure the long months on the claim. When her plans are thwarted, she is portrayed negatively with phrases such as "heartbroken," "out of her head," "wept pitifully," "losing her mind." The article says nothing about Mamie's skill at managing a homestead or her contributions to settlement. Instead, her home-steading venture is seen as incidental to the loss of a potential hus-band. There is a subtle warning, as well, that independent women jeopardize their chances for marriage.

If one continues to the end of the article, however, one reads that Mamie recovered her composure rapidly, leaving for her homestead *the next day.* It is unlikely that such an incident would be considered newsworthy if the roles had been reversed, that is, if Mr. Pickering had been the object of scorn.

Contrast this account with excerpts from Pauline Neher Diede's book *Homesteading on the Knife River Prairies.*[1] In this volume, she reports that her Uncle Martin confessed to crying many times and related an incident that showed his brother's frustration with life on the plains.

On the particular Sunday after the horse episode, Neher sat on the stone near his unfinished sod house, eating his brined side pork and bread. He fell to his knees, clutching the stone, and screamed. He was not thinking about his sufferings in the Russo-Japanese war, or of the persecution of the Russian people he knew was going on, he simply was very homesick. He did not really enjoy North Dakota's stony prairie.

This account by Diede is unusual for the glimpse of male vulnerability it provides. Crying and screaming are not actions associated with men of the prairie. These are manifestations of emotion normally reserved for women. In this case, however, the circumstances are laid out so that the reader can understand the men's frustration as both reasonable and temporary. Diede does not suggest that these men were "out of their heads." The most important difference between the two accounts lies in the fact that in the first case a woman's distress is used as the object of amusement and thus trivialized while in the second a serious description is presented that furthers our understanding of the everyday frustrations of the early pioneers, be they men or women.

The dichotomy of gender roles presented in the first account still seems to hold sway over public opinion. Since frontier women in general are characterized as being secondary figures in the public sphere, dependent, and overly concerned with marriage, these same labels have been applied to women who took claims. Their contributions are downplayed, and they are portrayed as figurehead homesteaders.

Since land ownership usually indicates participation in the public sphere, not the domestic one, the skeptic must manipulate the marriage, madness, and marginality syndrome in such a way as to explain this inconsistency within a traditional framework.

Skeptics assume that if women filed claims, it was probably at the bidding of a man who wanted to extend his acreage. Some women did take land with the idea they would sell it to the highest bidder as soon as it was proved up, but women are more likely than men to be seen as pawns in the process while men are characterized as speculators.

Skeptics suggest women were seeking to improve their chances of marriage by acquiring land. In other words, a piece of land would make an enticing dowry. Historian Everett Dick reinforces this idea with this comment: "A marriageable lady with a homestead certainly was not unattractive in a land of unlimited bachelors who, batching in dugouts and very sorry figures at stag housekeeping, readily succumbed to the wiles of these prairie sirens."[2]

Because of their alleged delicate nature, women are thought to have been less able to cope with the rigors of frontier life, resulting in a marked tendency to lose their mental faculties ("go out of their heads"). Given this situation, how could women expect to meet government requirements for proving up the land?

Finally, skeptics simply revert to the general judgment that "they didn't really homestead," implying that women did only women's work, which does not count as homesteading.

To assess the validity of these common assumptions and stereotypes, I examined the material from my case studies to determine attitudes of these women toward marriage, their reasons for taking land, and the division of labor. This information severely challenges entrenched gender stereotypes, although it does not overturn them completely.

The public perception that frontier women were primarily interested in finding a mate and settling down is not supported by the actions of women who took land. Marriage was a goal for many of them, but it was seen as a part of life, not its only focus. The roles of wife and mother were not rejected but rather postponed for awhile, allowing for extensive participation in the public arena through both occupational pursuits and land ownership.

Many women expressed a reluctance to marry and resisted efforts of others to have them marry at an early age. Many did not marry until their late twenties or early thirties, and some chose to remain single. Their days on the claim were likely to be coordinated with time spent pursuing an occupation, which many women found in the areas of teaching, housekeeping, and sewing.

Although comments about women who "lost their minds" owing to an inability to cope with the harsh conditions on the prairies abound, stories of this kind seem to be based mostly on hearsay rather than rooted in reality. Insanity as a reaction to difficult situations did not figure in the accounts of the women in my sample. I had only one report of a homesteading woman "gone mad," and this report could not be verified.

This does not mean that insanity was entirely unknown on the plains, but the real question is how frequent. The lives of women settlers often are depicted as lonely, isolated, and filled with drudgery and tragedy. This bleak description does not correspond to the situation of most of the women in my sample. Although they may have suffered greatly at times, their lives were filled with purpose, determination, and a light heartedness that often is overlooked. During this time in history, few men or women led lives of complete isolation for long. Most were a part of a network of family, friends, and neighbors. If we judge their lives as more tragic or trying than our own and assume that "madness" was a frequent consequence of hard times, particularly for women, we may err.

It seems that some characteristics of the lives of homesteading women functioned as an effective buffer against the oppressive aspects of the plains. Through their paid occupations, these women had more contact with the "outside" world than many of their counterparts who married and started families at a younger age.

"Did women 'really' homestead?" When people ask this question, I believe they have two thoughts in mind: (1) Were these women "in charge" of their homesteads? and (2) Did they work in the fields? The underlying assumption that homesteading women were following the directives of men, and therefore, took little interest in their land or that women's physique would not allow them to work in the fields perpetuates the idea that women were simply helpmates, and that, in some cases, even though they may have worked themselves to death, they had little control over their fates except in the domestic realm. Scholars have questioned this subordinate position of women and suggested that earlier historians failed to see variations in the division of labor and the subtle, and sometimes not so subtle, power and influence pioneer women exerted. Katherine Harris proposes that some men and women defined their relationships in terms of partnership rather than male domination and female domestic support.[3]

Who was in charge of the homestead is quite clear. As mentioned before, 94 percent of the women in the study oversaw the operation of their land.

Overall, however, the assignment of tasks did tend to follow a traditional pattern. Women saw to the household chores: cooking, cleaning, sewing, laundry, and so on. Men cultivated the fields, constructed buildings, and went for supplies. Some of the women interviewed mentioned a stigma attached to families who allowed their women to work in the fields. If women had to work in the fields, it was evidence that the men of the house were not providing adequately for "their women." (This notion ignores the backbreaking work demanded of women in the home.) Though the traditional roles were generally the ideal, the actual division of labor is complex and confusing. Ethnicity, circumstance, and choice modified the ideal pattern considerably.

The "ideal" was not the same in all ethnic groups or even within groups. German-Russians often expected women to work in the fields as well in the household.[4] The aversion to having women in the fields appears to have been stronger among Anglo-Americans and Scandinavians; but even among these groups, women did do field work by necessity or choice. Unfortunately my sample was not ethnically representative, prohibiting an accurate comparison of the practices of various ethnic groups.

Agnes Lamb. Women usually took care of domestic tasks. Courtesy Kathy Crary.

In the case study files, the traditional division of labor had many exceptions. Under certain circumstances, women did all the tasks men usually did; and, in some instances, men took care of the household chores. Both men and women had to be flexible, altering their normal activities according to what was practical in a given situation. Not all bachelors were able to find a woman to do domestic work, and not all women were able to or wanted to hire someone to do field work. Considering the range of activities of both genders, however, it appears that women were more likely to assume traditionally male tasks than men were to assume traditionally female tasks.

M.J. Vandeberg did his own domestic work before he married Lucy Goldthorpe. Courtesy Vernon Vandeberg.

As one relative remarked about Caroline May, a widow whose son helped her homestead until he married: "She helped build fence, milk cows, raise chickens, and a

216

garden. They had to mine their own coal for winter. She helped with the haying. She helped outside but never got much help inside."

Whatever the actual division of labor was, many women who chose to take homesteads seemed to support the idea that the cooperation of the genders represented a partnership instead of a dominant male with helpmate. This perception of equality was eloquently expressed by Anna Koppergard when she said, "Uncle helped us a lot," and then added emphatically, "but we helped him too." Anna and her cousin did all the household chores; and, in return, her uncle cultivated her land. Anna felt that the division of labor was practical and that her contributions were just as important as her uncle's. Louise Karlson was keenly aware of the advantages of a division of labor when she explained her decision to marry. Her neighbor was homesteading on the opposite quarter section; "[he] needed a cook and I needed a farmer."[5]

Caroline May with her son, Herman. She "helped outside but never got much help inside ." Courtesy Herman and Luella May.

One hardly ever finds evidence that women were frustrated by men and their lack of skill, but I did come across a couple of remarks. Eliza Crawford, impatiently waiting for a man to come to dig a well, wrote in her diary, "Our well is still in 'Status Quo'. Men never seem to get anything done in this country."[6] Gunda Ryen Haga took matters into her own hands when her husband and his uncle could not agree on how to butcher a cow. "The cow had been killed and bled but the men could not agree how to open it up. Gunda sent them into the house for lunch and coffee, and while they were there, she opened up the cow, removed the innards and it was ready to be cut up, when they returned."

Even though some sharing and partnership seemed to characterize the division of labor between women and men on the plains, overestimating the equality of men and women should be avoided. Sharing and partnership may have been more prevalent than previously thought, but there are many indications of the constraints that regulated women's activities and the lesser evaluation of their talents.

Fannie Overstreet and her husband, George Henry. For them, homesteading was a joint effort. Courtesy Pat Henry.

The "cult of true womanhood" provided a powerful blueprint even for frontier women, perpetuating the idea that men and women occupied "separate spheres." The woman's world was private and domestic while the man's was public and active. True womanhood was defined by the four cardinal virtues of poetry, purity, domesticity, and submissiveness.[7] The crossover of both women and men into the other's sphere was not acceptable to everyone.

Anna Jacobson's daughter recalled, "As a young woman mother wanted to be a doctor. Women doctors were not popular in those days and not with her father. She read medical books when available and helped the doctor occasionally. I remember she would chuckle every time she cleaned a chicken for she carefully examined all its organs."

Even nursing, which was accepted as a women's profession, was considered by some to be unfit for a woman. Louise Trenne

Louise Trenne wanted to be a nurse, but her father did not approve. Courtesy Helen and Vernon Porth.

commented, "I would like to have been a nurse but my father did not consider that a very nice profession."

Women played a central role in the establishment of churches in their communities, but gender divisions were here, too. Kari Skredsvig helped to organize a neighborhood church and was an active participant. She could not be considered a charter member of that church, however, since only men in the congregation could be so designated. Women were allowed to be charter members of the Ladies Aid.

Hanna Amanda Boesen Anderson showed her sensitivity to community reac-

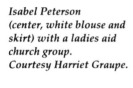

Isabel Peterson (center, white blouse and skirt) with a ladies aid church group. Courtesy Harriet Graupe.

tion when she wrote in a letter, "I have learned to handle a saw so I have made window sills and a door sill. My neighbor came over and said that it was 'well done for a woman'. I wear Jens' shirt and suspenders and a pair of boys overalls. . . . And you can believe that my neighbor laughed, so I said, 'Why shouldn't I be the man in my own house.' I expect to wear this habit until I am finished with my building and I don't care if anyone laughs." Then she added, "Very few people come this way and I am a good ways from the road."

Top: Fannie Overstreet, like some women, did field work. Courtesy Pat Henry.

Bottom: Johanna Kuhn. Her husband, Oscar Peterson, often mentioned that his best hired man was Johanna's sister, Lena, an expert horsewoman and good at rounding up cattle and checking fences. Courtesy Lena Nelson.

Christine Larson Tollefson's remarks show the ambiguity of women's position. Though she obviously contributed a great deal to "outdoor" work on the farm and had faith in her own abilities, she nonetheless considered her husband "pretty much the boss":

> We just enjoyed working together. He was pretty much the boss but we worked together all the time.... I'm not worse off than those who didn't do anything outside. And I believe a woman should have something to say.

The frustration pioneer women faced, not because of the climate or terrain but simply because they were women, is aptly expressed by Kaja Kurz who exclaimed, "Oh, if I were a man, I surely could do so many things!"

Returning to the original question, "Did they 'really' homestead?", with few exceptions the women who took claims were, in many instances and to some degree, willing to cross traditional gender boundaries. Their reasons for homesteading were many and sometimes complicated, but the possibility to achieve some measure of independence as a result of land ownership was a strong incentive. These women, many of whom had occupations as well as responsibility for their claims, were not tied to a role that dictated early marriage and dependence on men. Yet they spent much of their lives carrying out domestic activities or following accepted careers for women.

Kaja Kurz. "Oh, if I were a man, I surely could do so many things." Courtesy Daisy Schuman.

Thus, before answering the question, what criteria should be used to judge a "real homesteader?" Does doing "women's work" disqualify one from this distinction? The answer now becomes a matter of definition and evaluation, taking

221

Top: Breaking sod. Courtesy Helga Norgard Anderson.

Bottom: Harvest 1911. Courtesy Ruth Hinkley.

into consideration the tendency of people to explain the actions of women using a different context from that applied to men. Women are seen as being dependent upon others and more concerned with home and family. Not only are women's actions viewed in a different context, but their contributions are often devalued. For example, references like the following are not unusual in historical accounts: "Generally, the young women located claims near relatives and on quarter sections adjoining if possible."[8] The statement itself is not inaccurate. Women did just that. The misinterpretation comes in the omission of a similar observation about men who also settled near relatives and on adjoining quarter sections.

Since men are not described in the context of family but rather in terms of their occupational activities, the subtle inference is that they were the ones doing the important work and further that they were independent and did not have to rely on others. Yet most men depended on women to take care of domestic needs. It was essential that this work be done. Domestic work, however, always has been devalued, and those doing it have been considered dependent and less important. The question, "Did they 'really' homestead?" reflects this evaluation. The question has no meaning unless "women's work" is defined as requiring little initiative and skill and as being less important than "men's work."

This interpretation has been used in many analyses, both in the past and today. Scholars and public opinion alike have cast men's plowing their fields in the role of the "real" pioneers. Women's supplying the work that sustained these men rarely received credit for their efforts, and their contributions to field work were ignored.

Although recent analyses have questioned the validity of this view, changing stereotypes is difficult. My study lends support to the idea that women took part in a variety of activities that usually included decision making, and, in many instances, field work as well and, further, that the work considered to be "women's work" was as vital to settlement as was "men's work" and should be considered so. In almost all cases, women who took homesteads managed their land. They made the decisions necessary to meet the government requirements, and the government recognized their accomplishments by issuing them title to the land.

Further, women were as likely as men to successfully prove up their claims. I collected data on the cancellation of claims for two counties in North Dakota. The percentages of those canceling or failing to prove up claims were remarkably similar for both genders. In Sheridan County, 28 percent of the men canceled their rights compared to 24 percent of the women. The figures for McIntosh County are 29 and 32 percent, respectively.

In light of these factors, the answer to the original question, "Did they 'really' homestead?" has to be "Yes!"

Caroline Wolfe May and her husband, Jacob May. Courtesy Carol and Bill May.

Alonzo and Amber Vrooman at work on their homestead near Anna Chermak's land. Courtesy Ruth Hinkley

8

The Legacy:
Strong Minds and
a Sense of Humor

A statement by Mari Sandoz, noted author of the plains, seems appropriate when we reflect upon the accounts and descriptions of the women included in this study: "We tend to forget that the homesteaders were not a type, not as alike as biscuits cut out with a baking-powder can. They varied—as much as their origins and their reasons for coming west.... Yet there was a certain repetition of characters in the homestead communities".[1] This statement describes what seems to be a paradox, the combination of unique with common characteristics. Yet the same paradox describes the women whose lives became a part of this work. The interviews and the accounts leave the impression that each woman was in some way unique; each related a tale different in content and circumstance. Underlying their individual experiences, however, were characteristics that all possessed.

The qualities that defined homesteading women are clearly illustrated in the following descriptions by relatives and friends.

Rosa Kateley Olstad— "She taught school, sometimes 3-4 month terms a year, for $30 a month. . . . She loved all aspects of education and learning. . . . Everyone consulted her for advice and information and she wrote letters for many neighbors. She was a good public speaker and attended every possible convention for school, P.T.A., farm organizations, and politics. . . . She was very active in church, Sunday School, and helped organize the Nonpartisan League for farmers. . . . Mother was an avid reader, but I can never remember seeing her just sitting and reading. She felt she couldn't waste time just reading so she would churn butter or knit socks or mittens while she read" (Olive Kately Sprague, daughter).

Sarah Jepson Saville— "Mom was a great promoter and supporter of advancing as times progressed" (Elsie Saville Weiser, daughter).

Tillie Mostad Smith— "She had a very sociable and outgoing personality. She was a very forceful and independent woman. She took part in everything the community offered all her life and started some of it herself" (Lorraine Smith, daughter).

Tillie Mostad.

Mary Roaldson—"I must have been about 11 when Aunt Mary died but she was my idol. She was slim and tall and I thought real fancy. I always liked to have her around. She had the look of someone frail but evidently she wasn't. She was one gutsy lady" (Pauline Roaldson Sirl, niece).

Emma Steles

Emma Steles Heidlebaugh— "She was a very capable person. She had the first pressure-cooker sold in Rugby.... A diligent worker for the Nonpartisan League and was a candidate for State Senator" (Helen Heidlebaugh, daughter-in-law).

Josephine Uleberg

Effie Vivian Smith Rogers Peterson—"She had an eager questioning mind. She read and studied extensively all her life" (Madge Rogers Hoppie, daughter).

Josephine Uleberg Anderson—"She had a keen mind and a wonderful, warm personality" (Avis Busse, daughter).

Lillie Tysver Ronnevik— "She hungered for knowledge and would read by lantern at the bedpost after the others went to bed" (Myrtle Ronnevik Lindstrom, daughter).

Sarah Knutson

Sarah Knutson Gryde—"Her support and encouragement and ideals made our accomplishments possible. All this in spite of the fact that she was a rather shy retiring person." (Olga I. Gryde, daughter).

Gurina Holkestad

Clara Rowe—"Very active in the Methodist Church .... A proud, spunky lady.... She was 'a strong mama'" (Ruth Rowe, granddaughter).

Gurina Sofie Holkestad Bolken—"She possessed a spirit of faith, courage and determination" (Alice Foreng, daughter).

229

Randi Garmann

Randi Garmann Stockman—"She was jolly and outgoing" (Elsa Stockman Ferguson, daughter).

Viola Stramblad Liessman— "She was a well educated woman. She organized the women of the Nonpartisan League and was the winner of the slogan contest with her 'We'll Stick, We'll Win'" (Thelma Liessman Vantine, daughter).

Janie Brew

Janie Brew Scott— "She was an avid reader, a poet, and had a strong will to make things go in spite of the odds" (Bill Scott, son).

Mary Mertes Engelhard—"She was the epitome of a real pioneer woman, with vision far beyond her time. Years on a farm in N.D. were difficult, fighting elements every inch of the way.... She could make things out of almost nothing" (Helen Engelhard Geiger, daughter).

Ella Curry Boise— "Mother was a manager. We were all lucky to inherit her ability.... She helped form the Nonpartisan League.... Supported the Women's Boarding Home in Fargo, active in Women's Suffrage.... A Langer supporter.... She was the 'kingpin' of what went on in the family" (Philip Boise, son).

Annie Budke

Lucy Gorecki

Annie Budke Zurburg—"She loved a joke. . . . Annie was a leader" (Aurora Seehofer, niece).

Cora Wilson— "She and her father were one of the first two families to winter in York. She helped to found the first school and was chosen as clerk. Also helped to start the church and served on the first Board of Trustees. A pioneer in any endeavor must be strong and endure, must be able to walk over obstacles, not around them" (Interviewer, State Historical Project).

Lucy Gorecki Blasky—"She was a better business manager than my father" (Mrs. Glenn Niedlinger, daughter).

Julia Pettingill—"She was very independent and always managed for herself and others. . . . She was a very special person and was able to do almost anything she wished to do. . . . She was always ready and a leader in many community activities. . . . She was jolly and full of fun and a wonderful story teller" (Margaret McNamara Holbach, granddaughter).

The legacy of these women is clear. They are remembered as capable, independent, strong, and courageous. A sense of adventure guided their decisions and commitments.

Along with these characteristics, which describe women who were purposeful and initiators of action, was another important attribute—a sense of humor. Margaret Holbach's characterization of her grandmother Julia Pettingill as "jolly and full of fun and a wonderful story teller" is typical of many statements about homesteading women. Besides being community leaders and decision makers, they tempered their tasks with lightheartedness. Being able to find humor in their situations undoubtedly helped them through the rough times and added zest to the good times. Their sense of humor was often droll and rather subtle.

With a twinkle in her eye, Flora Whittemore told me of the time she and a friend dined out: "Lorna Sanford worked at an attorney's office when I had my shop. We were great friends. She was short and stout, and I was tall and thin. I remember one day we exchanged clothes and went out to dinner."

Janie Brew Scott used poetry to warn against the consequences of taking life too seriously. This poem was written during the drought and depression of the 1930s, but the outlook it expresses undoubtedly was present during her homesteading days.

> If your nose is close
> To the grindstone rough,
> And you hold it down
> There long enough.
>
> In time you'll say
> There's no such thing
> As brooks that babble
> And birds that sing.
>
> These three will all
> Your world compose,
> Just you, and the grindstone
> And your darned old nose.[2]

A sense of humor must have been a saving grace for many a pioneer, male or female, particularly those who came from the city and had to learn such unfamiliar skills as milking cows, shoveling manure, and harnessing horses. Marie Burns chuckled as she recalled the time the horses ran away when she got out of the buggy to open the gate. It was serious business when she was running wildly after them, shedding her coat to improve her speed, but she laughed when her arms were around Fatty's neck, realizing how ridiculous she must have looked.

As we look more closely at the lives of women who chose to take land during the settlement period, we find that their experiences do not bear out the old descriptions that portrayed them as secondary and often reluctant pioneers. Women must be recognized as main characters in the settlement drama. Women as well as men showed initiative, strength, and courage, and both no doubt experienced fear and disappointment. Through it all, they shared the burdens and joys of building new communities.

Reflecting back on Walter Prescott Webb's description of men and their relationship to the plains, given earlier in the Preface, I was struck with how accurate his observations would have been had he applied them to women as well as men. The women whose lives are portrayed in the pages of this book found "zest to the life, adventure in the air, freedom from restraint." They, too, "developed a hardihood" which, coupled with a sense of humor, allowed them to endure the hardships and lack of refinements that the plains offered.[3]

Although much work still must be done before the story of women on the plains is complete, several conclusions can be stated.

Thousands of women acquired public lands in North Dakota. Their success rate at proving up was comparable to that of men. Women tended to combine their homesteading endeavors with other paying jobs. "Working out" as a teacher, seamstress, nurse, domestic worker, or in some other capacity helped to finance the expenses of the claim. Partly because of their occupational interests, these women tended to marry later than many of their counterparts, and some chose to remain single.

233

Although the majority took land between the ages of 21 and 30, older women sometimes took advantage of the investment in land. Women who were widowed, divorced, or deserted found homesteading a practical investment. Financial gain was the primary motivation for taking land. Some women sold their land as soon as they proved up and used the cash to invest in other enterprises. A number of them remained on the land for many years, some for the rest of their lives.

Many women as well as men formed strong bonds to the soil. Most were an integral part of an active and growing community composed of relatives, neighbors, and friends. Although a general division of labor existed for men and women, the specific tasks assigned to each depended on circumstance, ethnicity, and choice. When the situation demanded, each sex assumed the other's role, although women performed men's tasks more frequently than vice versa. Almost all women who chose to homestead managed the affairs related to their land.

This study has been devoted to examining the lives of women who took land in their own names, a particular group of courageous women who history largely ignored. It seems fitting to conclude with one final account. Pauline Shoemaker Crowley represents the adventuresome spirit that led many women, young and old, single, widowed, divorced, and deserted, to take land in their own names and thus become forever a part of the history of North Dakota.

THE STORY OF PAULINE

Pauline Shoemaker in New York, 1903. Courtesy Sheila Robinson.

Pauline Shoemaker home-steaded along the Knife River north of Hebron, North Dakota, in Mercer County. She was raised in Pennsylvania and graduated in 1897 from the State Normal School in East Stroudsburg with a Bachelor's in the Elements. In 1900, she received the State Normal School Diploma for having practiced the profession of teaching two full years. Her training included languages, and she was proficient in Latin and Greek.

What prompted Pauline to go west is unknown, but in later years she remarked to her daughters that she remembered looking at maps of the West. They sparked her curiosity because there was "sort of a blank in the middle," and she wondered what was there. Her family was well educated and well read. Though they did not accompany her in her travels, they must have been supportive of her desire for adventure. While still in Pennsylvania, she and a friend, Helen Cook, planned a train trip to California. In the end, Helen's father would not allow her to go, so Pauline made the trip by herself.

Pauline first came to North Dakota in 1902 to teach at the Will School in Bismarck. A cousin probably helped her get this first job, but it is not known how long he stayed in the area. Otherwise she had no family in the state. After teaching for a few years in North Dakota, she again traveled to California and taught school there.

The schoolhouse where Pauline Shoemaker taught. Courtesy Sheila Robinson.

Other adventures included a tour of Yellowstone Park. Pauline and her friends took 10 days to tour the park, traveling by spring wagons with an accompanying supply wagon. She spent one summer with a young couple, following their flock of sheep in the Sierra Nevada mountains. But North Dakota still beckoned, and she finally returned to teach again in the Bismarck area. There she soon became acquainted with Ralph Ward, owner of the 101 Ranch, located 90 miles north of Bismarck. In May 1910, he invited her to bring some friends and join the annual horse roundup. Pauline wrote to her sisters in Pennsylvania describing the experience:

> We girls left all unnecessary clothing at the ranch and took such as was positively needed, such as divided skirts, boots, felt hats, men's heavy woolen shirts, some shirtwaists which we did not use, heavy gloves and all wore spurs. . . . Needing some more supplies for the prospective trip four of us went in the auto to a ranch five miles away to get the butter supply. There was a large sod house at this place and we were invited in and found the interior as cheerful

236

as tho the house were built of the best lumber. The
inside was papered and there happened to be a very
jolly crowd assembled and they were enjoying music
on the piano, cornet, mandolin and phonograph
which shows that life is not so dull even in a sod
house. . . . There were two wagons in the outfit, one a
medium light spring wagon which carried the tents,
stoves, baggage, water keg, kodaks, etc. A large
heavy wagon was loaded with provisions and that
was a veritable grocery store with cases of tomatoes,
corn, peas, beans, beef, salmon, dried beef, plums,
peaches, pears, cherries, pineapple, olives, pickles,
apricots, eggs, milk (evaporated), one hundred
pounds of pickled pork, bacon, hams, potatoes, syrup,
chocolate, sugar, coffee and cornmeal. . . . That afternoon we came into the Shell Creek country and a
most beautiful country it is. After winding around
coulees for a few miles we came out upon a level
stretch of country with the Missouri River beyond. . . .
There will probably be but one more round up in this
section of the country as the Reservation will be
opened up next year. I am more than glad that I
seized the opportunity and went regardless of the
possibility of snow storms which are liable to over-
take one at that time of year. . . . Altogether about
seven hundred horses were gathered in. . . . The
reservation is forty miles square. The round up
covered about all of the sixteen hundred square miles
in eight days.[4]

About a year after the roundup, in 1911, Pauline, at the
age of 31, filed on her claim in Mercer County. To add to her
income, she taught five students from two families in her
shack. When company came on weekends, she set the chil-

237

dren's desks outside. The first winter, she was alone one evening during a blizzard. All was quiet except for the wind howling outside. When she heard movement and a brushing against the house, she put out the light, went to the loft with her gun, and looked out the window. A couple of horses were seeking shelter in the lee of the shack.

In 1914, Pauline married a neighbor, Matt Crowley, who had a ranch nearby. She proved up in 1916, and eventually the couple moved to Matt's ranch. Throughout her life, Pauline remained interested in adventure and wider community concerns. She read profusely, keeping up to date on current affairs and participating in state politics. Pauline was the first woman to be appointed to the State Board of Higher Education, serving from 1939 to 1943. She and her husband were both mindful of community needs, and their daughters remember them as empathetic with those in trouble or need.

Pauline died in 1970 at the age of 91. Her venturesome and courageous spirit reflects the high hopes and determination that she and many women like her brought with them to North Dakota, helping to provide for the needs of growing communities and to build a state with strong foundations. As her daughter, Sheila, proudly reflected, "After Mother came West, she never rode side-saddle, she always rode astride."

*Pauline Shoemaker (center) and her friends
Helen Cook (left) and Constance Schaffner
(right), 1913. Courtesy Sheila Robinson.*

Appendix

Information in the following appendix includes names of women in the case study sample, and when available, locations of their land, ethnic backgrounds, ages, dates they took land, dates of initial and final land transactions, birth dates, and marital status when the land transactions were initiated. An asterisk (*) by a name indicates women the author interviewed or with whom she corresponded.

The names are listed alphabetically, according to the name used when a land transaction was initiated. Any name changes, usually from marriage, are listed below the original name.

Location of land is designated by section, township and range. Specific location within the section is not given. Most allotments were 160 acres, but some were 80 acres and others were as small as 40 acres.

Dates not designated as FC (Final Certificate) or PAT (Patent) for the date of final land transaction most likely are the dates of final certificate. For those who took preemptions, no date appears in the column showing when the land transaction was initiated. Some inaccuracies may occur in the dates given, since determining the handwritten numbers found in the land tract books sometimes was difficult.

Name	Location Section-Township N-Range W	Ethnic Background M = Mother, F = Father	Age, Land Transaction Initiated
Abbott, Ruth Haug	McHenry Co. 18-157-80 Kottka Valley Twp.	M New England Yankee F New England Yankee	23
Amdahl, Sena Rendahl	Benson Co. 9-154-71 Impark Twp.	M Norwegian F Norwegian	24
Anderson, Alma	Mountrail Co. 11-156-94		
Anderson, Amanda Isakson	Sargent Co. 20-131-55 Dunbar Twp.	M Swedish F Swedish	
Anderson, Anne Hovde	McKenzie Co. 6-150-100 Arnegard Twp.	M Norwegian F Norwegian	21
Anderson, Christiane Oslie	Golden Valley Co. 4-144-105 Henry Twp.	M Norwegian F Norwegian	52
Anderson, Emma	Sargent Co 17-131-55		
Anderson, Mary	Richland Co. 10-132-49 Morton Twp.	M Norwegian F Norwegian	46
Andin, Annie Scurlock	Ward Co. 14-152-85 Rice Lake Twp.	M Swedish F Swedish	28
Asch, Ada H. Rush	Emmons Co. 18-129-74 Selz Twp.	M English F German	18
Aslakson, Betsy	Williams Co. 5-154-95 Unorganized Twp.	M Norwegian F Norwegian	34
Banner, Jennie Bryant	McKenzie Co. 4-149-102 Moline Twp.	Black American	
*Barnfather, Cora Meglasson	Williams Co. 10-154-95	M Scottish, Irish, Canadian F English Canadian	21
Berg, Anna Mathilda	Eddy Co. 14-150-63 Eddy Twp.	M Swedish F Swedish	34
Bergan, Anna Marie Forsberg	Dickey Co. 31-131-59 Bear Creek Twp.	M Norwegian F Norwegian	24
Berge, Gunhild Nesheim	Mountrail Co. 6-155-91 Purcell Twp.	M Norwegian F Norwegian	21

Date, Land Transaction Initiated	Date of Final Land Transactions	Birth Date	Marital Status, Land Transaction Initiated
5-17-1901	9-11-1906 FC	1-1-1878	Single
4-15-1899	12-11-1901	12-27-1874	Single
9-18-1909	7-7-1911 3-11-1912 PAT		Single
1-7-1887	3-15-1892 FC		Single
3-7-1910	11-18-1911 FC 4-29-1912 PAT	1-11-1889	Single
4-19-1912	6-21-1916 FC 7-17-1916 PAT	3-25-1860	Separated
5-29-1883	3-13-1885		Single
5-8-1879	10-30-1885 FC	1-11-1833	Widow
1-28-1908	7-6-1909 2-11-1910 PAT	1-1-1880	Single
3-9-1903	4-1-1908	8-16-1884	Single
10-31-1907	4-24-1909 12-1-1909	9-8-1873	Widow
5-6-1907	12-5-1910 FC		
8-8-1906	10-10-1907	7-1-1885	Single
8-7-1905	8-18-1906	7-7-1871	Single
7-13-1882	11-22-1888 FC	12-9-1857	Single
5-11-1905	10-1-1907	12-4-1883	Single

241

Name	Location Section-Township N- Range W	Ethnic Background M = Mother, F = Father	Age, Land Transaction Initiated
Bergsgaard, Aagdt	Benson Co. 23-157-69 South Viking Twp.	M Norwegian F Norwegian	28
Beske, Emma Grimes	Stutsman Co.	M German F German	
Bjirka, Iverte Johnson	Ward Co. 31-154-84 Burt Twp.	M Norwegian F Norwegian	22
Blegen, Clara Odegard	Rollette Co. 26-159-71 Rice Twp.	M Norwegian F Norwegian	21
Boesen Anderson, Hanna Amanda Taylor	Burke Co. 8-162-90 Carter Twp.	M Norwegian F Norwegian	22
Breckenridge, Bertha C. Walch	Adams Co. 18-130-98	M English, Scottish, Irish F Scottish, Irish	22
Brennon, Amelia Jacobsen	Mountrail Co. 33-156-94 Myrtle Twp.	M Irish F Irish	30
Brennon, Lena	Mountrail Co. 3-155-94 Robinson Twp.	M Irish F Irish	25
Brew, Janie Scott	Dunn Co. 6-143-95	M English F English	22
Brorby, Gina Stadum	Burke Co. 27-162-93 Fay Twp.	M Norwegian F Norwegian	21
Brumwell, Elizabeth Ball	Cavalier Co. 20-163-64 Cypress Twp.	M (From Canada) Anglo-American F Anglo-American	
*Bublitz, Emma Freitag	Slope Co. 4-133-100 Mineral Spring Twp.	M German F German	23
Budke, Annie Zurburg	Renville Co. 17-162-85 Hamerly Twp.	M French F German	26
Budke, Caroline Pepke	Renville Co. 21-162-85 Hamerly Twp.	M French F German	24
*Burns, Marie Jensen	Dunn Co. 12-142-91	M Norwegian F Norwegian	30
Burud, Dora Gagnum	Mountrail Co. 6-157-89 & 1-157-90 Redmond Twp.	M Norwegian F Norwegian	25

Date, Land Transaction Initiated	Date of Final Land Transactions	Birth Date	Marital Status, Land Transaction Initiated
7-27-1907	11-28-1908	2-5-1879	Single
1904	1906	1-15-1885	Single
4-4-1901	8-23-1904	3-5-1879	Single
5-24-1900	7-15-1905	3-25-1879	Single
5-12-1899	4-24-1902	1877	Married; widowed before land was proved up
11-7-1906	1-30-1908	2-10-1884	Single
8-26-1907	11-4-1908 6-24-1909 PAT	7-22-1877	Single
8-26-1907	5-17-1910 9-19-1910 PAT	3-26-1882	Single
1-15-1910	8-5-1913	3-29-1887	Single
4-18-1903	7-18-1904	7-28-1881	Single
1-3-1902	11-1-1904		Single
7-1-1908	11-11-1909 11-7-1910 PAT	10-14-1884	Single
6-21-1901	8-10-1907	5-11-1875	Single
7-2-1901	3-24-1905	12-27-1876	Single
8-22-1913	4-24-1917 8-30-1917	10-29-1882	Widow
10-19-1903	8-9-1905	12-20-1877	Single

Name	Location Section-Township N-Range W	Ethnic Background M = Mother, F = Father	Age, Land Transaction Initiated
*Carkin, Theona Taylor	Hettinger Co. 5 miles from New England	F Anglo-American	20
Carlson, Lena Swanson	Benson Co. 5-152-70 Hesper Twp.	M Swedish F Swedish	27
Carns, Leah B. Smith	Dunn Co. 20-143-92	M Irish, English F Irish, English	21
Cavett, Harriette A.	Williams Co. 28-156-96 West Bank Twp.	M Anglo-American F Anglo-American	23
Chermak, Anna Swanson	Slope Co. 10-133-105 Hughes Twp.	M Bohemian F Bohemian	26
Clausen, Mary Uran	Mountrail Co.	M Norwegian F Norwegian	23
Cleary, Margret	Logan Co. 12-134-72 Starkey Twp.	F Irish	
Cleary, Mary	Logan Co. 12-134-72 Starkey Twp.	F Irish	
Cobb, Bess	Grant Co. 14-132-90 Lorim Twp.	F Anglo-American	
Collier, Mary	Dickey Co. 13-129-59	F Anglo-American	
Corneliusen, Sjannette	Pierce Co. Torgerson Twp.	M Norwegian F Norwegian	24
Crane, Rannie Fedje Alcok	Ward Co. 34-154-84 Burt Twp.	M Norwegian F Norwegian	33
Crawford, Eliza Hagerty	Adams Co. 9-130-97 Bucyrus Twp.	M Scottish, Irish, English F Scottish, Irish, English	38
Cumming, Clara Dounelly	Ward Co. 27-160-87 Sauk Prairie Twp.	M Scottish (Canadian) F Scottish (Canadian)	
Cumming, Mary	Ward Co. 27-160-87 Sauk Prairie Twp.	M Scottish (Canadian) F Scottish (Canadian)	
Curry, Ella Boise	Steele Co. 34-144-56 Carpenter Twp.	M English F Irish	21

244

Date, Land Transaction Initiated	Date of Final Land Transactions	Birth Date	Marital Status, Land Transaction Initiated
1906		5-3-1886	Single
9-7-1898	11-5-1903	9-12-1870	Single
10-28-1903	8-24-1909 FC 4-4-1910 PAT	10-18-1882	Single
12-17-1907	9-15-1909 6-16-1910 PAT	12-29-1883	Single
5-7-1910	8-24-1916 FC 12-12-1916 PAT	10-25-1883	Single
1907		9-29-1884	Single
2-23-1906	7-20-1907		
2-23-1906	6-20-1907		
10-18-1906	5-8-1912 FC 7-29-1912 PAT		Single
	12-10-1884		
1897		6-23-1873	Single
4-28-1904	8-9-1907	1871	Widow
5-25-1906	9-25-1907	5-16-1868	Widow
4-10-1900	8-2-1906		Single
4-10-1900	10-4-1905		Single
11-4-1885	10-3-1889	8-21-1864	Single

Name	Location Section-Township N-Range W	Ethnic Background M = Mother, F = Father	Age, Land Transaction Initiated
Danielson, Josephine	Williams Co. 4-154-95	F Anglo-American	
Davis, Alta Eberle	Divide Co. 1-160-101 Sioux Trail Twp.	M Anglo-American F Anglo-American	
Delong, Josephine Ferebee	Dunn Co. 22-145-92	F Anglo-American	31
Deming, Annie McCombs	McHenry Co. 3-158-76	M Anglo-American F Anglo-American	23
Deming, Bernice	Dunn Co.	M Anglo-American F Anglo-American	
Deming, Dora Hazeltine	Dunn Co.	M Anglo-American F Anglo-American	
Deming, Josephine Mineah	Dunn Co.	M Anglo-American F Anglo-American	34
Dill, Mary Garrity	Pierce Co.	M Scottish F Scottish	24
Divet, Edith L.	Grant Co. 9-130-90	M French Canadian F Irish	32
*Dooley, Mary Bartels	South Dakota	M Irish F Irish	21
Doolittle, Carrie J.	Ward Co. 3-155-86 Mandan Twp.	F Anglo-American	
Dunlava, Clara A. Fuller Seager	McKenzie Co. 5-149-101 Antelope Twp.		58
Eldred, Ann Davis	Renville Co. 28-162-84 Hurley Twp.	F Anglo-American	
Elliott, Nell Robinson	Bowman Co.	F Anglo-American	27
Ellis, Maude Hammond	Logan Co. 20-135-70	F Anglo-American	25
Enright, Sister Mary Augustine	Near Stump Lake	M Irish American F Irish American	
Enstulen, Anna Skedsvold	McKenzie Co. 12-147-103 12-147-103 Additional Homestead	M Norwegian F Norwegian	22
Erickson, Anna	Hettinger Co.	M Swedish F Norwegian	
Erickson, Annetta E.	Burleigh Co. 6-143-78 Estherville Twp.	M Swedish F Swedish	21

246

Date, Land Transaction Initiated	Date of Final Land Transactions	Birth Date	Marital Status, Land Transaction Initiated
10-29-1906	2-11-1908		Single
11-22-1910	6-8-1911 PAT	4-21-1885	Single
8-15-1907	3-15-1909 FC 12-1-1909 PAT	4-18-1876	Single
5-20-1907	11-1908 FC 6-1909 PAT	6-6-1883	Single
			Single
			Single
1906	11-1907	12-5-1872	Single
1904		10-9-1880	Single
8-8-1906	8-30-1912 FC 11-12-1912 PAT	12-28-1873	Single
1909	1910	1-14-1888	Single
10-8-1900	10-6-1902		Single
4-26-1906	3-11-1912 PAT	11-19-1847	Widow
10-26-1901	6-8-1907		Single
1909		10-29-1882	Single
2-27-1907	3-16-1914	3-18-1881	Single
8-24-1883	Transferred title to Sister Louise		
8-5-1912	11-13-1916 FC	11-25-1889	Single
9-5-1913	11-13-1916		
1909	7-1911		Single
11-1-1900	3-28-1906	10-25-1879	Single

Name	Location Section-Township N-Range W	Ethnic Background M = Mother, F = Father	Age, Land Transaction Initiated
Erickson, Hildur Hanson	McLean Co. 27-149-86	M Swedish F Swedish	26
Espeseth, Berget Hendrickson	McHenry Co.	M Norwegian F Norwegian	27
Espeseth, Betsey	Bottineau Co. 11-162-79 Eidsvold Twp.		
Espeseth, Gurina Lund	McHenry Co. 2-154-78	M Norwegian F Norwegian	21
Espeseth, Julia	Bottineau Co. 35-163-79 Scotia Twp.		
Evenden, Eva May Burow	Pierce Co. 24-158-72 Springlake Twp.	M (born in USA) F English	19
Evenson, Matilda Esoline Zackerson	Adams Co. 22-129-93 Gilstrap Twp.	M Norwegian F Norwegian	24
Farland, Andrea	Williams Co.	M Norwegian F Norwegian	53
Fedje, Ella	Ward Co. 34-154-84 Burt Twp.	M Norwegian F Norwegian	46
Ficker, Susan Holzemer	Slope Co. 20-135-100 White Lake Twp.	M German F German	22
Fjelde, Margaret Madsen	Burleigh Co. 20-143-77 Canfield Twp.	M Danish F Danish	
Fleckten, Annie Olson	Near Niobe Elmdale Twp.		21
Fuller, Georgia	Mountrail Co. 25-154-93	Black American	
Furnberg, Anne Jensen	Cass Co. 32-139-49 Barnes Twp.	M Norwegian F Norwegian	38
Garmann, Randi Stockman	Williams Co. 7-154-95 Unorganized Twp.	M Norwegian F Norwegian	29
Gerhardt, Wilhelmina Dohrmann	Stark Co.	M German F German	
Gjellstad, Anne O. Seyton	McHenry Co. 8-154-80 North Prairie Twp.	M Norwegian F Norwegian	21

Date, Land Transaction Initiated	Date of Final Land Transactions	Birth Date	Marital Status, Land Transaction Initiated
8-24-1907	7-9-1909 7-11-1910 PAT	1-26-1881	Single
1900	1906	2-14-1873	Single
10-16-1899	1-26-1905		Single
10-10-1903	10-28-1908 FC 6-10-1909 PAT	10-5-1882	Single
2-7-1900	3-15-1905		Single
2-10-1902	10-14-1907 FC	10-9-1882	Single
9-9-1907	1-30-1909	5-3-1883	Single
1908		9-14-1855	Widow
9-25-1905	8-9-1907	3-24-1859	Single
6-26-1908	10-30-1912 FC 2-3-1913 PAT	7-21-1886	Single
10-23-1901	4-16-1907 FC 8-27-1907 PAT		Widow
1898		1877	Single
1907	11-5-1909 FC 6-9-1910 PAT		
5-25-1875	7-16-81 FC 5-20-1882 PAT	1837	Widow
7-6-1910	7-19-1916 FC 11-3-1916 PAT	3-9-1881	Single
11-28-1899	7-18-1905	5-12-1878	Single

Name	Location Section-Township N-Range W	Ethnic Background M = Mother, F = Father	Age, Land Transaction Initiated
Gjellstad, Marie Hauge	McHenry Co. 35-154-79 Hendrickson Twp.	M Norwegian F Norwegian	21
Glynn, Eunice Divet	Grant Co. 9-130-90	M French Canadian F Irish	33
Goldsberg, Ella	Ramsey Co. 19-158-62 Northfield Twp.	M Scottish, English F Scottish, English	47
Goldthorpe, Lucy Vandeberg	Williams Co. 26-156-99 Marshall Twp.	F Anglo-American	22
Gorecki, Lucy Blasky	Burke Co. S. of Bowbells	M Polish F Polish	26
Graham, Lotta Elizabeth Maddock	Mountrail Co. 27-154-88 Osloe Twp.	M Scottish	
*Gramling, Katie Stewart	Burleigh Co. 20-142-77 Rockhill Twp.	M English, Irish F Penn. "Dutch"	21
Green, Eleanor Hasselstrom	Divide Co. 15-161-99 Burg Twp.	M English F Irish	33
Gryde, Jane (Joraand K.)	Walsh Co. 29-158-54 Glenwood Twp.	M Norwegian F Norwegian	57
Gunvaldson, Caroline Hall	Ward Co. 30-157-85 Mayland Twp.	M Norwegian F Norwegian	26
Hagel, Juliana	Pierce Co. 26-153-74	German-Russian	
Hagen, Emma Foster	Williams Co.	M Norwegian F Norwegian	26
Halverson, Christina Matson	Burke Co. 3-160-90 Roseland Twp.	M Swedish F Swedish	52
Hanson, Bessie Hove Peterson	Oliver Co. 32-143-83 Nebo Twp.	M Norwegian F Norwegian	32
Hanson, Florence Jacobson	Slope Co. 8-136-102	M English F English, Welsh	21
Hanson, Mary Belle Pierson	Benson Co. 7, 18-155-69 Beaver Twp.	M Norwegian F Norwegian	21

Date, Land Transaction Initiated	Date of Final Land Transactions	Birth Date	Marital Status, Land Transaction Initiated
8-5-1902	5-22-1909 FC	7-25-1881	Single
8-8-1906 refiled 1-2-1909	10-9-1907 relinquished 1-24-1913 FC	7-7-1873	Separated
4-16-1898	7-3-1903	11-1850	Widow
11-9-1905	8-10-1907	3-23-1883	Single
1906		3-14-1880	Single
11-25-1904	12-28-1909 FC 7-7-1910 PAT		Single
5-3-1909	3-27-1913	6-24-1887	Single
3-10-1909	7-27-1915	8-26-1875	Single
	5-27-1881 Inherited by heirs.	9-11-1822	Widow
7-30-1902	4-24-1907	10-21-1875	Single
4-27-1901	10-30-1907 FC 6-11-1908 PAT		Single
1910	1913	12-30-1884	Single
1-17-1903	12-16-1908 FC 7-22-1909 PAT	9-9-1850	Widow
8-12-1905	9-13-1911 FC 9-19-1912 PAT	1873	Widow
7-13-1916	4-25-1921 FC 9-20-1921 PAT	4-13-1895	Single
1-11-1897	7-14-1902	1-2-1876	Single

Name	Location Section-Township N- Range W	Ethnic Background M = Mother, F = Father	Age, Land Transaction Initiated
Haug, Bertha Storberget	Towner Co. 22-160-68 Grainfield Twp.	M Norwegian F Norwegian	23
Haug, Maren Storberget Olson	Towner Co. 26-160-68 Grainfield Twp.	M Norwegian F Norwegian	24
Heide, Rebecca Rolfsrud	McKenzie Co. 32-152-96 Keene Twp.	M Norwegian F Norwegian	28
Helland, Anna Kantrud	McLean Co.	M Norwegian F Norwegian	27
Henderson, Elsie Mountain	Cavalier Co.	M Scottish	23
Hensel, Anna	Hettinger Co. 10-132-91	M German-Russian F German-Russian	68
Hewson, Ann Newton	Dunn Co.	M English F English	21
Hildremyer, Anna Hanson	Williams Co. 13-154-98 Truax Twp.	M Norwegian F Norwegian	22
Holen, Karoline	Williams Co. 11-157-98 Oliver Twp.	M Norwegian F Norwegian	64
Holen, Marie Nelson	Williams Co. 19-159-99 Rock Island Twp.	M Norwegian F Norwegian	22
Holkestad, Gurina Sofie Bolken	McKenzie Co. 22-151-101 15-151-101 Additional Homestead Timber Creek Twp.	M Norwegian F Norwegian	28
Holseth, Clara Potter	Bowman Co. 23-130-104 Nebo Twp.		
Honens, Cornelia Beeson	Sheridan Co. 28-146-77 McClusky Twp.	M German F German	22
Humberstad, Julianna	Williams Co. 28-158-97 New Home Twp.	F Norwegian	
Humberstad, Louise	Williams Co. 27-158-97 New Home Twp.	F Norwegian	
Hvinden, Marie Nelson	Benson Co. 29-152-69 North Viking Twp.	M Norwegian F Norwegian	28

252

Date, Land Transaction Initiated	Date of Final Land Transactions	Birth Date	Marital Status, Land Transaction Initiated
3-16-1887	3-7-1894	1864	Single
11-6-1886	6-15-1892	1862	Single
5-31-1904	10-14-1909 FC 5-9-1910 PAT	10-11-1875	Single
1902	1906	11-17-1875	Single
1895		10-4-1872	Single
6-20-1903	1-24-1910	9-26-1834	Widow
1909	1912	11-7-1888	Single
3-1-1909	6-15-1911	10-24-1886	Single
10-23-1906	10-20-1910 7-1911	9-10-1842	Widow
10-31-1904	5-31-1907	5-3-1882	Single
12-14-1911	3-1-1915	7-6-1883	Single
11-19-1913	3-1-1915		
6-26-1907	9-14-1913 FC		Single
12-10-1901	12-28-1903	5-5-1879	Single
6-19-1902	12-14-1908		Widow
4-5-1905	6-16-1909		Single
4-27-1897	4-25-1903	2-29-1869	Single

Name	Location Section-Township N-Range W	Ethnic Background M = Mother, F = Father	Age, Land Transaction Initiated
Hylden, Hannah Anderson	McKenzie Co. 33-150-100 Arnegard Twp.	M Norwegian F Norwegian	21
*Isaacson, Sara Ingle	McKenzie Co. 4-149-95	M Norwegian	21
Jacobsen, Grace Nelson	Grant Co. 8-136-86	M Norwegian, Swedish F Norwegian	21
Jacobson, Anna Aaberg	McKenzie Co. 21-152-100 Banks Twp.	M Norwegian F Norwegian	40
Jallo, Betsey (Bergit) Helgeson	Walsh Co. 32-155-57 Cleveland Twp.	F Norwegian	
Jennings, Margaret McDermott	Stark Co.	M Irish F Irish	33
* Jensen, Anna Matilda Warke	Ward Co. 33-151-87 Hiddenwood Twp.	M Norwegian F Norwegian	22
Jepson, Sarah Saville	Emmons Co. 18-136-75	M English-Irish-Scottish F Danish	21
Johanson, Mathilde Vannebo	Divide Co. 2-161-93 Daneville Twp.	M Norwegian F Norwegian	
*Johanson, Thora Olson	Divide Co. 10-161-103 Daneville Twp.	M Norwegian F Norwegian	22
Johnson, Carrie	Burleigh Co. 28-137-77 Morton Twp.		
Johnson, Emily Bakke	Mountrail Co. 28-155-92 Alger Twp.	M Swedish F Swedish	24
Johnson, Gertie	McKenzie Co. 10-149-102 Moline Twp.	Black American	
Johnson, Kaia Lindblom	Sheridan Co. 18-149-77 Highland Twp.	M Norwegian F Norwegian	25
Johnson, Nora Rust	Divide Co. 11-162-102 Westby Twp.	M Norwegian F Norwegian	22

Date, Land Transaction Initiated	Date of Final Land Transactions	Birth Date	Marital Status, Land Transaction Initiated
12-28-1906	7-6-1912	3-30-1885	Single
6-7-1910	12-23-1915 FC 3-27-1916 PAT	3-12-1889	Single
4-15-1912	11-11-1916 FC 4-7-1917 PAT	4-7-1891	Single
12-20-1913	11-16-1917 FC 4-5-1918 PAT	10-30-1873	Widow
10-15-1885	10-7-1892 cancelled		Single
1907	1908	3-18-1874	Widow
10-2-1912	10-5-1914	1890	Single
2-21-1905	4-18-1910 FC 2-12-1911 PAT	1-11-1884	Single
2-10-1912	12-21-1916 FC 9-15-1917 PAT		Widow
2-21-1913	11-23-1916 FC 7-9-1917 PAT	1891	Single
1907			Widow
2-25-1907	5-15-1908	12-15-1882	Single
7-23-1906	11-22-1907		
1-2-1907	10-18-1909	4-4-1881	Single
2-12-1913	12-7-1916	6-11-1890	Single

255

Name	Location Section-Township N- Range W	Ethnic Background M = Mother, F = Father	Age, Land Transaction Initiated
Johnson, Sarah	McKenzie Co. 30-149-102 Moline Twp. 31-149-102 Additional Homestead	Black American	
Jones, Hattie A. O'Kins	Ward Co. 21-154-85 Rolling Green Twp.	M Irish F Irish	21
Jorgenson, Aase Holen	Williams Co. 17-157-98 Oliver Twp.	M Norwegian F Norwegian	21
Kapseng, Ingrid Dybing	Wells Co. 3-150-71 Fram Twp.	M Norwegian F Norwegian	28
Karlson, Louise Wike	Billings Co.	M Norwegian F Norwegian	29
Kateley, Rosa Olstad	McHenry Co. 10-151-76 Spring Grove Twp.	M Scottish, Irish F Scottish	24
Kelsey, Ada	McKenzie Co.	F Anglo-American	25
Kline, Lenora D. Kamps	Mountrail Co. 31-152-91 Van Hook Twp.	M Scottish, English, Dutch F Dutch	22
Knudsen, Kirsten Alida Moller	Mountrail Co. 18-155-94 Robinson Twp.	M Norwegian F Norwegian	27
Knudson, Ingeborg	McHenry Co. 4-151-79 Olivia Twp.	M Norwegian F Norwegian	62
Knutson, Amelia Erickson	Williams Co. 22-157-99 Dublin Twp.	M Swedish F Swedish	22
Knutson, Sarah C. Gryde	McHenry Co. 11-151-79 Olivia Twp.	M Norwegian F Norwegian	25
Koehmstedt, Annie Elizabeth Hanggi	Cavalier Co. 33-162-63 Grey Twp.	M German F German	22
*Koppergard, Anna Strand	Divide Co. 30-162-99 Twin Butte Twp.	M Norwegian F Norwegian	29

Date, Land Transaction Initiated	Date of Final Land Transactions	Birth Date	Marital Status, Land Transaction Initiated
9-24-1909	8-12-1915 FC		
9-7-1913	8-12-1915 FC		
9-5-1902	9-7-1904	9-5-1881	Single
11-3-1909	1-8-1912	6-20-1888	Single
3-28-1894	4-17-1899	10-3-1865	Single
1909	3-1914	1880	Single
4-23-1900	7-18-1905	8-3-1875	Single
1908		1883	Single
8-12-1912	7-7-1916 FC	6-14-1890	Single
7-1-1912	7-27-1916 FC 11-3-1916 PAT	7-13-1884	Single
6-28-1900	1-23-1905	12-30-1837	Single
2-5-1910	6-15-1911 10-30-1911 PAT	2-11-1887	Single
7-11-1907	1-4-1909 FC 10-14-1909 PAT	2-18-1882	Single
2-20-1902	2-9-1909	4-6-1879	Single
9-21-1909	3-22-1910	7-15-1880	Single

Name	Location Section-Township N-Range W	Ethnic Background M = Mother, F = Father	Age, Land Transaction Initiated
Kringen, Anna	Williams Co. 35-157-103 Strandahl Twp.	M Norwegian F Norwegian	30
*Krueger, Hulda Olsen	McLean Co. 30-149-88 Deepwater Twp.	M German F German	21
Kuhn, Johanna Peterson	Adams Co. Haynes Area	M German F German	21
Kurz, Kaja Togstad	Benson Co.	M Norwegian F German	
Lamb, Agnes McEvoy	Near Washburn		
Lamb, Viola Edwards	Near Washburn		
Larsen, Mathilda Froslie	McLean Co. 9-150-80	M Norwegian F Norwegian	
*Larson, Christine Tollefson	Divide Co. 21-160-99 Garnet Twp.	M Norwegian F Norwegian	21
Larson, Emma Eastby	Benson Co. 34-155-71 Iowa Twp.	M Norwegian F Norwegian	46
Larson, Ingebor	Nelson Co. 8-152-57 Petersburg	M Norwegian F Norwegian	
Larson, Lizzie Olson	Burke Co. 6-159-93 Colville Twp.	M Norwegian F Norwegian	22
Larson, Louisa Oberg	Oliver Co. 20-142-84 Lincoln Twp.	M Swedish F Swedish	51
Lauzon, Nellie Oslund Feland	Morton Co. 8-136-86	M Swedish F Swedish	24
Lavalle, Lydia	Bottineau Co. 34-161-79 Tacoma Twp.	M French F French	32
Lavalle, Minnie Shipton	Bottineau Co. 34-161-79 Tacoma Twp.	M French F French	30
Lee, Anna J.	Mountrail Co. 17-158-92 Powers Twp.		
Lee, Ina Mary (Marie) Berkman	Benson Co. 18-155-69 Beaver Twp.	M Norwegian F Norwegian	21

Date, Land Transaction Initiated	Date of Final Land Transactions	Birth Date	Marital Status, Land Transaction Initiated
4-13-1905	2-25-1908	1875	Single
6-12-1916	10-10-1917	1-9-1895	Single
1907	4-24-1908	1-24-1886	Single
1899			Single
		3-17-1884	Single
		7-1-1885	Single
4-26-1904	1-17-1910 6-23-1910 PAT		Single
2-21-1913	3-29-1917 FC 8-14-1917 PAT	10-19-1891	Single
4-10-1899	11-11-1905	1-13-1853	Widow
	10-11-1884	7-15-1839	Widow
6-27-1905	4-8-1911 FC 9-12-1911 PAT	8-19-1882	Single
2-26-1906	6-19-1911 FC 4-27-1912 PAT	5-1854	Widow
10-27-1910	2-2-1914	10-19-1886	Widow
11-18-1900	9-2-1902	9-7-1868	Single
11-18-1900	Relinquished	3-7-1870	Single
11-20-1908	1-28-1913 FC		Single
1-25-1900	11-6-1907 cancelled	11-3-1878	Single

Name	Location Section-Township N-Range W	Ethnic Background M = Mother, F = Father	Age, Land Transaction Initiated
Lewis, Hester Swift	Renville Co. 34-159-85 Callahan Twp.	M Irish F English, Irish	26
Lien, Mary Dale	Walsh Co. 31-155-56 Medford Twp.	M Norwegian F Norwegian	23
Lindsay, Mrs. William	Walsh Co. Near Minto	M from Canada F from Canada	
Lindsley, Addie	Mountrail Co. 3-156-93 Manitou Twp.	F Anglo-American	38
Lindstrom, Engeborg	Benson Co. 4-151-67 Oberon Twp.	M Norwegian F Norwegian	52
Linn, Elise	McLean Co. 34-150-83 Economy Twp.	M Norwegian F Norwegian	24
Linn, Emelia	McLean Co. 35-150-83 Economy Twp.	M Norwegian F Norwegian	
Linn, Inga Louise	McLean Co. 28-150-83 Economy Twp.	M Norwegian F Norwegian	
Linn, Lena Johnson	McLean Co. 35-150-83 Economy Twp.	M Norwegian F Norwegian	26
Loraas, Grethe Edholm	Cavalier Co. 34-160-62 Gordon Twp.	M Norwegian F Norwegian	43
Lynch, Sarah Jane Murphy	Burke Co. 30-163-90 Richland Twp.	M Irish F Irish	33
Lyngen, Gelina Hilden	Adams Co. 6-130-98 Reeder Twp.	M Norwegian F Norwegian	22
Lyngen, Julia A. Hilden	Adams Co. 30-130-98 Reeder Twp.	M Norwegian F Norwegian	31
Lynner, Hilda M.	McKenzie Co. 18-149-100 Elsworth Twp.	M Norwegian F Norwegian	32
McCombs, Cora Green	McHenry Co. 11-157-76	M Scottish, Irish F Scottish	20

Date, Land Transaction Initiated	Date of Final Land Transactions	Birth Date	Marital Status, Land Transaction Initiated
10-19-1901	4-27-1908 FC	5-21-1875	Single
6-10-1886	6-5-1894	3-31-1863	Single
6-19-1903	9-16-1905	12-4-1864	Married; widowed before land was proved up Single
	10-21-1884	7-10-1832	Divorced
9-26-1902	10-16-1907	5-20-1878	Single
6-19-1905	11-6-1907		Single
2-6-1906	7-31-1908 4-5-1909 PAT		Single
9-26-1902	10-16-1907	3-2-1876	Single
7-20-1902	12-28-1903	6-23-1859	Single
3-30-1903	3-27-1906	3-16-1870	Single
5-1-1906	8-14-1907	6-2-1883	Single
5-2-1906	8-14-1907	7-13-1874	Single
8-1-1907	10-7-1913 FC	11-4-1874	Single
5-11-1902	11-9-1908 FC 10-1909 PAT	3-24-1882	Single

Name	Location Section-Township N- Range W	Ethnic Background M = Mother, F = Father	Age, Land Transaction Initiated
McCombs, Hattie Evelyn Chamberlain	McHenry Co. 6-157-76	M Scottish, Irish F Scottish	21
McDonald, Emma Graham	Cavalier Co. 1-163-64 Cypress Twp.	M Scottish (Canadian) F Scottish (Canadian)	
McElwain, Maria Jane Gallagher	McLean Co. 31-149-85 Platt Twp.	M English F Scottish, Irish	23
McGuire, Edith Thompson	Renville Co. 33-159-85 Callahan Twp.	M Irish F Irish	20
McInnis, Euphemia Potter	Burke Co. 1-163-88 Lakeview Twp.	M Scottish F Scottish	23
Maresh, Stealla Swab	Williams Co. 2-154-102 Judson Twp.	M Bohemian F Bohemian	21
Marshall, Anna C.	McHenry Co.		
May, Caroline Wolfe	Dunn Co. 6-147-95	M Italian F Austrian, Hungarian	53
Mertes, Mary Engelhard	Renville Co. 10-158-84		21
Moen, Julia Gunvaldson	Ward Co. 26-157-86 Carpio Twp.	M Norwegian F Norwegian	26
Mogren, Ebba Lotty Johnson	Burke Co. 33-160-90 Roseland Twp.	M Swedish F Swedish	21
Mostad, Tillie Smith	Ward Co. 35-153-83 Freedom Twp.	M Norwegian F Norwegian	22
Murray, Mary Ann	Slope Co. 12-133-104 Crawford Twp.	M Irish F Irish	49
Murray, Olive Shaw	Slope Co.	M Irish F Irish	24
Naismith, Jennie MacLean	Cavalier Co. 6-163-64 Cypress Twp.	M Scottish F Scottish	21
Nelson, Anna Morland	Slope Co. 22-133-99	M Swedish F Swedish	26
Nelson, Emma Thingvold Johnson	Rolette Co. 33-159-73 South Valley Twp.	M Norwegian F Norwegian	23

Date, Land Transaction Initiated	Date of Final Land Transactions	Birth Date	Marital Status, Land Transaction Initiated
7-19-1904	9-13-1907 FC 7-8-1910 PAT	7-2-1883	Single
7-11-1902	11-1-1904		Single
12-17-1912	6-26-1916 FC 10-2-1916 PAT	1-29-1889	Single
10-9-1901	3-21-1904	3-17-1881	Single
6-16-1900	10-10-1905	10-13-1876	Single
5-4-1904	12-14-1907	12-4-1882	Single
			Widow
5-21-1932	10-28-1937	11-19-1878	Widow
8-7-1905	11-26-1906	7-12-1884	Single
5-27-1901	10-6-1906	11-1-1874	Single
11-15-1904	6-12-1907	5-9-1883	Single
11-15-1909	7-21-1913	11-26-1886	Single
11-12-1907	6-7-1914	3-30-1858	Widow
1910		6-17-1886	Single
5-27-1897	8-18-1902 FC	8-6-1875	Single
5-8-1908	10-3-1912 FC	4-21-1882	Single
5-7-1901	12-10-1906 FC	12-6-1877	Widow

263

Name	Location Section-Township N-Range W	Ethnic Background M = Mother, F = Father	Age, Land Transaction Initiated
Nelson, Helma	Northwest of Velva		
Newnam, Cora	Mountrail Co. 35-154-90 Austin Twp.	M Irish	26
Nickelson, Cecil McMillan	McKenzie Co. 31-150-100 Arnegard Twp.	M Norwegian F Norwegian	22
Nickelson, Susie Snell	McKenzie Co. 30-150-100 Arnegard Twp.	M Norwegian F Norwegian	24
Norby, Lena M. Olson	McKenzie Co. 1-152-96, 6-153-95 Hawk Valley Twp.	M Norwegian F Norwegian	20
Nott, Carrie Ott	Mountrail Co. 28-158-88 Lowland Twp.	M English F English	22
O'Connor, Maggie	Eddy Co. 7-149-67 Munster Twp.	M Irish F Irish	25
Olimb, Caren	McHenry Co. 21-151-77 Land Twp.	M Norwegian F Norwegian	34
Olimb, Petra	McHenry Co. 21-151-77 Land Twp.	M Norwegian F Norwegian	33
Olsen, Jonetta Odegaard Narum	Sargent Co. 4-130-54 Ransom Twp.	M Norwegian F Norwegian	22
Olsen, Karen Kittleson Erickson	Towner Co. 22-160-68 Grainfield Twp.	M Norwegian F Norwegian	36
Olson, Anna Strand	Williams Co. 17-157-102 Bonetrail Twp.	M Norwegian F Norwegian	32
Olson, Mary Digre	Williams Co. 32-158-102 Good Luck Twp.	M Norwegian F Norwegian	31
Olson, Olga Thompson	McLean Co. 14-146-79 Mercer Twp.	M Norwegian F Norwegian	23
Ott, Minnie Sullivan	Ramsey Co. 34-158-63 Royal Twp.		24

Date, Land Transaction Initiated	Date of Final Land Transactions	Birth Date	Marital Status, Land Transaction Initiated
1901 or 1902			
6-23-1902	9-9-1907	9-12-1875	Single
6-21-1907	9-23-1908 4-5-1909 PAT	10-23-1884	Single
10-4-1906	1-31-1908	5-13-1882	Single
1-29-1905	8-30-1912	10-8-1884	Single
2-24-1902	9-16-1908 FC	4-26-1879	Single
7-8-1891	3-17-1900	7-15-1865	Single
5-31-1899	6-6-1904	1-18-1865	Single
5-25-1900	7-12-1906	4-19-1867	Single
11-11-1893	9-24-1890	7-25-1871	Married-Widowed before land was proved up
7-8-1892	11-21-1898 FC 10-23-1901 PAT	11-18-1855	Widow
11-18-1905	3-21-1907	8-17-1873	Single
3-24-1905	7-25-1906	8-17-1873	Single
2-25-1907	6-25-1910 FC 5-18-1911 PAT	5-4-1883	Single
12-19-1898	9-23-1905	1-31-1874	Single

265

Name	Location Section-Township N-Range W	Ethnic Background M = Mother, F = Father	Age, Land Transaction Initiated
Overbeck, Ellen Elizabeth Hanson Dickinson	Billings Co. 34-137-102	M English F English, Welsh	31
Overstreet, Fannie Henry	McKenzie Co. 11-150-102 Randolph Twp. 12-150-102	M English F English	23
Paquin, Nellie McCarty	Billings Co. 24-137-100 Rocky Ridge Twp.		58
*Paulson, Hilda Oakland	McKenzie Co. 10-149-104 Estes Twp.	M Norwegian F Norwegian	22
Pederson, Johanna Lee	Sheridan Co. 12-146-78		
Peterson, Anna Borgeson	Walsh Co. 7-156-57 Norton Twp.	M Swedish F Swedish	26
Peterson, Caroline S.	McHenry Co. 14-151-79 Olivia Twp.	M Norwegian F Norwegian	21
Peterson, Ida Wingerd	Williams Co. 8-159-97 Hazel Twp.	M Norwegian F Norwegian	20
Peterson, Isabel Legge	Williams Co. 21-159-103 Grenora Twp.	M Norwegian F Norwegian	21
Peterson, Mathilda	McKenzie Co. 14-150-95 Grail Twp.	M Norwegian F Norwegian	
Peterson, Sophia	Williams Co. 8 & 9-159-97 Hazel Twp.	M Norwegian F Norwegian	24
Pettingill, Julia	Mountrail Co. 30-153-90 Wayzetta Twp.	M Irish F Irish	56
Pettingill, Sadie McNamara	Mountrail Co. 30-153-90 Wayzetta Twp.	M Irish F Irish	28
*Pfundheller, Nora King Lenartz	Mountrail Co. 24-151-92	M German F German	20
Popp, Eva A. Henry	Bowman Co. 32-132-101 Grainbelt Twp.	M German F German	24

Date, Land Transaction Initiated	Date of Final Land Transactions	Birth Date	Marital Status, Land Transaction Initiated
8-28-1915	6-27-1922	1-6-1884	Widow
5-4-1914	11-15-1917 FC 8-24-1918 PAT	12-4-1890	Single
3-24-1915	11-15-1917 FC 8-24-1918 PAT		
4-8-1907	6-16-1908	4-2-1849	Widow
1-16-1914	8-17-1917 FC 4-5-1918 PAT	2-1-1891	Single
5-15-1900	12-9-1909		Single
	7-25-1883	1857	
6-13-1904	6-21-1909 FC 6-14-1910 PAT	9-3-1882	Single
8-9-1906	3-29-1908	8-23-1885	Single
6-4-1910	7-23-1915	4-3-1889	Single
3-5-1912	7-29-1916 FC 11-31-1916 PAT		Single
8-9-1906	9-16-1911 Inherited by heirs	11-30-1881	Single
4-15-1905	3-6-1912 6-20-1912 PAT	1849	Widow
7-6-1905	7-6-1912 FC 10-4-1912 PAT	7-29-1876	Single
7-11-1913	7-14-1915 FC	5-31-1893	Single
9-12-1906	12-21-1907	10-1-1881	Single

Name	Location Section-Township N- Range W	Ethnic Background M = Mother, F = Father	Age, Land Transaction Initiated
Popp, Ida J. Joyce	Bowman Co. 32-132-101 Grainbelt Twp.	M German F German	21
Potter, Viola Maynard	Bowman Co.	F Anglo-American	21
Prideaux, Ethel Louella Twist	Dunn Co. 20-142-91	M English F English	22
Raaen, Gurine T. Weltzin	McKenzie Co. 25-151-100 Patent Gate Twp.	M Norwegian F Norwegian	22
Rafter, Sister Mary Stanislaus	Near Stump Lake	M Irish American F Irish American	
Ralyea, Libbie	Dickey Co. 14-129-59 Lovell Twp.	F Anglo-American	
Redahlen, Valberg Welstad	Divide Co.	M Norwegian F Norwegian	25
Reetz, Ella Erbstoesser	Mercer Co. 34-141-90	M German F German	21
Reidy, Lizzie	McKenzie Co. 18-151-101 Timber Creek Twp.	Black American	
Roaldson, Mary	Foster Co. 8-145-62 Eastman Twp.	M Norwegian F Norwegian	23
Robertson, Pearl	Renville Co. 20-162-85 Hamerly Twp.	F Anglo-American	
*Rodenbaugh, Luella LeBarron	Logan Co. 18-136-72 Glendale Twp.		20
Roneberg, Mina Helstad	Williams Co.	M Norwegian F Norwegian	30
Ronning, Karen	Ramsey Co. 17-154-66 Norway Twp.	M Norwegian F Norwegian	44
Roterud, Olive McElwain	McLean Co. 35-150-86 Bluehill Twp.	M Norwegian F Norwegian	23
Rowe, Clara	Dickey Co. 27-129-59 Lovell Twp.	M Anglo-American (Wales) F Anglo-American (Wales)	40
Rude, Sophie Sanderson	Divide Co. 27-162-101 Clinton Twp.	M Norwegian F Norwegian	30

Date, Land Transaction Initiated	Date of Final Land Transactions	Birth Date	Marital Status, Land Transaction Initiated
5-14-1907	11-22-1907 7-15-1909 PAT	8-6-1885	Single
1910		8-4-1889	Single
11-14-1911	6-17-1915	9-20-1889	Single
11-6-1907	2-19-1914	3-16-1885	Single
8-24-1883			
8-11-1884	Heir of Elisha Ralyea 9-28-1889 FC		
1908	1911	4-4-1883	Single
11-3-1910	1-5-1914	10-28-1889	Single
2-28-1906	5-18-1914		
7-26-1895	9-17-1900	5-16-1872	Single
8-27-1901	1-16-1909		Single
3-7-1903	11-27-1908 FC 7-12-1909 PAT	11-5-1882	Single
10-1908	6-1911	1-13-1878	Single
7-28-1888	8-9-1901 FC 5-27-1902 PAT	1844	Widow
8-18-1909	10-10-1911 5-13-1912 PAT	9-5-1885	Single
8-26-1886	6-27-1899	1846	Widow
3-23-1906	10-12-1907	3-9-1876	Single

Name	Location Section-Township N-Range W	Ethnic Background M = Mother, F = Father	Age, Land Transaction Initiated
Russell, Dorothy	Benson Co. 22-156-69 York Twp.	M Irish, English F Irish, English	64
Ryen, Gunda Haga Erickson	McHenry Co.	M Norwegian F Norwegian	24
Ryen, Mathilda	Williams Co. 21-157-99 Dublin Twp.		32
Sanda, Hege Berjuven	Mountrail Co. 26-155-89 McAlmond Twp.	M Norwegian F Norwegian	36
Sanda, Thora Norgard	Mountrail Co. 35-155-89 McAlmond Twp.	M Norwegian F Norwegian	18
Schanche, Tyra Mattson	Williams Co. 8-154-95	M Swedish F Swedish	34
Schlapman, Emma	Stark Co. 26-140-94	M German F German	21
Schwartz, Bessie	Bowman Co.	M Jewish (Romanian)	20
Shaski, Margaret Madson	McKenzie Co. 26-146-102	M English F English	26
*Sheidamantel, Gertrude Wenck	Slope Co. 10-133-103 Deep Creek Twp.	M German F German	19
Sheridan, Mae Ulwelling	Renville Co. 13-162-84 Hurley Twp.	M Irish F Irish	29
Sheridan, Margaret	Renville Co. 14-162-84 Hurley Twp.	M Irish F Irish	28
Sheridan, Nell Hopkins	Renville Co. 13-162-84 Hurley Twp.	M Irish F Irish	21
Shoemaker, Pauline Crowley	Mercer Co. 4-142-90	M Dutch F German	31
Sindalson, Ida Christensen	Grant Co. 26-133-85 Raleigh Twp.	M Danish F Danish	41
Sisco, Leone	Emmons Co. 12-136-74 Campbell Twp.	M English F Scottish	
Sisco, Mayme Ryan	Emmons Co. 2-136-74 Campbell Twp.	M English F Scottish	

Date, Land Transaction Initiated	Date of Final Land Transactions	Birth Date	Marital Status, Land Transaction Initiated
4-20-1893	9-24-1898	6-21-1828	Widow
1899		9-15-1875	Single
4-6-1911	6-23-1915 FC	1879	Single
6-27-1904	9-11-1907 3-9-1908	8-4-1867	Widow
9-30-1908	12-21-1909 6-23-1910 PAT	12-11-1889	Single
7-6-1910	11-20-1916 FC 2-13-1917 PAT	1876	Widow
6-27-1905	11-18-1909 5-26-1910 PAT	7-21-1883	Single
1906		1886	Single
7-28-1916	8-12-1921	5-14-1890	Separated
10-31-1907	9-11-1913	6-15-1888	Single
11-29-1901	6-21-1907	3-8-1872	Single
11-29-1901	6-21-1907	10-8-1873	Single
11-29-1901	10-7-1903	4-11-1880	Single
3-17-1911	7-31-1916 FC 10-12-1916 PAT	5-1879	Single
8-8-1907	9-23-1912 FC	12-1-1865	Single
7-17-1903	10-23-1908		Single
7-17-1903	10-19-1908		Single

271

Name	Location Section-Township N-Range W	Ethnic Background M = Mother, F = Father	Age, Land Transaction Initiated
Skredsvig, Kari	Burke Co. 35-160-90 Roseland Twp.	M Norwegian F Norwegian	38
Smith, Effie Vivian Rogers Petersen	Burke Co. 3-160-91 Diamond Twp.	M English F English	21
Smith, Martha Ann Walker	Golden Valley Co. 12-138-105	M Irish, Scottish F Irish	20
Smith, Nancy Hollenbeck	Golden Valley Co. 12-138-105	M Irish, Scottish F Irish	25
Smith, Nellie	Logan Co. 30-134-71 Red Lake Twp.	F Anglo-American	
Steles, Emma Heidlebaugh	Pierce Co. 30-158-71 Juniata Twp.	M English F English, German	22
Stenehjem, Anna Drovdal	McKenzie Co. 1-149-100 Ellsworth Twp.	M Norwegian F Norwegian	25
Stenehjem, Gertrude Mitten	McKenzie Co. 7-149-99	M Norwegian F Norwegian	27
Stevens, Gertrude Cushing	McKenzie Co. 34-149-100	M English, Scottish	20
Storberget, Karen Olsen	Towner Co. 35-160-68 Grainfield Twp.	M Norwegian F Norwegian	64
Stracker, Barbara	Slope Co. 6-134-103 Harper Twp.	M German F German	50
Stramblad, Viola A. Liessman	Kidder Co. 30-144-73 Stewart Twp.	M Swedish F Swedish	33
Swanson, Hilma Van Vorst	Mountrail Co. 28-158-91 Lostwood Twp.	M Swedish F Swedish	28
Taipe, Sarah Elizabeth Cordner	Burleigh Co.	M (born in Mass.)	28
Taylor, Rachel Martin	McKenzie Co. 12-151-102 Charbonneau Twp.		21
*Thedin, Josephine Bostrom	Divide Co. 19-161-99 Burg Twp.	M Swedish F Swedish	21

Date, Land Transaction Initiated	Date of Final Land Transactions	Birth Date	Marital Status, Land Transaction Initiated
6-21-1900	2-25-1907	10-14-1861	Widow
3-14-1905	8-26-1908	1-21-1884	Single
12-15-1903	9-16-1910	3-20-1883	Single
12-15-1903	12-23-1910	1-28-1878	Single
11-6-1905	10-25-1911		Single
8-22-1901	11-2-1903	6-2-1879	Single
9-25-1911	6-5-1915	1-17-1886	Single
1-21-1908	8-28-1911	8-19-1880	Single
1-16-1906	3-28-1911	11-21-1885	Single
	10-4-1889	10-29-1826	Widow
8-1-1911	7-14-1915	12-1860	Single
9-20-1902	4-16-1909	1-13-1869	Single
8-2-1905	10-29-1906	1877	Single
1883		1-17-1855	Single
11-30-1903	8-21-1909 FC 3-10-1910 PAT	1882	Single
4-10-1908	12-15-1909 FC 6-23-1910 PAT	5-28-1886	Single

Name	Location Section-Township N-Range W	Ethnic Background M = Mother, F = Father	Age, Land Transaction Initiated
Thingvold, Anna Henry	Rolette Co. 26-159-73 South Valley Twp.	M Norwegian F Norwegian	29
Thingvold, Thina Charbonneau	Williams Co. 15-157-102 Bonetraill Twp.	M Norwegian F Norwegian	22
Thompson, Amanda Stensland Olsen	Ramsey Co. 18-157-60 Newland Twp.		
Thompson, Leone Haskett	Williams Co. Near Barr Butte Twp.		
Thompson, Margret Kirsch	Logan Co. 24-134-72 Starkey Twp.		
*Thompson, Thea Johnson	Williams Co. 26-157-101 Blacktail Twp.	M Norwegian F Norwegian	22
Thoreson, Tomena Whiting	McLean Co. 9-150-85 Douglas Twp.	M Norwegian F Norwegian	21
Timboe, Lena Jorgenson	Williams Co. 21-157-98 Oliver Twp.	M Norwegian F Norwegian	32
Tolsby, Caroline Larson	McKenzie Co.	M Norwegian F Norwegian	21
Tompte, Anna	Divide Co. 29-163-99 Ambrose Twp.	M Norwegian F Norwegian	19
Tompte, Helga Almos	Divide Co. 19-163-99 Ambrose Twp.	M Norwegian F Norwegian	21
Tool, May	Morton Co. 21-136-79	M German, Irish F German, Irish	25
Trenne, Louise Porth	Divide Co. 31-163-99 Ambrose Twp.	M German F French, German	23
Troska, Clara Eaton	Burke Co. 34-160-92 Lucy Twp.	M Polish F Polish	23
Trygstad, Olga Hauge	Grant Co. 22-132-88 Fisher Twp.	M Norwegian F Norwegain	26
Tysver, Lillie E. Ronnevik	Mercer Co. 28-144-86 Hazen Twp.	M Norwegian F Norwegian	24

Date, Land Transaction Initiated	Date of Final Land Transactions	Birth Date	Marital Status, Land Transaction Initiated
3-1-1900	3-7-1903	8-14-1870	Single
9-17-1904	12-26-1905	10-24-1881	Single
5-24-1898	11-25-1904		Widow
			Single
3-9-1908	2-5-1910 FC 9-8-1910 PAT		
9-19-1910	3-8-1912	12-25-1887	Single
9-13-1902	11-2-1904	4-6-1881	Single
2-6-1908	12-8-1909 6-16-1910 PAT	6-27-1875	Single
1907		3-8-1886	Single
11-16-1904	6-25-1907	1885	Single
11-16-1904	6-25-1907	1883	Single
7-24-1906	1-13-1908	5-1881	Single
5-9-1907	3-16-1909	12-17-1883	Single
9-5-1905	12-27-1906	5-10-1882	Single
7-30-1913	9-30-1918	2-11-1887	Single
9-22-1913	8-4-1917	5-7-1889	Single

275

Name	Location Section-Township N- Range W	Ethnic Background M = Mother, F = Father	Age, Land Transaction Initiated
Uleberg, Josephine Anderson	Mountrail Co. 15-156-94 Myrtle Twp.	M Norwegian F Norwegian	22
Uleberg, Kari	Burke Co. Near Columbus	M Norwegian F Norwegian	
Underdahl, Anna Osteroos	Ward Co. 12-153-86 Linton Twp.	M Norwegian F Norwegian	22
Vaughn, Bessie	Burke Co. 32-159-91 Vanville Twp.		
Von Readen, Bertha Henry	Bottineau Co. 8-161-79 Kane Twp.	M German F German	22
Von Readen, Lena Wyman	Bottineau Co. 12-161-80 Brander Twp.	M German F German	25
Warren, Luella	Benson Co. 19-156-70 Knox Twp.	F Anglo-American	29
Wells, Susie Nelson	Oliver Co. 20-143-82 Marysville Twp.	F Anglo-American	25
West, Miriam Coburn	Stutsman Co. 22-143-67	M English F Scottish	60
Wheeler, Minnie	McKenzie Co. 11-150-95 Grail Twp. 2-150-95	F Anglo-American	
*Whittemore, Flora Walter	Mountrail Co. 26-157-94 White Earth Twp.	M English F English	22
Wilson, Cora	Benson Co. 20-156-69 York Twp.	M Anglo-American F Anglo-American	23
Wingust, Hilma	McHenry Co. 31-155-77	M Swedish F Swedish	21
Wood, Mary E. Lynch	Burke Co. 5-163-90 Richland Twp.	M Irish F Irish	21
Zimmerman, Anna Hammel	Dunn Co. 10-146-94	F German	
Zirbes, Marie	Mountrail Co. 26-156-94 Myrtle Twp.		

Date, Land Transaction Initiated	Date of Final Land Transactions	Birth Date	Marital Status, Land Transaction Initiated
4-24-1909	9-26-1910 7-13-1911 PAT	10-15-1886	Single
5-1-1906	10-30-1907	5-12-1883	Single
4-17-1906	6-1-1908		Single
1-20-1900	12-3-1906	2-12-1877	Single
6-15-1899	6-22-1905	1-14-1874	Single
9-21-1900	1-20-1906	1-7-1871	Single
9-12-1901	7-28-1908 FC 2-1-1909 PAT	4-18-1876	Single
10-16-1906	10-30-1913	5-10-1846	Widow
3-21-1912	12-1917 FC 12-18-1918 PAT		Single
6-19-1913	12-1917 FC 12-18-1918 PAT		
4-16-1907	12-24-1912	1-19-1885	Single
	7-16-1889	1866	Single
2-18-1901	1-5-1908	1-6-1880	Single
7-22-1902	5-5-1905 FC 12-12-1905 PAT	6-27-1881	Single
2-24-1910	8-16-1915 FC		Single
12-17-1900	11-21-1901		

Notes

Most of the research in this book is based on primary data collected during the years 1983 and 1984, which eventually will be deposited in and cataloged by the North Dakota Institute for Regional Studies, North Dakota State University, Fargo. Until then, access to the materials is possible by contacting the author through the North Dakota Institute for Regional Studies. Materials include transcribed interviews with sixteen women; questionnaires filled out by relatives and friends of 290 additional women; and miscellaneous documents, including recollections, letters, naturalization papers, homestead patents, newspaper articles, and diaries. Citations for materials that have been published are included in the Notes or cited within the text. The source and time frame of some unpublished material is included in the text; otherwise, the reader can assume the information has been selected from the unpublished sources, usually recollections. In the Appendix, an asterisk is included by the names of those interviewed; it also includes information on initiating and finalizing land transactions for each woman. This enables the reader to determine an approximate time frame for all uncited references.

Preface

1. Carol Fairbanks, *Prairie Women: Images in American and Canadian Fiction* (New Haven: Yale University Press, 1986), pp. 5-6.

2. For a discussion of the concept of the plains as "the garden of the world," see Henry Nash Smith, *Virgin Land: The American West As Symbol and Myth* (Cambridge: Harvard University Press, 1950).

Chapter 1: They Staked Their Claims

1. Verne Benedict, "Homesteading Was Contagious," *Old West* (Fall 1967): 24, 25, 42.

2. Mary Dunlava Tellefson, "My Biography and Recollections of Pioneer Days in McKenzie County," in *From Dreams to Reality*, Hedvig Clawsen Svore (Bismarck: Bismarck Tribune Co., 1954), pp. 76-77.

3. *Stories and Histories of Divide County*, [S.l.: s.n.], (Marceline, Mo.: Walsworth, 1964), p. 408.

4. Ted Upgren, "The Murray Place: A Bicentennial Sketch of Sod Houses, Settlers, and Prairie Tails," *North Dakota Outdoors* (November 1976): 20-25.

5. Ibid., p. 22.

6. Mrs. Morris Kauffman, "As I Remember." *Ranger Review*, (Glendive, Montana), Sunday, Februrary, 15, 1970, no. 2 in a series of six articles.

7. Carol Fairbanks, *Prairie Women: Images in American and Canadian Fiction* (New Haven: Yale University Press, 1986), pp. 5-6.

8. *New York Daily Tribune*, June 6, 1862. Cited in Roy M. Robbins, *Our Landed Heritage: The Public Domain 1776-1936* (Princeton: Princeton University Press, 1942), p. 206.

9. *They Planted Their Roots Deep: Horace 100 Years*, [S.l.:s.n.] 1973, p. 60; and additional notes from her grandson, Oscar Furnberg.

10. *Annals of the Ursuline Nuns of Grand Forks, Dakota Territory*, Bishops House, Fargo.

11. H. Elaine Lindgren, "Ethnic Women Homesteading on the North Dakota Plains," *Great Plains Quarterly 9*, no. 3 (July 1989).

12. This data comes from unpublished research of William C. Sherman, North Dakota State University, Fargo.

13. Thomas Newgard and William Sherman, *African-Americans in North Dakota: Sources and Assessments*. (Bismarck, N.D.: Mary University Press, 1996).

14. May Shipton Girard, *The Cruel Cold Land* (Portland, Oregon: Metropolitan Press, 1980), pp. 36-7.

15. From the diary of Eliza Crawford, reprinted in the *Adams County Record*, series of four articles beginning November 4, 1981. The original diary is in a family collection.

16. *Sunday Argus* (Fargo), August 19, 1883, p. 7.

17. Grace Hudson, "Linda Warfel Slaughter," in *Women of North Dakota - Hall of Fame*, [Fargo, N.D.]: Hudson, 1977, pp. 1-2.

18. Mrs. Linda W. Slaughter, *The New Northwest* (Bismarck: Burleigh County Pioneers' Association, 1874).

19. Roberta M. Starry, "Petticoat Pioneer," *The West 7*, no. 5 (October 1967): p. 8.

20. "Mrs. Wike Leaves Messages of Courage, Faith and Hope," *Belfield News*, October 12, 1961.

21. Enid Bern, ed., "They Had a Wonderful Time: The Homesteading Letters of Anna and Ethel Erickson," *North Dakota History* (Fall 1978): 4-31.

22. Leonard Lund, "Early Day Memories Survived on Scraps of Paper," *Minot Daily News*, September 19, 1981.

Notes

23. McIntosh and Sheridan Counties: *United States Bureau of Land Management Tract Books*, also called *Federal Land Office Homestead Tract Books*, Chester Fritz Library, University of North Dakota, Grand Forks. Foster County: *A History of Foster County* [Carrington, The Committee] 1983. Burke County: *Burke County and White Earth Valley Historical Society, 1971* [Bismarck, N.D.: Quality Printing Service] 1972. Williams County: *The Wonder of Williams* 1. Compiled and published by the Williams County Historical Society, Marlene Eide, Coordinator [S.l.] 1975. Grand Forks County: earliest map available from Register of Deeds Office, Grand Forks County, Grand Forks. Kidder County: map compiled by Robert Thompson, Bismarck. McKenzie County: map compiled by Mary Dunlava Tellefson, Cupertino, Calif. Pembina County: map compiled by Laura Mitchell and the Pembina County Pioneer Daughters.

24. Sheryll Patterson-Black, "Women Homesteaders on the Great Plains Frontier," *Frontiers* (Spring 1976); and Katherine Llewellyn Hill Harris, "Women and Families on Northwestern Colorado Homesteads, 1873-1920" (Ph.D. diss., University of Colorado, Boulder, 1983).

25. Emma Haddock, "Women as Land-Owners In the West" in Association for the Advancement of Women, *Proceedings. . . Fourteenth Annual Convention, Louisville, Kentucky, 1886.* (Louisville, 1886), pp. 12-27.

26. Elaine Lindgren and William Sherman, "Drive Your Oxen, Ride Your Plows: Homesteading Women in North Dakota," in *Day In, Day Out: Women's Lives in North Dakota*, eds. Bjorn Benson, Elizabeth Hampsten, and Kathryn Sweney (Grand Forks: University of North Dakota, 1988), pp. 219-35.

Chapter 2: The Land and the Law

1. Parts of four government circulars were used as basic references for legislation regarding preemption, homesteading, and timber culture.

a. *Circular from the General Land Office showing the Manner of Proceeding to Obtain Title to Public Lands*, August 23, 1870 (Washington, D.C.: Government Printing Office, 1870), pp. 1-28.

b. Henry N. Copp, comp., *Public Land Laws, Passed by Congress from March 4, 1875, to April 1, 1882, with the Important Decisions of the Secretary of the Interior and Commissioner of the General Land Office, the Final Opinions of the Attorney General, and Circular Instructions. . . .* (Washington, D.C.: Henry N. Copp, 1883), pp. 247-303.

281

c. *Circular from the General Land Office showing the Manner of Proceeding to Obtain Title to Public Lands Under the Homestead, Desert Land, and other laws,* July 11, 1899 (Washington, D.C.: Government Printing Office, 1899), pp. 1-35.

d. U.S. Department of the Interior, *Decisions of the Department of the Interior in Cases Relating to the Public Lands,* vol. 39 (Washington, D.C.: Government Printing Office, 1911), pp. 232-53.

Information not specifically cited in the text comes from one or more of these sources. These references contain a great deal of additional information that has not been included in my discussion but may be of interest to those who wish to learn more about specific regulations.

More general discussions of public land laws and policies can be found in Benjamin Hibbard, *A History of the Public Land Policies* (New York: Macmillan, 1924); Roy M. Robbins, *Our Landed Heritage: The Public Domain 1776-1936* (Princeton: Princeton University Press, 1942); Everett Dick, *The Lure of the Land* (Lincoln: University of Nebraska Press, 1970); and Howard W. Ottoson, ed., *Land Use Policy and Problems in the United States* (Lincoln: University of Nebraska Press, 1963).

2. Paul W. Gates, "The Homestead Act: Free Land Policy in Operation, 1862-1935," in *Land Use Policy and Problems in the United States,* ed., Howard W. Ottoson (Lincoln: University of Nebraska Press, 1963), p. 31.

3. Correspondence with James Muhn, Land Law Historian, Bureau of Land Management, U.S. Department of the Interior, Denver, Colorado, February 16, 1989. A statement made by the acting commissioner of the General Land Office, Luther Harrison, to the editor of *Saturday Night* on November 20, 1883, indicated, "a widow, who was under 21 years of age, and was the head of a household [a household according to John Bouvier and Francis Rawle in *Bouvier's Law Dictionary* (new ed. [Boston: The Boston Book Co., 1897], 1: 965) being " 'those who dwell under the same roof and constitute a family' "] could make a Homestead entry. However, if she was a single widow—without dependents—she would not be the head of a household, and therefore, could not, as stated in the Homestead Act of May 20, 1862, make an entry."

4. Dick, *The Lure of the Land,* pp. 67-68.

5. Biography of Dr. Josephine Lindstrom Stickelberger, Historical Data Project, Benson County, State Historical Society, North Dakota Heritage Center, Bismarck.

6. Map of squatters in Lovell Township, Dickey County, Register of Deeds.

7. Dick, *The Lure of the Land*, p. 55.

8. Robbins, *Our Landed Heritage*, pp. 89-91.

9. *5 U.S. Statutes at Large,* p. 455.

10. Dick, *The Lure of the Land,* p. 113.

11. U.S. General Land Office, *Report of the Commission of the General Land Office of the year 1867* R.S. 2259 (Washington, D.C.: Government Printing Office, 1867), pp. 80-81.

12. *12 U.S. Statutes at Large,* p. 392.

13. Rachel Taylor Martin, "First Teacher in Alexander," in *From Dreams to Reality,* ed. Hedvig Clausen Svore (Bismarck: Bismarck Tribune Co., 1954), p. 57.

14. Mary Collier, publication notice, *Jim River Journal,* October 10-November 14, 1884. Caroline Budke, news clipping, source unknown.

15. *26 Statutes at Large,* Sec. 7, p. 1098.

16. Muhn correspondence, June 5, 1988.

17. Cited in Hibbard, *A History of the Public Land Policies*, p. 387.

18. Ibid.

19. Muhn correspondence, June 5, 1988. *The United States Bureau of Land Management Tract Books*, also called *Federal Land Office Homestead Tract Books*, are available for North Dakota on microfilm at the Chester Fritz Library, University of North Dakota, Grand Forks.

20. *37 U.S. Statutes at Large,* Pt. 1, p. 123.

21. *37 U.S. Statutes at Large,* Pt. 1, p. 132.

22. Dick, *The Lure of the Land,* pp. 295-97.

23. Cited in Gates, "The Homestead Act" p. 34.

24. *17 U.S. Statutes at Large,* p. 333.

25. Mrs. William Lindsay, "My Pioneer Years in North Dakota," Manuscript collection B20, no. 357, State Historical Society, North Dakota Heritage Center, Bismarck.

26. Elisha Ralyea, Archival file, Civil Archives Division, National Archives, Washington, D.C.

27. Susan Jackel, introduction to *Wheat and Women*, by Georgina Binnie-Clark (1914; reprint, Toronto: University of Toronto Press, 1979), p. xx.

28. Ibid., p. xxv.

29. Binnie-Clark, *Wheat and Women*, p. 300.

30. U.S. General Land Office, *Report of the Commission of the General Land Office for the year 1864* (Washington, D.C.: Government Printing Office, 1864), p. 10.

31. Henry N. Copp, comp., *Public Land Laws passed by Congress From March 4, 1869 to March 3, 1875, Important Decisions of the Secretary of the Interior, and Commissioner of the General Land Office, the Opinions of the Assistant Attorney General and the Instructions. . .* (Washington, D.C.: Henry N. Copp, 1875), p. 287.

32. Ibid., p. 656.

33. Ibid., p. 656. Muhn correspondence, June 28, 1989.

34. Daniel M. Greene, *Public Land Statutes of the United States* (Washington, D.C.: Government Printing Office, 1931), pp. 204-5. Cites legislation approved June 6, 1900 (31 Stat. 683, U.S.C., Title 43, Sec. 166). Muhn correspondence, June 28, 1989.

35. Greene, *Public Land Statutes*, p. 205. Cites legislation approved April 6, 1914 (38 Stat. 312).

36. Ibid., pp. 205-6. Cites legislation approved Oct. 17, 1914 (38 Stat. 740, U.S.C., Title 43, Sec. 168) and Oct. 22, 1914 (38 Stat. 766, U.S.C., Title 43, Sec. 170).

37. Robbins, *Our Landed Heritage.*

38. Gates, "The Homestead Act,"pp. 31-2.

39. From the diary of Eliza Crawford, reprinted in the *Adams County Record*, series of four articles beginning November 4, 1981. The original diary is in a family collection.

40. As a legal secretary, Cornelia Honens took down the contest proceedings in shorthand. The transcript is in a family collection.

41. Julianna Hegel, Archival file, Civil Archives Division, National Archives, Washington, D.C.

Chapter 3: The Shack

1. Angela Boleyn, "Quarter Sections and Wide Horizons," *Fargo Forum,* July 5, 1931.

2. Ted Upgren, "The Murray Place: A Bicentennial Sketch of Sod Houses, Settlers, and Prairie Trails," *North Dakota Outdoors* (November 1976): 22.

3. *Prairie Tales* (Bowman County, N. D.: Rural Area Development Committee, 1965), p. 253.

4. Biography of Mrs. Carl J. Olstad of Drake, North Dakota, and diary of R. D. Kateley, now Mrs. Carl J. Olstad, Historical Data Project, State Historical Society, North Dakota Heritage Center, Bismarck.

5. Angel Kwolek-Folland, "The Elegant Dugout: Domesticity and Moveable Culture in the United States, 1870-1900," *American Studies* 25, no. 2 (Fall 1984): 21-37.

6. Evan J. Jenkins, *The Northern Tier: Or Life Among the Homestead Settlers* (Topeka, 1880), pp. 150, 154. Cited in Kwolek-Folland, "The Elegant Dugout," p. 25.

7. Mrs. Morris Kauffman, "As I Remember," *Ranger Review,* (Glendive, Montana), Sunday, February 15, 1970, no. 2 in series of six articles.

8. Roberta M. Starry, "Ice In the Bucket," *The Dakota Farmer,* April 19, 1969.

9. From the diary of Eliza Crawford, reprinted in the *Adams County Record,* series of four articles beginning November 4, 1981. The orginal diary is in a family collection.

10. *Stories and Histories of Divide County,* [S.l.: s.n.], (Marceline, Mo.: Walsworth, 1964), p. 447.

11. May Shipton Girard, *The Cruel Cold Land* (Portland, Oregon: Metropolitan Press, 1980), p. 37.

Chapter 4: Patterns of Life

1. U.S. Bureau of the Census, *Historical Statistics of the United States: Colonial Times to 1970*, pt. 1 (Washington, D.C.: U.S. Government Printing Office, 1975), p. 19.

2. "Nell Elliott Robinson," *Pioneer Women Teachers of North Dakota*, ed. Nellie R. Swanson and Eleanor C. Bryson. Ward County Independent (Minot) 1965, pp. 45-46.

3. Roberta M. Starry, "Petticoat Pioneer," *The West* 7, no. 5 (October 1967): 48.

4. *Prairie Tales* (Bowman County, N. D.: Rural Area Development Committee, 1965), p. 253.

5. Mrs. Morris Kauffman, "As I Remember: Mrs. Nancy Hollenbeck," *Ranger Review* (Glendive, Montana), no. 6 in a series of six articles, March 1970.

6. Bessie Schwartz, "My Own Story," file SC1055, Institute for Regional Sudies, North Dakota State University, Fargo, p. 5.

7. From the diary of Eliza Crawford, reprinted in the *Adams County Record*, series of four articles beginning November 4, 1981. The original diary is in a family collection.

8. Starry, "Petticoat Pioneer," pp. 11, 48-49.

9. Diary of Eliza Crawford.

10. From the diary of Grace Jacobsen, 1912. The diary is in a family collection.

11. Excerpts from a letter written by Bess Cobb, Guide to Manuscripts 1364, State Historical Society, North Dakota Heritage Center, Bismarck.

Chapter 5: Fear, Frustration, Fun

1. *Prairie Tales* (Bowman County, N. D.: Rural Area Development Committee, 1965), p. 253.

2. Family records include newspaper clippings covering this incident, but dates of publication were not recorded. Papers reporting the incident included the

Minneapolis Journal and the *Fargo Forum*. The incident occurred in March 1902. Helma Nelson dated her response to the *Minneapolis Journal* April 2, 1902. Papers carrying retractions included the *Minneapolis Journal, Fargo Forum, Norwich Pioneer, Enderlin Independent, Fingle Herald, Valley City Alliance,* and *Times Record-Valley City.*

3. Angela Boleyn, "Quarter Sections and Wide Horizons," *Fargo Forum,* July 5, 1931.

4. "Nell Elliott Robinson," *Pioneer Women Teachers of North Dakota,* ed. Nellie R. Swanson and Eleanor C. Bryson. *Ward County Independent,* (Minot), 1965, pp. 45-46.

5. Enid Bern, "They Had A Wonderful Time: The Homesteading Letters of Anna and Ethel Erickson," *North Dakota History 45,* no. 4 (Fall 1978): p. 7.

6. Bessie Schwartz, "My Own Story," file SC1055, Institute for Regional Studies, North Dakota State University, Fargo, pp. 3-6.

7. From the diary of Eliza Crawford, 1906-07, reprinted in the *Adams County Record,* series of four articles beginning November 4, 1981. The original diary is in a family collection.

8. Mrs. Renhold Hammel, formerly Anna Zimmerman, "My Life In the Early Days of Dunn County, North Dakota," Gladys Webster's Papers, A-143 Box 1, Folder 2, State Historical Society, North Dakota Heritage Center, Bismarck.

9. Carrie J. Doolittle, *Berthold 75th* (Berthold, N. D., 1975).

Chapter 6: Returns on the Investment

1. Mountrail County Historical Society Publication Committee, *Tales of Mighty Mountrail* (Dallas: Taylor Publishing Company, 1979), 1:195.

2. From the diary of Eliza Crawford, 1906-07 reprinted in the *Adams County Record,* series of four articles beginning November 4, 1981. The original diary is in a family collection.

3. May Shipten Girard, *The Cruel Cold Land* (Portland, Oreg.: Metropolitan Press, 1980), pp. 86-87.

4. *Prairie Tales* (Bowman County, N. D.: Rural Area Development Committee, 1965), p. 254.

5. *Burke County and White Earth Valley Historical Society, 1971* (Bismarck, N.D.: Quality Printing Service, 1972), p. 1174.

6. "99-year-old U graduate recalls early childhood," *Alumni Review*, University of North Dakota, Grand Forks, (June 1985): 5.

7. Girard, *The Cruel Cold Land*, pp. 260-62.

8. Leonard Lund, "Early-Day Memories Survived on Scraps of Paper," *Minot Daily News*, September 19, 1981.

9. Rachel Taylor Martin, "First Teacher in Alexander," in *From Dreams to Reality*, ed. Hedvig Clausen Svore (Bismarck: Bismarck Tribune Co., 1954), p. 57.

Chapter 7: The Gender Factor

1. Pauline Neher Diede, *Homesteading on the Knife River Prairies* (Bismarck: Germans from Russia Heritage Society, 1983), p. 47.

2. Everett Dick, *Sod-House Frontier* (New York: Appleton-Century Co., 1937), pp. 129-30.

3. Katherine Llewellyn Hill Harris, "Women and Families on Northwestern Colorado Homesteads, 1873-1920" (Ph.D. diss. University of Colorado, Boulder, 1983).

4. Timothy J. Kloberdanz, "Volksdeutsche, The Eastern European Germans," in *Plains Folk: North Dakota's Ethnic History*, ed. William C. Sherman and Playford V. Thorson (Fargo: North Dakota Institute for Regional Studies, 1988), p. 150.

5. Bea Peterson, "Mrs. Wike Leaves Message of Courage, Faith and Hope," *Belfield News*, October 12, 1961.

6. From the diary of Eliza Crawford, reprinted in the *Adams County Record*, series of four articles beginning November 4, 1981. The original diary is in a family collection.

7. Elizabeth Jameson, introduction to "Coming to Terms With the West," pp. 143-44, and "Women as Workers, Women as Civilizers: True Womanhood in the American West," pp. 145-64. in *The Women's West*, ed. Susan Armitage and Elizabeth Jameson (Norman: University of Oklahoma Press, 1987).

288

8. Lewis M. Puffer, "Pioneer Days in Area Recalled: Early Settler In Guelph Section Writes of Experiences During Period 1870-1910." Dickey County, N. D. (San Luis Obispo, Calif: Lewis M. Puffer, Date Unknown).

Chapter 8: The Legacy

1. Mari Sandoz, "The Homestead in Perspective," *Land Use Policy and Problems in the United States*, ed. Howard W. Ottoson (Lincoln: University of Nebraska Press, 1963), pp. 49-50.

2. This poem is printed courtesy of Bill Scott, a son of Janie Brew Scott.

3. Cited in Carol Fairbanks, *Prairie Women: Images in American and Canadian Fiction*, (New Haven: Yale University Press, 1986), pp. 5-6.

4. The complete account appeared in "Trails and Smoke Signals," North Dakota Historical Society, Inc., Newsletter, vol. 4, no. 2, 1970.

Index

J

K

L

M

N

O

Made in the USA
Las Vegas, NV
13 January 2023

65417682R00187